AF598925

Emma Sdegno

IN VENICE WITH RUSKIN

Marsilio Arte

Acknowledgements
Thanks are due to the following institutions that granted publication of the photographic materials and the people at these institutions who helped to facilitate loans: Abbot Hall, Lakeland Arts Trust; Ashmolean Museum, Oxford; Birmingham Museums and Art Gallery; The British Museum, London; The Fitzwilliam Museum, Cambridge; Fogg Museum, Harvard Art Museums; Guild of St George Collection, Ruskin Gallery, Museums Sheffield; Gallery Oldham; Ken and Jenny Jacobson, Great Bardfield; Manchester Art Gallery; The Metropolitan Museum of Art, New York; The Morgan Library & Museum, New York; Royal Collection Trust; The Ruskin at Lancaster University; South London Gallery; Tate, London; Victoria and Albert Museum, London.

So many people have participated in different ways in this publication with valuable advice, opinions, guidance. My heartfelt thanks go to the late James Dearden, first curator of the Ruskin archives and keeper of a profound knowledge he shared until his last days, whose transcription of Hobbs's manuscript diary remains a commitment to be fulfilled. I would particularly like to thank his successor, Stephen Wildman, for his great generosity in always responding promptly and competently to my many inquiries; Sarah Bunney who enthusiastically made available materials and images to which she holds the rights; as ever for their time, encouragement and observations Jeanne Clegg, André Hélard, Sarah Quill, Paul Tucker. I am grateful to the publisher Marsilio, for proposing this project and particularly to Martina Mian, Carmen Malafronte, Alice Montagnin, and Rosanna Alberti. Finally, a heartfelt thank you goes to the colleagues at the FoRS Centre, who wisely and passionately animate our workshop of ideas and initiatives on the sensitive topic of Ruskin and Venice. This book is dedicated to my mother, Michelina Loffredo.

Cover
The Fondamente Nove, circa 1876
Private collection (courtesy of Lowell Libson & Jonny Yarker Ltd)

Translation
Richard Sadleir

Design and layout
Carmen Malafronte

Editing
Rosanna Alberti

First edition October 2023
ISBN 979-12-5463-122-5

Marsilio Editori s.p.a.
Santa Marta, fabbricato 17
30123 Venice
www.marsilioeditori.it

CONTENTS

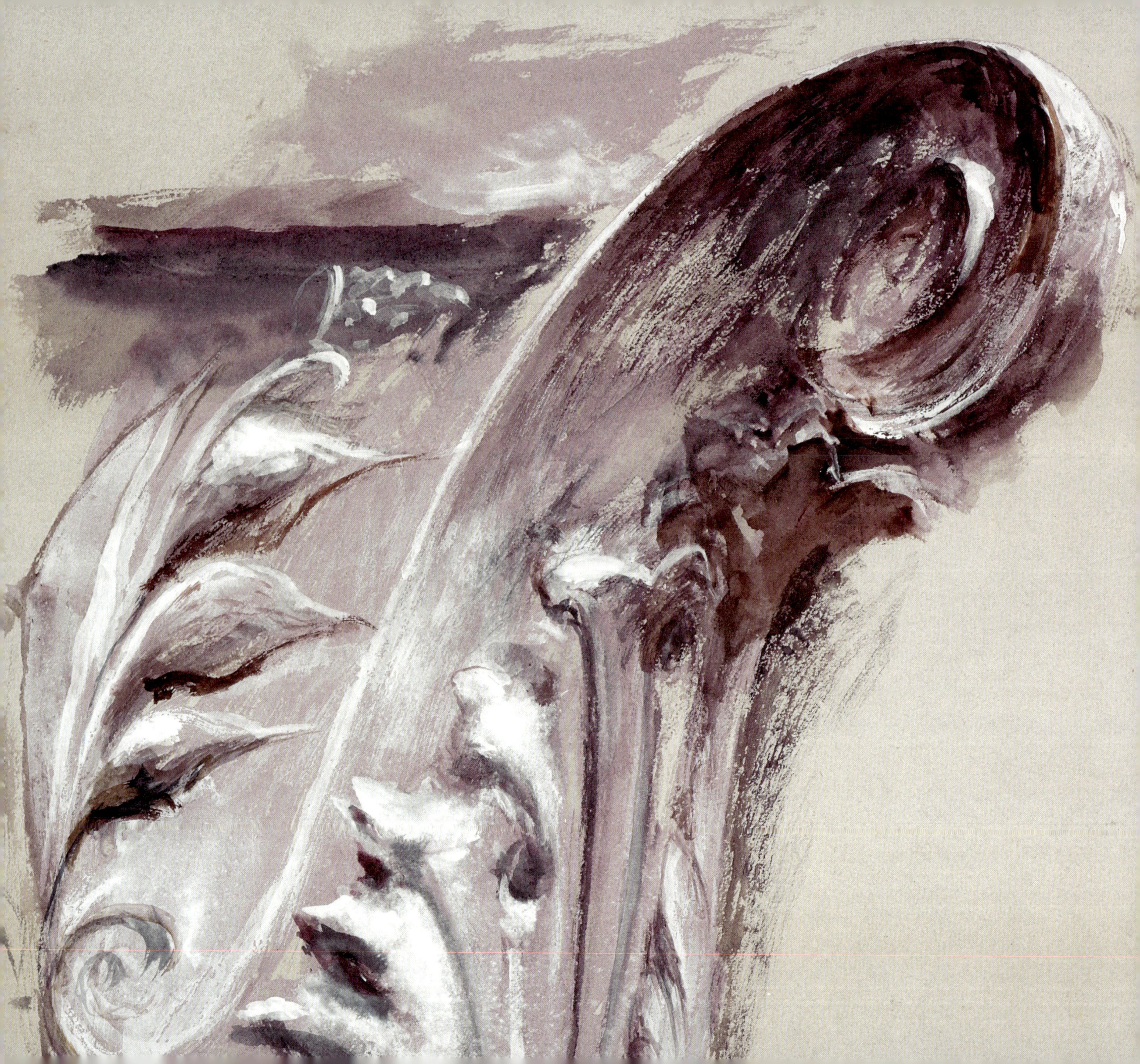

A BIOGRAPHY IN PICTURES

Emma Sdegno

I should like to draw all St. Mark's, and all this Verona, stone by stone, to eat it all up into my mind, touch by touch.
John Ruskin's letter to his father, June 1852[1]

The collection of drawings presented here tells the story of John Ruskin's relationship with Venice, a relationship that extended over a period of more than fifty years, during his eleven stays travelling on the Continent. Following a beaten track, Ruskin repeatedly headed to Italy through Northern France, Germany, Switzerland and the Alps, visited Rome and Naples, went once as far as Sicily in 1874, to Assisi, and several times to Tuscany. He recorded his encounters with places through writing and numerous drawings that he only partly published in his works (pp. 8, 25), and which form a wonderful gallery of his "cultural as well as affective geography of Europe".[2] Venice was a place he particularly cherished, calling it "the Paradise of cities."[3] The periods he spent in the city marked the fundamental moments of his life as artist and critic, up to his last, very brief stay in 1888, of which only the last broken words in his personal diary remain.

This biography in pictures takes the reader into the Venice that Ruskin represented through a variety of expressive forms and techniques, from which the interests and aims assigned to drawing over the years emerge. The images are organised according to the subject order followed in Volume 38 of the Library Edition, the penultimate one of Cook and Wedderburn's monumental undertaking partly devoted to Ruskin's enormous graphic and pictorial work. Referring back to the alphabetical and thematic criteria that Ruskin adopted in his numerous catalogues, this subdivision arranges the sections according to the subjects that Ruskin dealt with over time, presenting in chronological order the various media he used, from drawing to watercolour, oil painting and the daguerreotype. Ruskin's use of a plurality of media simultaneously in his study of the object constitutes an important feature of his approach to seeing. Other peculiarities surface, such as his greater interest in the Doge's Palace and St. Mark's Basilica – the main centre of research through the five decades, particularly in the years of work for *The Stones of Venice* (1849–52) – as well as the preponderance of civil over religious architecture, from the private dwellings on the Grand Canal to the Fondaco dei Turchi; and finally the number of views of the Grand Canal and the lagoon, which are mostly found in the later years, offering the occasion for some reflections.

Unlike similar selections of works by painters and artists, such as the volume *Venice with Turner* (Tate 2020), an anthological collection of Ruskin's Venetian themes that excludes the context of the written work risks attributing an autonomy to the graphic work which it does not have. And this is not so much because of the "amateur" nature of Ruskin's drawing, since Ruskin held that the only difference between the

VENETIAN RENAISSANCE CAPITAL, 1876–77
watercolour, bodycolour on purple card
faded to cream, 280 × 222 mm
Harvard, Harvard Art Museums / Fogg Museum
transfer from the Fine Arts Department
Harvard University, inv. 1926.33.116

amateur and the artist was a different degree of ability. Sharing the same intentions,[4] the artist produces a work that is valid in itself, while the amateur is condemned to the dissatisfaction of seeing his/her efforts repaid by results that are not permanent and excellent, but eminently moral in its engagement with beauty.[5] To state that Ruskin saw the essence of drawing as an "invaluable stimulus to knowledge of the world around us ... devoid of intrinsic value" is correct only if we clarify the cognitive and ethical significance that he attributed to drawing.[6] If the morality of art is a cliché of Victorian culture, for Ruskin the emphasis is on the intellectual as well as the manual processes leading to the creation of the artwork and not on its edifying effects.[7] Drawing is therefore a privileged means of observing both the physical reality and the art of the old masters, which Ruskin subjected to careful study, intended for his own training and that of his numerous students, artists or "laymen," to whom he gave lessons until the last years of his life.

It is necessary, albeit briefly in the space of this introduction, to clarify the principles that underlie Ruskin's practice of drawing, in order to put his graphic and pictorial works into perspective, recognising their educational value, while highlighting their extraordinary uniqueness. His visual works in Venice tell the story of an affective relationship with the city that had bewitched him. Inscribed in the Anglo-American and European tradition of the myth of decadent Venice, that relationship was built and matured through the practice of drawing. It harked back to Lord Byron – "my Venice," Ruskin would say in his autobiography, "like Turner's had been mainly created by Byron" –[8] and epigones such as Samuel Rogers, the author of the influential *Italy, a Poem* (1830), illustrated by Turner, that Ruskin received for his sixteenth birthday. In his first trip to Venice in 1835, the young Ruskin's reaction was charged with the enthusiasm modelled on Byron's fourth canto of *Childe Harold's Pilgrimage*, producing verses as passionate and acerbic as his drawing of the Piazzetta (p. 65). It would be his subsequent trip in 1841 to effect a qualitative shift, where we glimpse the signs of progress in his quest for representation, following new paths and producing different outcomes through words and drawing.

The encounter with J. M. W. Turner's paintings dates back to 1836. It would profoundly determine Ruskin's life and inspire *Modern Painters*, the magnum opus in five volumes written between 1843 and 1860, whose purpose was to examine the landscape painting of the European tradition in relation to Turner's unparalleled model. Venice was a subject of utmost importance for Turner and would be the occasion for Ruskin's continuous engagement with the English painter, up to the final results in the 1870s, as we shall see.

In order to prepare himself for his second trip to the Continent, Ruskin turned to the drawing master James Duffield Harding, whose teaching articulated the language of the picturesque by orienting it prevalently towards form and chiaroscuro, in preference to the teachers whose approach was more colouristic. This choice thus confirms the formative importance he attributed to drawing and results in a greater focus on architectural themes.[9] The diaries of this Venetian stay extensively record the emotions related to his drawing, the expectations, the frequent disappointments, the small satisfactions. But leafing through the travel diaries of 1841 reveals a "discrepancy between written text and drawing."[10] If the diary can rightly be called a "verbal sketchbook,"[11] with descriptions that emphasise colour effects and atmospheric variations, the drawings of this period represent different subjects. The descriptions are admirable translations into words of Turner's paintings, whose play of light and tonal contrasts seem to constitute the filter through which Ruskin perceives the city and which he can render through the verbal medium. Drawing, on the other hand, only occasionally gives him some pleasure and the sense of limitation and frustration is predominant. This divergence between drawing and writing, very marked in the 1841 journal, is also evident in the diary pages of the following years. In the mid-1840s, drawing became for Ruskin an instrument of research and investigation that he applied to the "mission" that he took on during his third trip to Italy. His 1845 stay in Venice was crucial, the last stage of his trip on the Continent made without his parents. It was a formative and transformative journey for the young man eager to dedicate his life to an aesthetically gratifying and spiritually edifying purpose. Such was the encounter with Tintoretto's painting in a memorable visit to the Scuola di San Rocco and the discovery, which came with the immediacy of a revelatory vision, of the poignant beauty of the city, whose heritage, severely degraded by destruction, modernisation and restoration, seemed close to being erased.

The drawings of this period have a documentary character, aimed at surveying and studying architecture and painting; they inaugurate a long season of feverish activity in the city. It is a very fertile phase, in which Ruskin elaborates his own figurative language, attaining autonomy from the example of Harding, with whom he shared the Venetian stay of 1845. He now recognises his drawing master to be too "simple,"[12] in comparison with the highly imaginative language of Tintoretto, "a painter from another planet" (pp. 108–10).[13] The priority still assigned to the architecture now has a documentary purpose and his meticulously detailed yet selective drawing, allowing the building to emerge from vast white areas of the sheet, in an evocative incompleteness, dates back to this period and would become a distinctive feature of his work (p. 33). He also dwells on certain elements, drawing them repeatedly, such as the two windows of Ca' Foscari (p. 29), part of a serial study with elements replicated at least three other times: a sign of an undoubted fascination with the Palace, of an interest in the Gothic moulding and the wild grass that framed it, whose possible theoretical scope remains undefined, since part of the series has been lost.[14]

It was this primary interest in observing and carefully reproducing buildings that led him to buy his first daguerreotypes of Venice from an unidentified "Frenchman said to be in distress,"[15] expressing to his father his enthusiasm for those reproductions of the palaces that he had hitherto struggled to depict correctly. Along with the astounding possibility of a faithful rendering of proportions – "It is very nearly the same thing as carrying off the palace itself" – Ruskin is fascinated by their aesthetic quality "some [are] most beautiful, though small."[16] He purchased numerous daguerreotypes in 1845, and on subsequent trips he either commissioned or personally directed many more (pp. 19, 38–39, 51). On the following journey in 1846, many of the daguerreotypes would be signed by himself and his valet John (called George) Hobbs (pp. 23, 43, 75). In the vast collection of Venetian daguerreotypes there are not only architectures and studio elements, but also images of everyday life that must have attracted Ruskin also by their dazzling unexpectedness (p. 39).[17] In time, Ruskin would publicly distance himself from this medium of representation, calling it an "adversity" above all because of its wide and indiscriminate use.[18] But the recently found daguerreotypes, now in the Ken and Jenny Jacobson vast collection, makes it possible to correctly evaluate the important part that this medium played for Ruskin, owing to its both documentary and aesthetic qualities. In the 1845 visit we thus find the essential elements of the approach that he would follow in his Venetian stays of 1849–50 and 1851–52 dedicated to the preparation of *The Stones of Venice*. Gathering an extraordinary profusion of meticulously drawn sketches, minimal fragments of architecture from a study that he would describe as by "useful bits,"[19] he developed a "membrology" of dilated details, producing thick notebooks and large-scale worksheets (pp. 89–105)[20]. These images, like the drawings of capitals, the corner sculptures of the Doge's Palace and the façade, are studies that have a cognitive purpose aimed at reconstructing the cultural and spiritual history of Venice, and at the same time possess a beauty of their own.

Ruskin's drawing during this stay develops into a personal language that is functional to the aims of a faithful rendering of the "truthfulness" of the object, and we notice a persistence of that divarication from his writing mentioned above. As one browses the pages of the 1846 Venetian diary, his intention to assign to words the recording of light effects, settings and impressions is evident. A comparison with the unpublished journal that Hobbs kept during the same period provides data that help reconstruct the plans and occupations that are passed over in silence by his master. It is mainly from Hobbs's diary that we learn of his intense daily schedule and the places that he sketched. Thus we know that at dawn, on the first days of his stay, they went to the cloister of San Gregorio (p. 86), crossing the Grand Canal by gondola from the Hotel Danieli where they were staying.[21] The place, which must have attracted Ruskin's attention due to its state of disrepair, is never mentioned in the diary, which records impressions of aspects of the lagoon at particular times of the day. See, for example, the entry for Sunday 17 May, describing St. Mark's Basin, in which the rippling of the surface of the water in the broad reach extending from the Redentore to the botanical garden, and the tones of colour that this assumes in reflecting the objects, the church and the boats are carefully observed:

> There is a bright sun and breeze from the east rippling the whole lagoon, except the channel between San Giorgio and the church of the Redentore, which is dead calm. The sky is blue in the distance and pale grey above. The lagoon is of a pale aquamarine green, reflecting near objects feebly, distant ones not at all, owing to the ripple. The seeming shadows of the ships fall on the rippled part distinctly, but the becalmed part behind San Giorgio reflects the sky clearly, and there is not a vestige of the shadow of the church or anything else upon it. This is looking across the sun-

light, i.e., south east at four afternoon. Looking east, however, towards the Botanic Garden, the water is calmer and reflects the sky and vessels; with this peculiarity, the sky which is pale blue is of the same kind of blue a little deeper in the water: the vessels' hulls, which are black, are reflected in pale sea green, the natural colour of the water under sunlight, which, however, comes dark against the blue of the reflected sky; while the orange masts of the vessels, wet with a recent shower, are reflected without change of colour, only not quite so bright as above. One ship has a white, another a red stripe – of these the water takes no notice. What is curious, a boat passes across with white and dark figures – the water reflects the dark in green and misses out all the white; this is chiefly owing to the dark images being opposed to the bright reflected sky.
On looking at the apparent shadow of a boat near me, I find that a boat swinging near the quay casts an apparent shadow on the rippled water. This appearance I find to be owing altogether to the increased *reflective* power of the water in the shaded space; for the farther sides of the ripples therein take the pale grey of the cloud, hardly darker than the bright green.[22]

This piece is one of the many examples of observations of the effects of light in nature that were reused in *Modern Painters* to prove Turner's "truths" in representing sky, vegetation and water. It was in fact taken up again, with minor modifications, from the third edition of *Modern Painters* I, published in 1846, showing Turner's unique ability to render the surface of water.[23] If, therefore, Ruskin in these years observed the lagoon with a Turnerian eye, his drawing turned to architectural spaces and details. The 1850s saw the publication of *The Stones of Venice* and the beginning of a very intense season in the field of teaching, as head of the drawing classes at the Working Men's College in London. The purpose of the classes was social and philanthropic, aimed at providing working men and young amateurs that did not aspire to be artists with an education, guiding them through the medium of drawing to vision – as "to see clearly" was to him "poetry, prophecy and religion, all in one."[24] Ruskin generously imparted his precepts, often original compared to the trends then current, and they then flowed into his manual *The Elements of Drawings* (1857). There he trained a team of pupils – improperly called "copyists"[25] – including J. W. Bunney, the young painter who spent twelve years in Venice. Ruskin commissioned him studies of details of Vittore Carpaccio's Saint Ursula cycle and St. Mark's Basilica in the late 1870s. The last great period, broadly represented by the drawings reproduced here, dates back to his long stay in Venice in the winter of 1876–77. It was a very important time for the development of Ruskin's critical thinking, as recent studies have highlighted.[26] He went there with the intention of writing a new edition of *The Stones of Venice* that would radically revise the ideological assumptions of the work by correcting its strongly anti-Catholic Protestant-evangelical approach. The project of a fourth volume of the *Stones* and of telling a different story of Venice was partly realised through the serial publication of *St. Mark's Rest* (1877–84) the *Guide to the Principal Pictures at the Academy of Fine Arts in Venice* (1877) and the letters written in those months for *Fors Clavigera*, the epistolary work addressed to the workers of England written discontinuously from 1871 to 1884. The visit had also the "restorative" purpose of soothing his pain at the early death of the young Rose La Touche, to whom he was bound by a tormented love, the last episode in an unhappy sentimental life. The drawings of Venice in these years present a variety of themes unparalleled in the Venetian corpus,[27] and interweave a deep and distressed relationship with the city that emerges from the correspondence and diaries. His intention was now to revisit the city and relive, as far as possible, a past that could be partly recovered through places. Ruskin was at work drawing the cycle of Saint Ursula by Carpaccio, the artist whose greatness he recognised in these years thanks to his friend Edward Burne-Jones, and whose *Dream* he drew in its entirety (p. 116) as well as some magnified details (p. 118). An honorary member of the Academy of Fine Arts, where the painting was exhibited, Ruskin obtained special permission to copy it in the seclusion of a room reserved for him. He thus cultivated a private relationship with the young martyr saint, whom he came to identify with his pious beloved Rose, to the point of seeing her as a mediating figure for messages from the beyond.[28] In this period, alongside the studies of Carpaccio's Saint Ursula, Ruskin made numerous drawings of views that seem to fit into a clearly defined programme. On 2 August 1876, the day after leaving Brantwood travelling "Venicewards," he wrote to his friend Charles Eliot Norton of his apprehension at the pain that the sight of places once associated with his happy past, now in ruins, would cause him. The decay would darken those memories, which, in pristine conditions, would have aroused in him the "exalting

SCUOLA GRANDE DI SAN MARCO, 1876
Frontispiece of *The Stones of Venice*, vol. III
in *The Complete Works of John Ruskin*, vol. XI

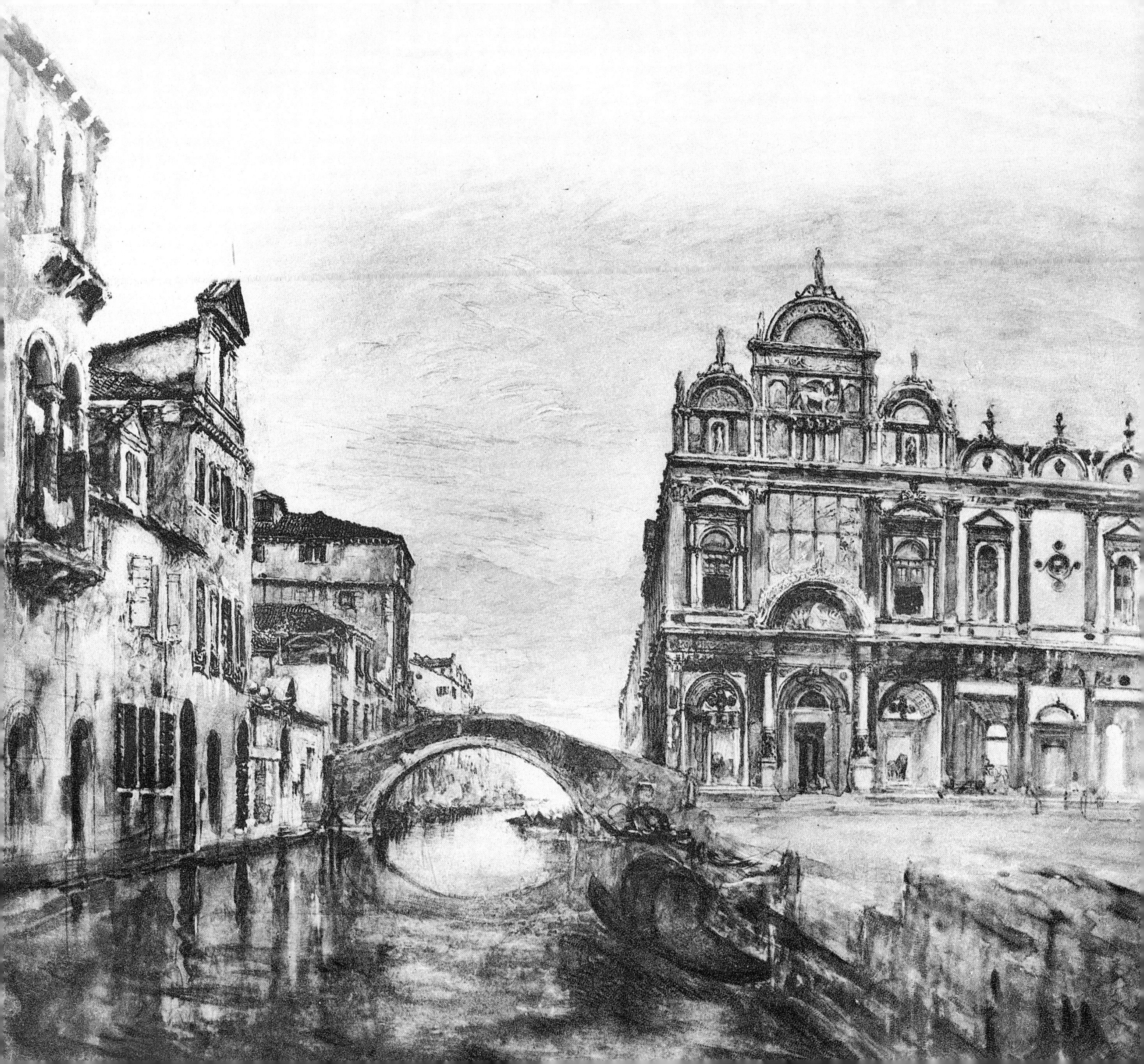

and thrilling pensiveness, as of some glorious summer evening in purple light."[29] But soon he overcame his distress resolving to draw what remained, to illustrate the new edition of the *Stones*. Instead of new engravings of old pictures, he told Norton, he would "make new drawings, giving some notion of [his] old memories of the place, in Turner's time, and get them expressed in line engraving, omit[ting] nearly all the architectural analysis."[30] Hence Ruskin intended to revisit and draw Turner's places for the revised edition of his history of Venice. Such a return would this time involve a new approach to the city, and a new figurative language. In a letter written some months earlier, he had announced to Norton his plan for the years to come. Regretting that he would no longer be able to make copies of the great Italian masters, he would concentrate, he said, given his remaining strength and the present circumstances, "no more on history, mythology, or literature," but on those occupations he felt he had a gift for, namely "on natural history, including sky, ... in connection with Turner's work only, and so end as [he] began."[31] Ruskin would now paint the views and atmospheres of Venice that he had previously explored, as we have seen, mainly through writing. The paucity of lagoon views (pp. 121, 122) made in the earlier years, finding compensation in the ecphrastic word, may betray a sense of inadequacy in comparison with Turner. In 1877 his return to the Venice of Turner's time through pencil and watercolour seems to coincide with a gained freedom of expression, in the awareness of his own abilities.[32] It is during this period that the diary entries are allied to the drawings in the themes and in the choice of a common essential language. As just one example among many possible ones, I will cite the entry for 9 September 1876: "this morning, entirely glorious scarlet dawn. I out on balcony in my nightgown, with bare feet; air quite delicious. I. Grand Canal Sketch begun" (p. 61).[33] The diary records the atmospheric hues, with particular attention to the sky, and the daily sketches render these visually. Ruskin regularly captures the sunrises and especially the sunsets; he regrets not remembering the setting of the sun two days earlier, always recording the colours of the sky and the sea, eschewing grey, which he feared most since it reminded him so much of the London sky. The broad luminous views of the Grand Canal (pp. 59, 60, 61), the Fondamente Nove (p. 129), the island of San Michele, the Arsenale (pp. 124-25), and the Euganean hills from the lagoon (p. 127) are rendered with a palette of light, often bright and vivid colours, bringing comfort to a weakened eyesight that Ruskin repeatedly mourns in the pages of his diary. The Venice that Ruskin paints in this late flourish is a Venice that privileges "the natural history" and the views of the Grand Canal take up the waterway in its extension, giving it the breadth of a great river. "The Deep River," Ruskin explains in *St. Mark's Rest*, is the translation of Rialto or Rivo Alto, referring back to the 1870 lesson of *Verona and its Rivers*, in which he had retraced the birth of Venice through the waterways that flow into the lagoon.[34] These are the last images of Venice that Ruskin gives us: in attempting to revisit the *Stones* he reconfigures them, turning his gaze to the water, to the sky, to its light, hues and colours. In a newly-found freedom of expression that does not fear comparison with Turner, his last visual traces of Venice compose the image of a natural, fragile, enchanting, fading place.

1 Cook, E. T. and Alexander Wedderburn (eds.), *The Works of John Ruskin*, Library Edition, 39 vols, London: Longmans, Green & Co., 1903–12, vol. x: 26. [hereafter *Works*].

2 Hélard, André, "Ce qui commence à Calais: l'Europe, terrain de jeu de Ruskin", Emma Sdegno, Martina Frank, Myriam Pilutti Namer, Pierre-Henri Frangne (eds.), *John Ruskin's Europe. A Collection of Cross-Cultural Essays*, Venice: Edizioni Ca' Foscari, 2020, 169–80: 176

3 Ruskin's diary entry dated Venice 6 May 1841. Evans, Joan and John Howard Whitehouse (eds.), *The Diaries of John Ruskin*, Oxford: Clarendon Press, 1959, 3 vols., vol. I: 183. [Hereafter *Diaries*]

4 Levi, Donata and Paul Tucker, *Ruskin didatta. Il disegno tra disciplina e diletto*, Venice: Marsilio, 1997, 12–13.

5 Ibid., 13.

6 Newall, Christopher, *John Ruskin. Artist and Observer*, Ottawa–London: Paul Olberton, 2014, 20. This outlook is essentially shared in the exhibitions that have presented a selection of Ruskin's drawings and watercolours as works of art. See Walton, Paul, *Master Drawings by John Ruskin. Selections from the David Thomson Collection*, London: Pilkington Press, 2000; Hewison, Robert, Ian Warrell and Stephen Wildman, *Ruskin, Turner and the Pre-Raphaelites*, London: Tate Gallery Publishing, 2000; Ottani Cavina, Anna (ed.), *John Ruskin. Le Pietre di Venezia*, Venice: Marsilio, 2018.

7 Levi and Tucker, *Ruskin didatta*, 14.

8 *Praeterita, Works* xxxv: 295. On Ruskin and Venice see the studies by Clegg, Jeanne, *Ruskin and Venice*, London: Junction Books, 1981; Hewison, Robert, *Ruskin and Venice*, London: Thames and Hudson, 1978; Unrau, John, *Looking at Architecture with Ruskin*, London: Thames and Hudson, 1978; id. *Ruskin and St. Mark's*, London: Thames and Hudson, 1984; Hewison, Robert, *Ruskin on Venice: "The Paradise of Cities"*, New Haven–London: Yale University Press, 2009; Quill, Sarah, *Ruskin's Venice: The Stones Revisited*, London: Lund Humphries, 2015.

9 Levi and Tucker, *Ruskin didatta*, 60.

10 Ibid., 62.

11 Ibid., 63.

12 Shapiro, Harold (ed.), *Ruskin in Italy. Letters to his Parents 1845*, Oxford: Clarendon Press, 1972, 189.

13 Letter to J. Severn of 21 September 1845, *Works* iv: 394. See Sdegno, Emma (ed.), *Looking at Tintoretto with John Ruskin. A Venetian Anthology*, Venice: Marsilio, 2018.

14 Clegg, Jeanne and Emma Sdegno, "Le pietre di Ca' Foscari: Ruskin e il Palazzo", Anna Cardinaletti, Laura Cerasi, Patrizio Rigobon (eds.), *Le lingue occidentali nei 150 anni di storia di Ca' Foscari*, Venice: Edizioni Ca' Foscari, 2018, 19–41.

15 Shapiro (ed.), *Ruskin in Italy*, 220. On Ruskin's daguerreotypes see Harvey, Michael, "Ruskin and Photography", *Oxford Art Journal* vol. 7, no. 2 (1984): 25–33; Costantini, Paolo and Italo Zannier, *I dagherrotipi della Collezione Ruskin*, Venice: Arsenale Editrice 1986; Wildman, Stephen, *"A noble invention": Ruskin's Daguerreotypes of Venice and Verona*, Lancaster: Library Exhibition Catalogues, 2013; Jacobson, Ken and Jenny, *Carrying off the Palaces: John Ruskin's Lost Daguerreotypes*, London: Bernard Quaritch Ltd, 2015.

16 *Ruskin in Italy*, cit., p. 220.

17 Frangne, Pierre-Henri, *John Ruskin, un œil européen. La photographie, la peinture, l'écriture et l'énigme de la visibilité*, in Sdegno, Frank, Pilutti Namer, Frangne (eds.), *John Ruskin's Europe*, 43-58: 51.

18 *Works* xxxv: 296.

19 Letter to G. Richmond, Lucerne, dated 30 August 1846, *Works* xxxvi: 64; Levi, and Tucker, *Ruskin didatta*, p. 89.

20 Kite, Stephen, *Building Ruskin's Italy. Watching Architecture*, Aldershot: Routledge, 2012, p. 69.

21 John Hobbs, *Diary* (unpublished), *1846, 1849*. Pierpont Morgan Library, New York, MA 2539.

22 *Diaries* iii: 337–38.

23 *Works* iii: 501.

24 *Modern Painters* iii, *Works* vi: 333.

25 Bunney, Sarah, *"John W. Bunney's 'Big Picture' of St. Mark's, and the Ruskin-Bunney Relationship", Ruskin Review and Bulletin* vol. iv, no. 1 (2007): 18–47.

26 See Paul Tucker's Introduction to J. Ruskin, *Guide to the Principal Pictures at the Academy of Fine Arts Venice (1877) with Other Texts*, Venice: Edizioni Ca' Foscari, 2023.

27 Wildman, Stephen, "'Scrawls and rags?' John Ruskin's Venetian Drawings of 1876–77," *Master Drawings* vol. xlvii, no. 3 (2009): 329–45, 329.

28 Burd, Van Akin, *Christmas Story. John Ruskin's Venetian Letters of 1876–1877. Edited with an Introductory Essay on Ruskin and the Spiritualists, His Quest for the Unseen*, Delaware: Associated University Presses, 1990.

29 Bradley, John and Ian Ousby (eds.), *The Correspondence of John Ruskin and Charles Eliot Norton*, Cambridge: Cambridge University Press, 1987, 384.

30 Ibid.

31 Ibid., 352.

32 In an 1878 exhibition Ruskin presented his "small visual autobiography," consisting of a heterogeneous selection of works alongside those of Turner; see Clegg, Jeanne, *John Ruskin. An Arts Council Exhibition*, exhibition catalogue (Sheffield, Mappin Art Gallery; Kendal, Abbot Hall; Oxford, Oxford Museum of Modern Art, 25 May–13 November 1983), London: Arts Council of Great Britain, 1983, 17; Levi and Tucker, *Ruskin didatta*, 11–12.

33 *Diaries* iii: 906.

34 It was to Rivo Alto that Ruskin intended to devote the second part of his manual for the Drawing School he founded in Oxford in 1870. As a complement to the *Laws of Fèsole*, on the teaching of the drawing principles, in the *Laws of Rivo Alto* he meant to deal with colour, as the lesson Venice had left to the world. See W. G. Collingwood, *Ruskin's Relics*, London: Isbister & Company Limited, 1903, 460–61.

IN VENICE WITH RUSKIN

November 23rd, 1849

The Verities of Venice. There is no town in Italy of which parts and detached groups of buildings are so perfect as some in Venice: but there is also no one which owes so much to the imagination. Between the Isola di San Giorgio and that of the Giudecca, the strong tide, divided on the quay of San Giorgio, curdles in smooth and sliding eddies into a triangular space where the water seems flowing all ways at once sweeping from a centre as it does from the swell of the [blank] of Spezia. Then a steady stream forms itself which runs out seaward between two banks of grey slime, smooth and level; the one extending far away to the south, the other to the foot of the dead wall which surrounds the gardens of San Giorgio. Dead it is – through its whole length not so much as a water door or a groined angle to break its perfect dullness. The campanile and dome are seen over it as the gondola glides with the tide towards the Lido, but the wall itself is unbroken, and forms the principal object in the view of Venice in this direction. Turning to the right after passing the Giudecca – and going by the back of the larger island – the view is still more melancholy.

The Diaries of John Ruskin, vol. II: 455.

BOATS

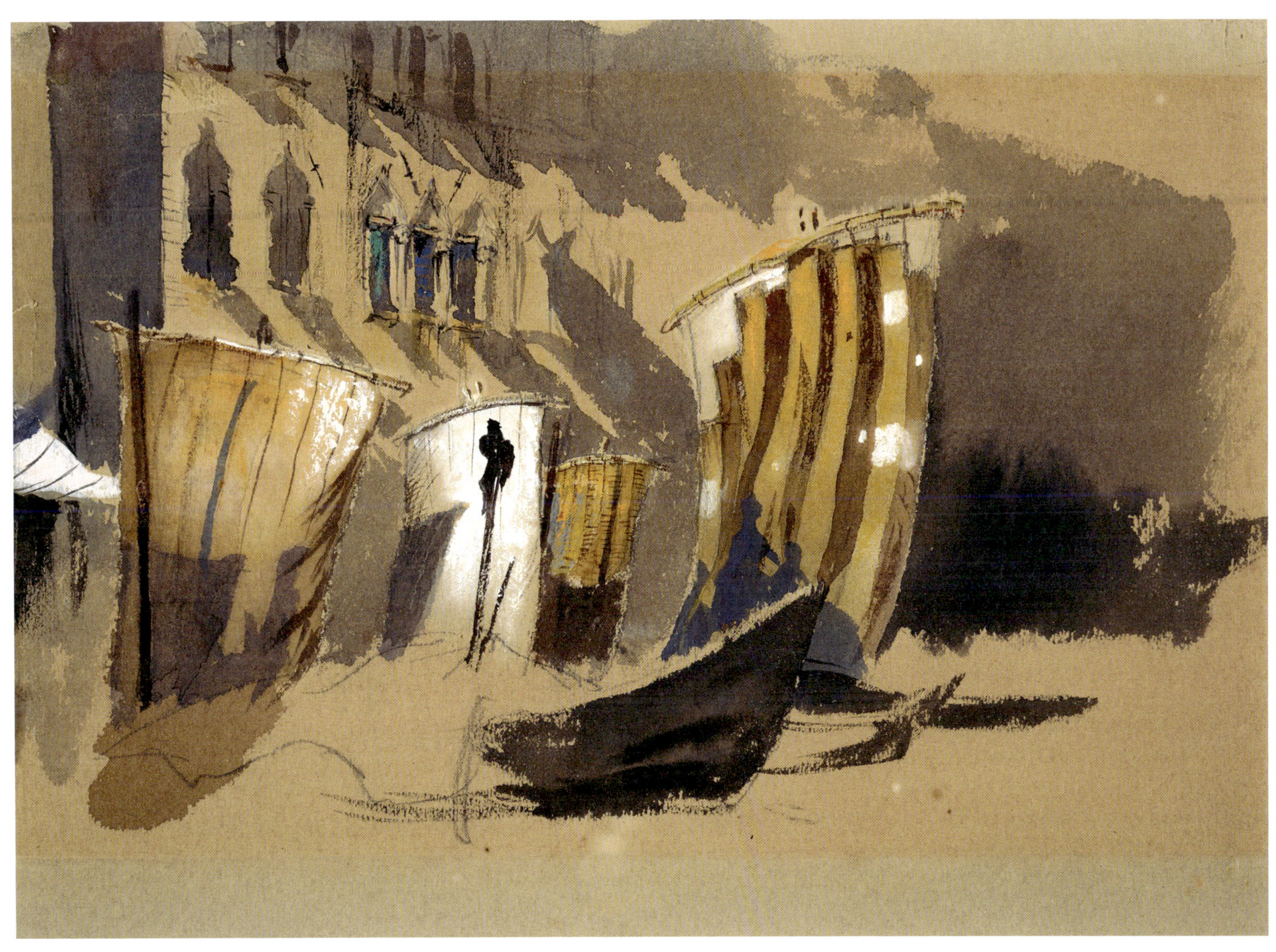

SAILS OF FISHING BOATS, 1845
pencil, watercolour and bodycolour on grey paper, 165 × 228 mm
recto: *Venice, Moonlight on the Lagoon* [page 122]
Lancaster, The Ruskin, Lancaster University, inv. 1996P1062

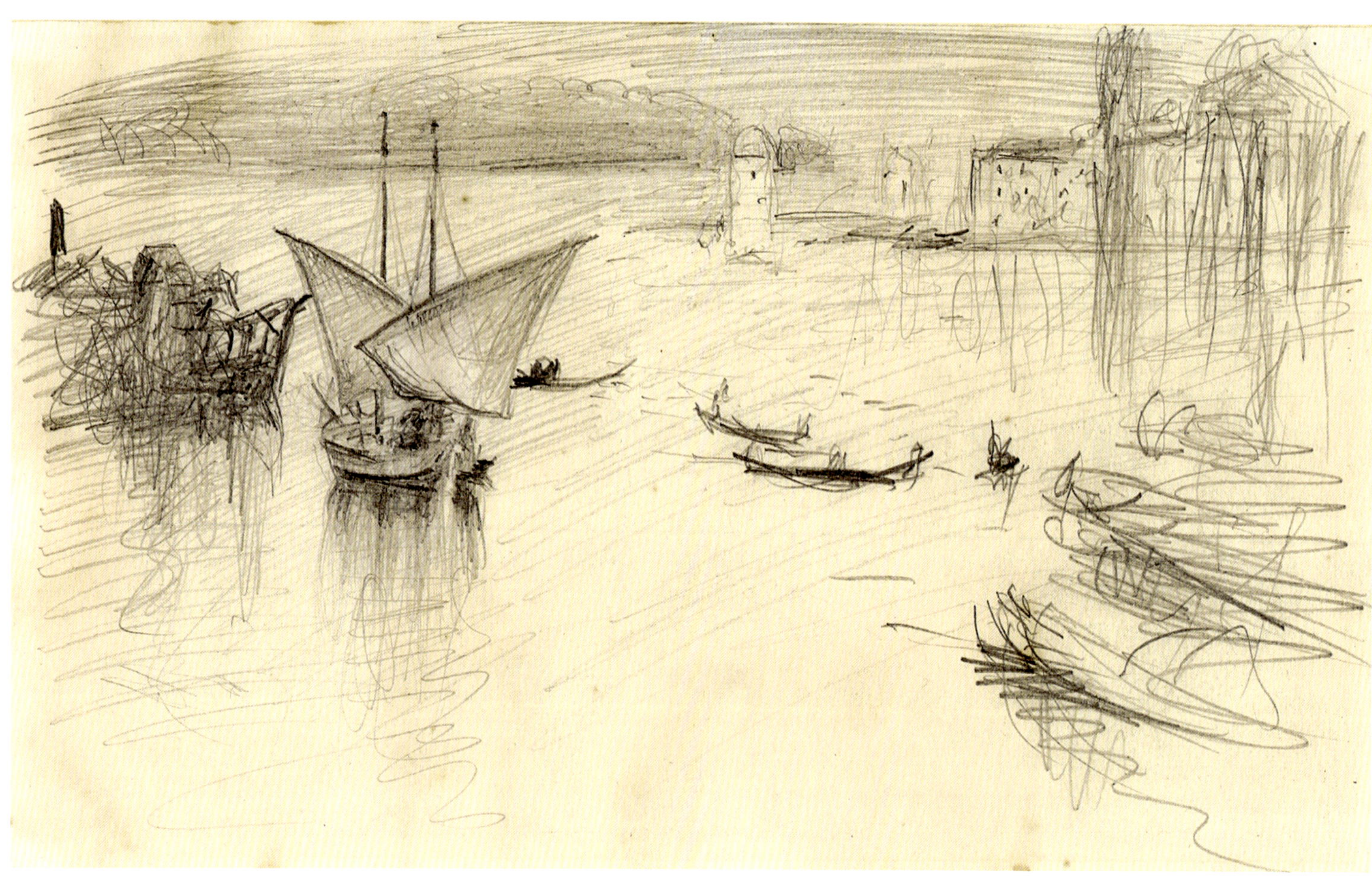

SAN GIORGIO MAGGIORE, DRAWN FROM THE DOGANA, 1876
pencil on paper, 139 × 230 mm
Lancaster, The Ruskin, Lancaster University, inv. 1996P1628

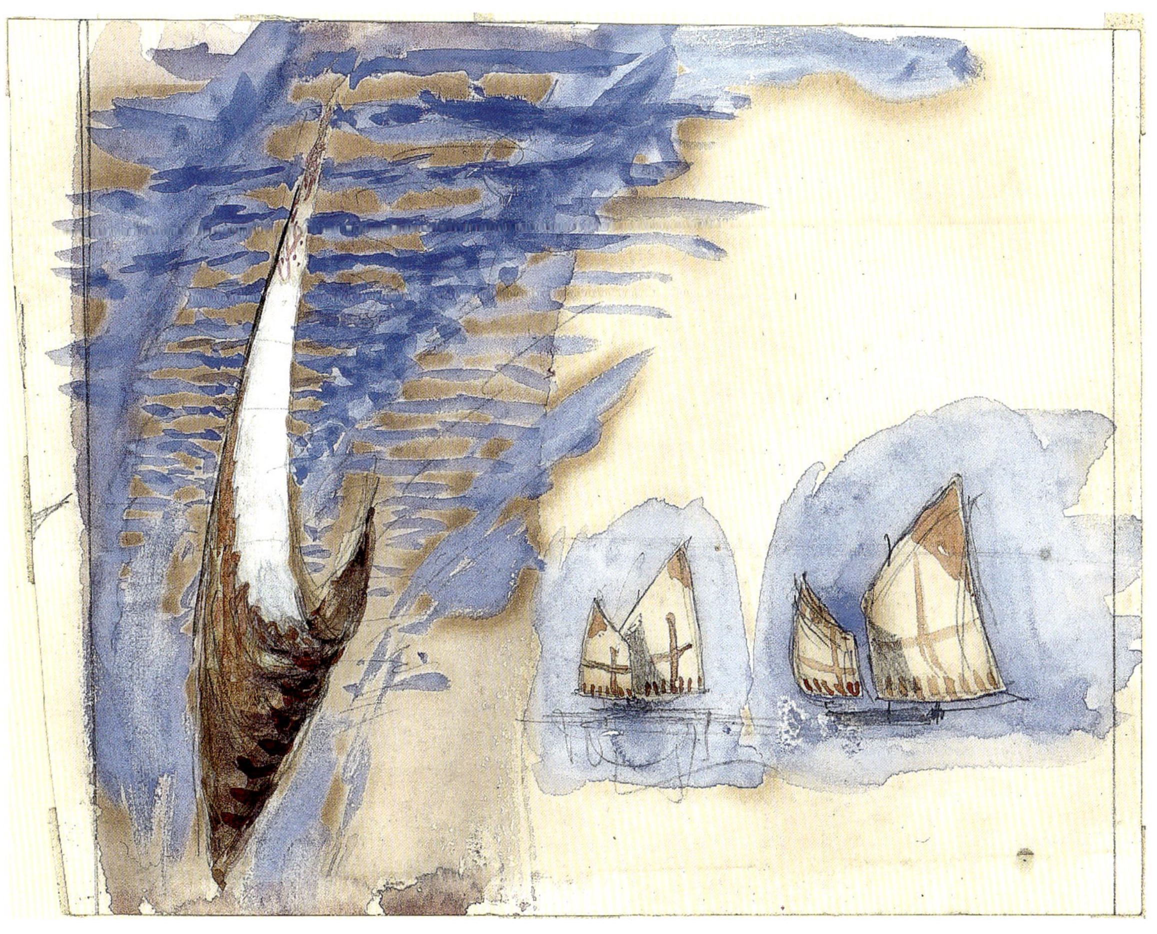

SAILING BOATS, undated
pencil, watercolour on paper, 140 × 182 mm
Lancaster, The Ruskin, Lancaster University
inv. 1996P1054

BRIDGES

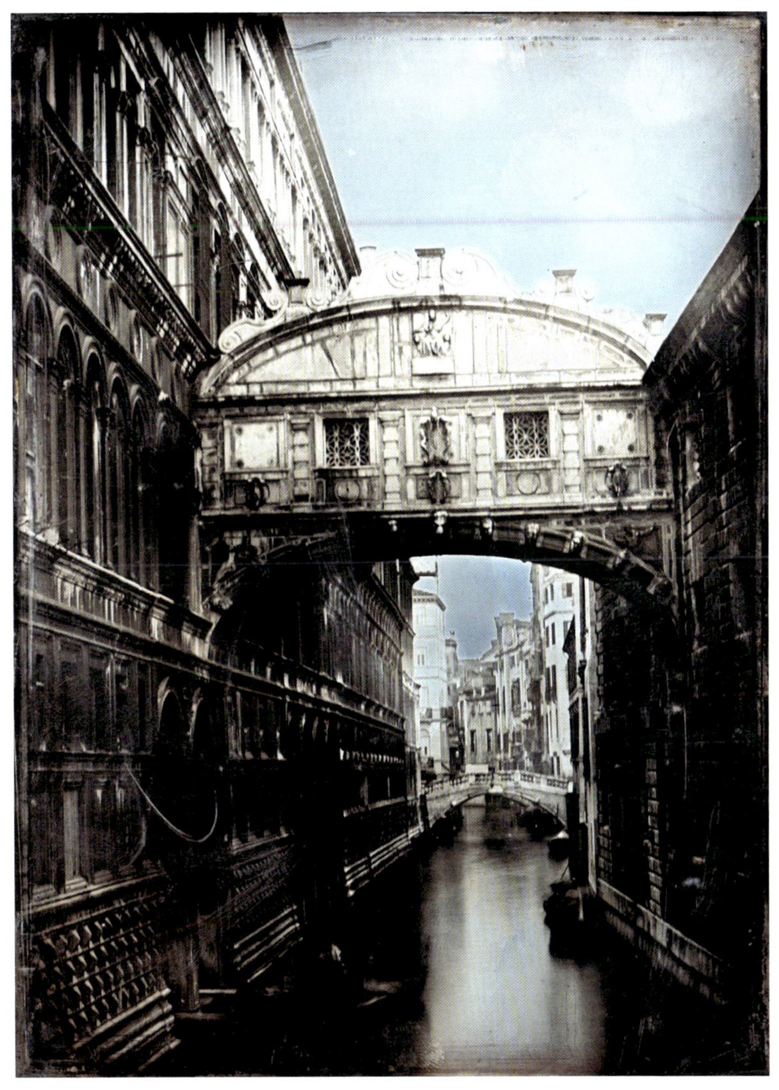

John Ruskin and Le Cavalier Iller
THE DUCAL PALACE AND THE BRIDGE OF SIGHS
circa 1846–52
half plate-daguerreotype, 161 × 120 mm
Courtesy of K&J Jacobson, UK

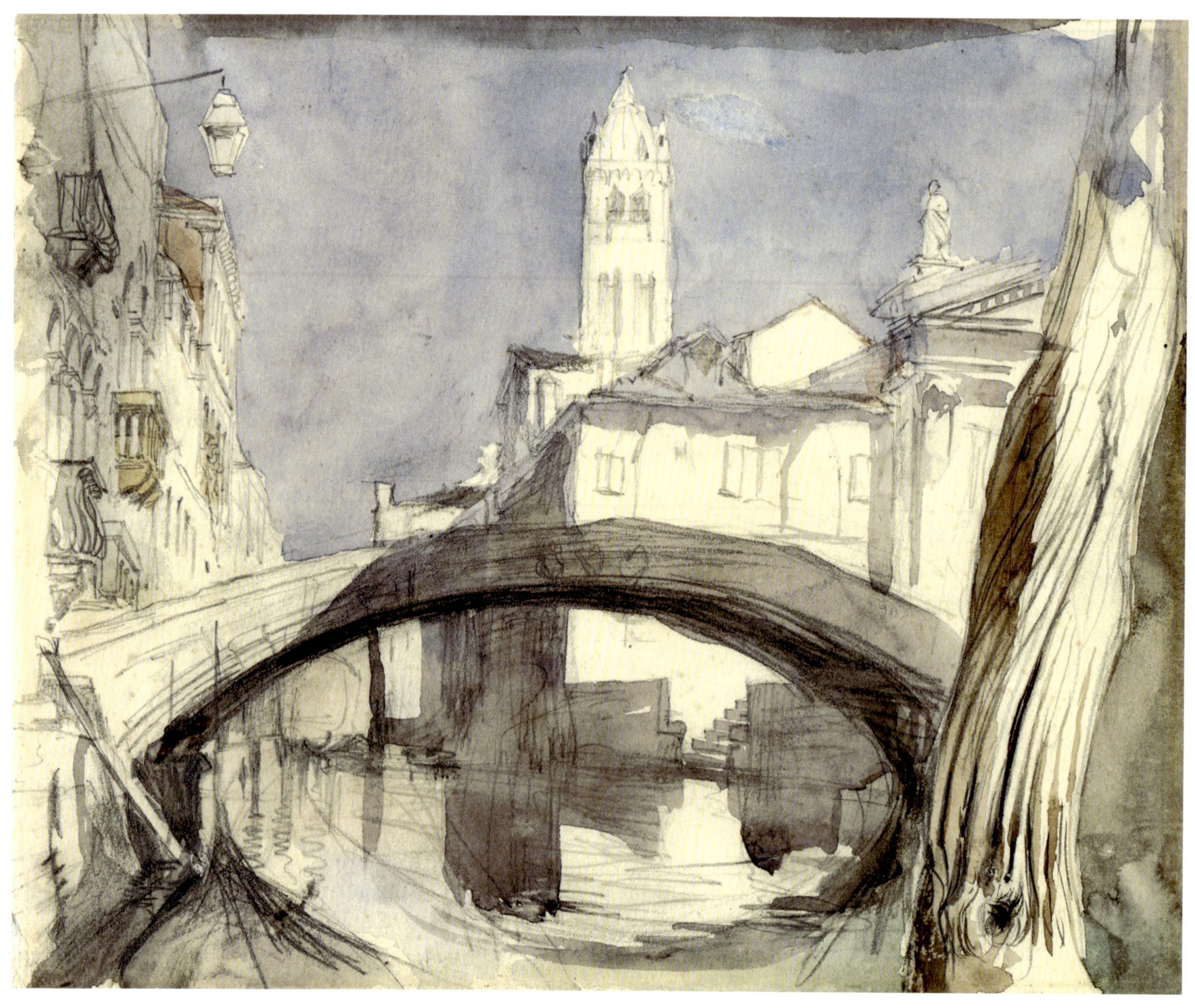

PONTE DEI PUGNI AT SANTA FOSCA, *circa* 1849
pencil, watercolour on paper, 180 × 223 mm
Lancaster, The Ruskin, Lancaster University, inv. 1996P1626

Wednesday January 17th, 1877

Yestarday found all manner of grand old things at the ponte del Paradiso and between it and the Rialto.

The Diaries of John Ruskin, vol. III, p. 931.

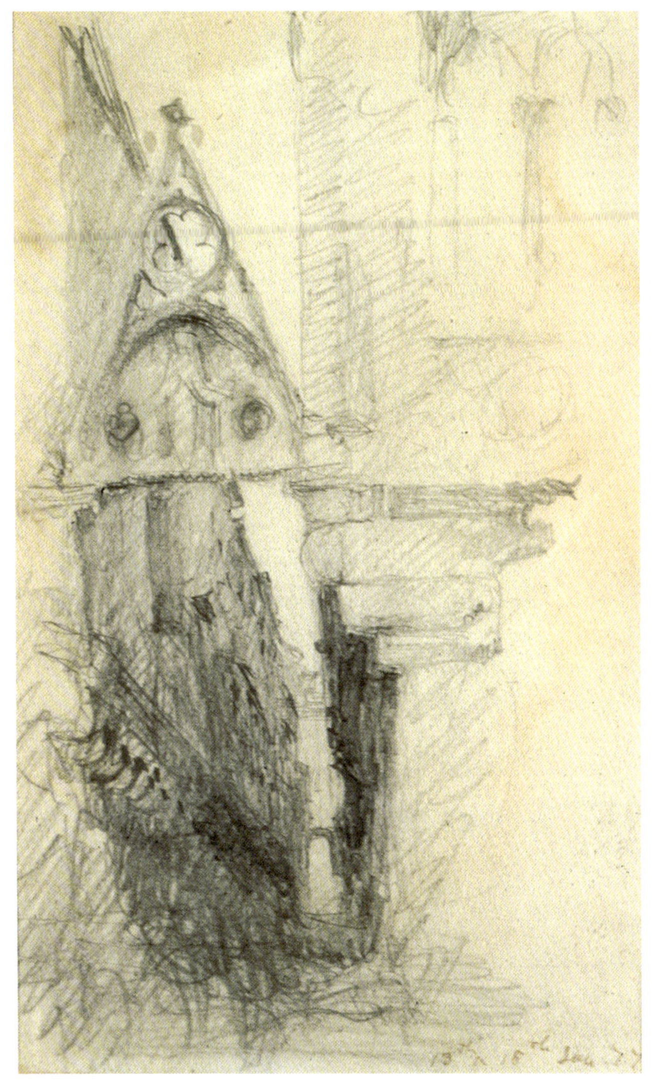

ARCHITECTURAL STUDIES (PONTE DEL PARADISO), 1877
ink and pencil on paper, 209 × 130 mm
London, South London Gallery Collection / Southwark Council
inv. GA0438

CAMPANILE

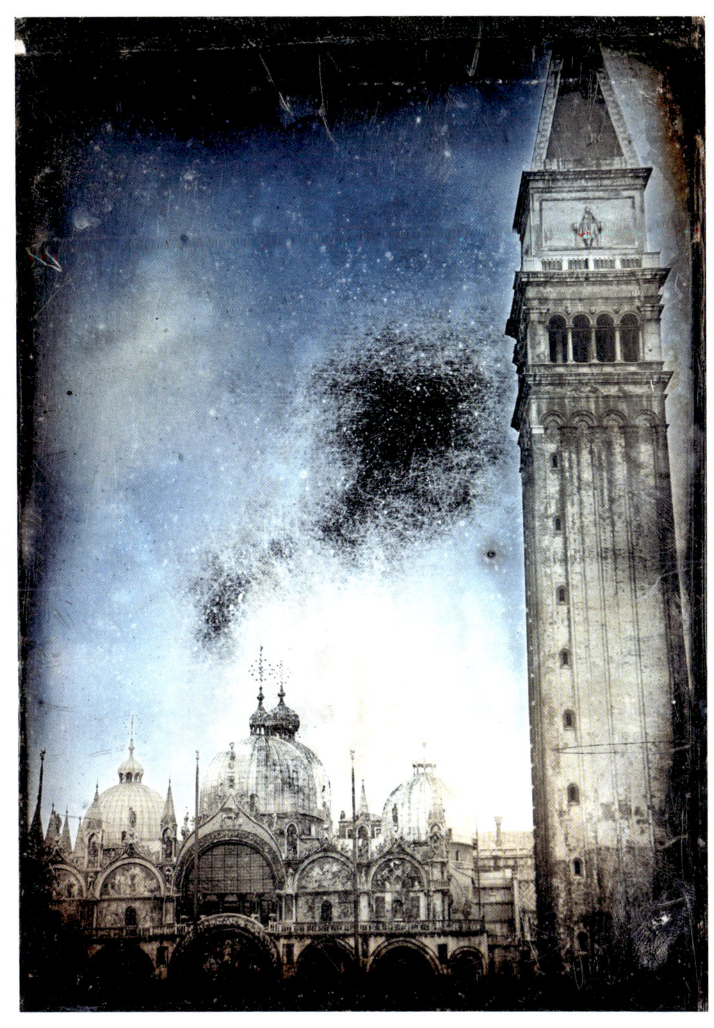

John Ruskin and John Hobbs (?)
ST. MARK'S AND THE CAMPANILE
circa 1850–52
half-plate daguerreotype, 162 × 121 mm
Courtesy of K&J Jacobson, UK

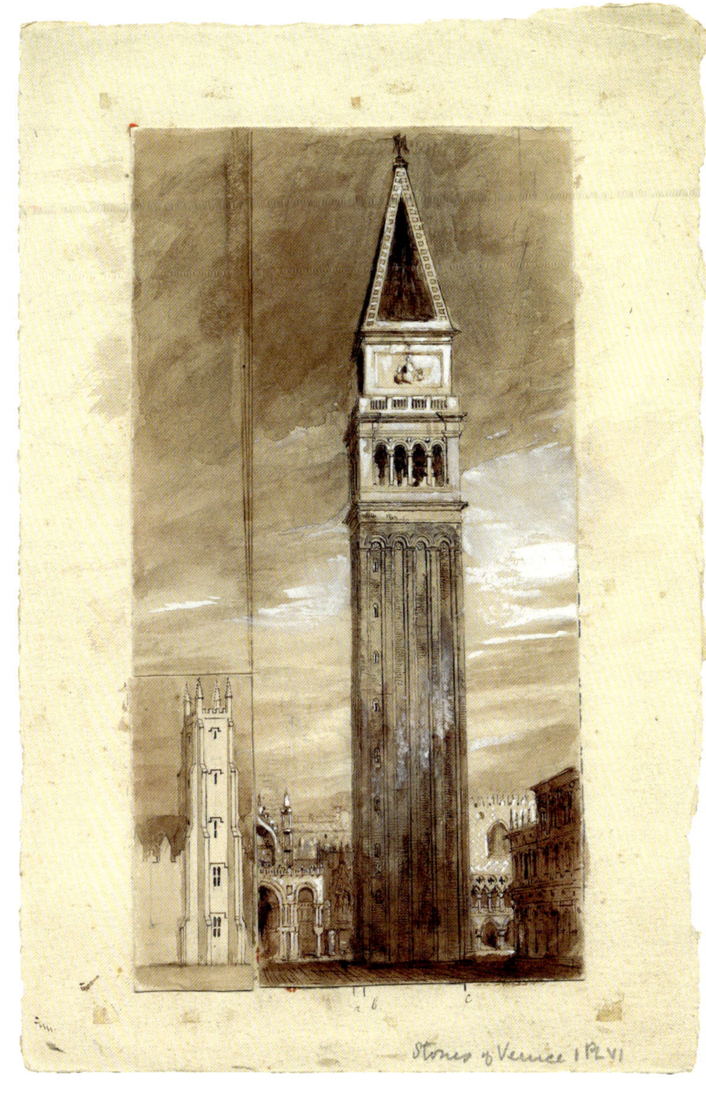

THE CAMPANILE, ST. MARK'S SQUARE; FIGURE AT CENTRE, BUILDING CASTING SHADOW ACROSS SQUARE AT R, BEYOND TOWER AND BUILDINGS, 1849–50
watercolour, white lead, pencil on grey paper, 163 × 126 mm
London, The British Museum, inv. 1946,1012.5

THE STONES OF VENICE: TYPES OF TOWERS, 1849–51
pencil, ink, ink wash, bodycolour on paper, 228 × 127 mm
inscription: "Stones of Venice I PL VI"
Lancaster, The Ruskin, Lancaster University, inv. 1996P2077

CA' / PALAZZO

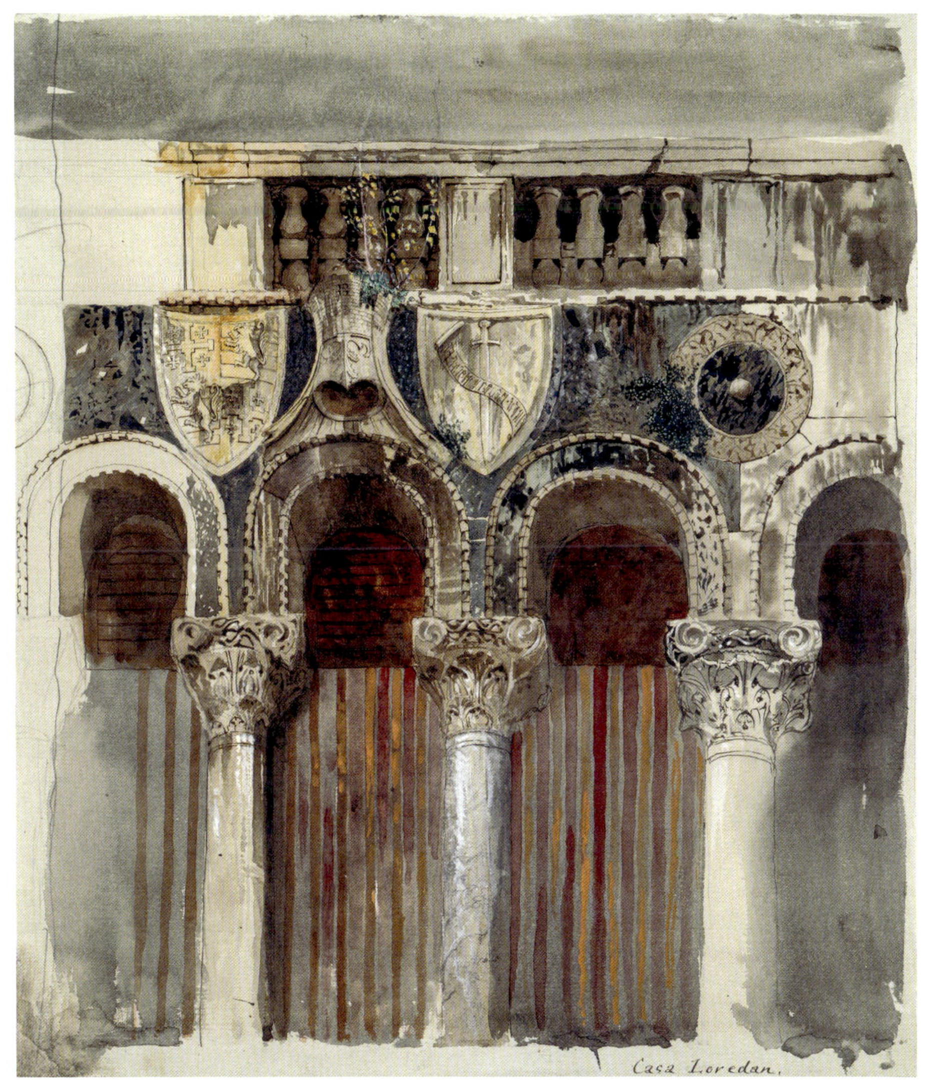

STUDY OF THE MARBLE INLAYING ON THE FRONT OF THE CASA LOREDAN, 1845
watercolour, bodycolour, pencil, ink on grey paper, 342 × 297 mm
inscription: "Casa Loredan"
Oxford, Ashmolean Museum, University of Oxford. Presented by John Ruskin to the Ruskin Drawing School (University of Oxford), 1875, inv. WA.RS.RUD.022

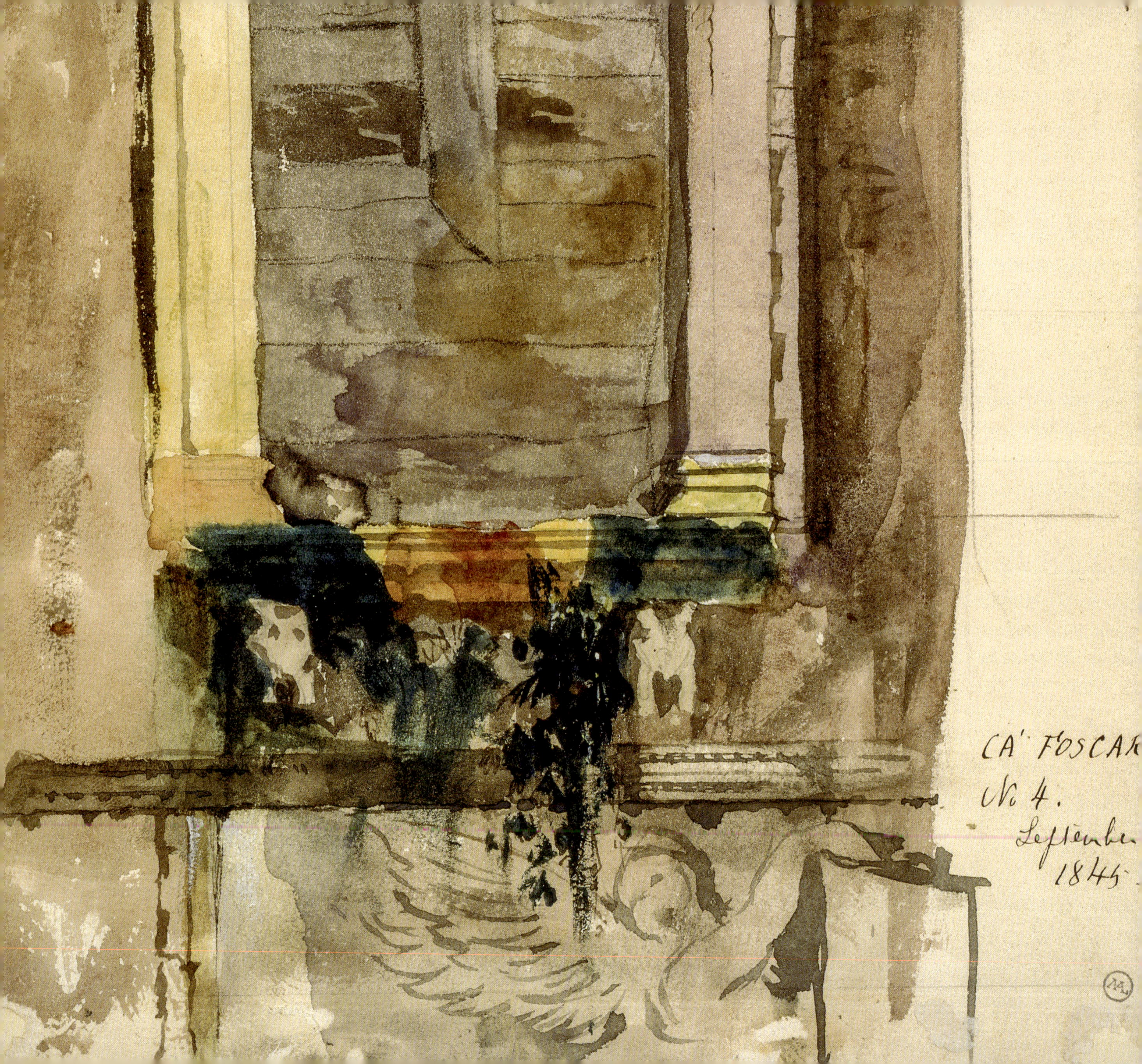
CA' FOSCAR
No. 4.
Septembe
1845

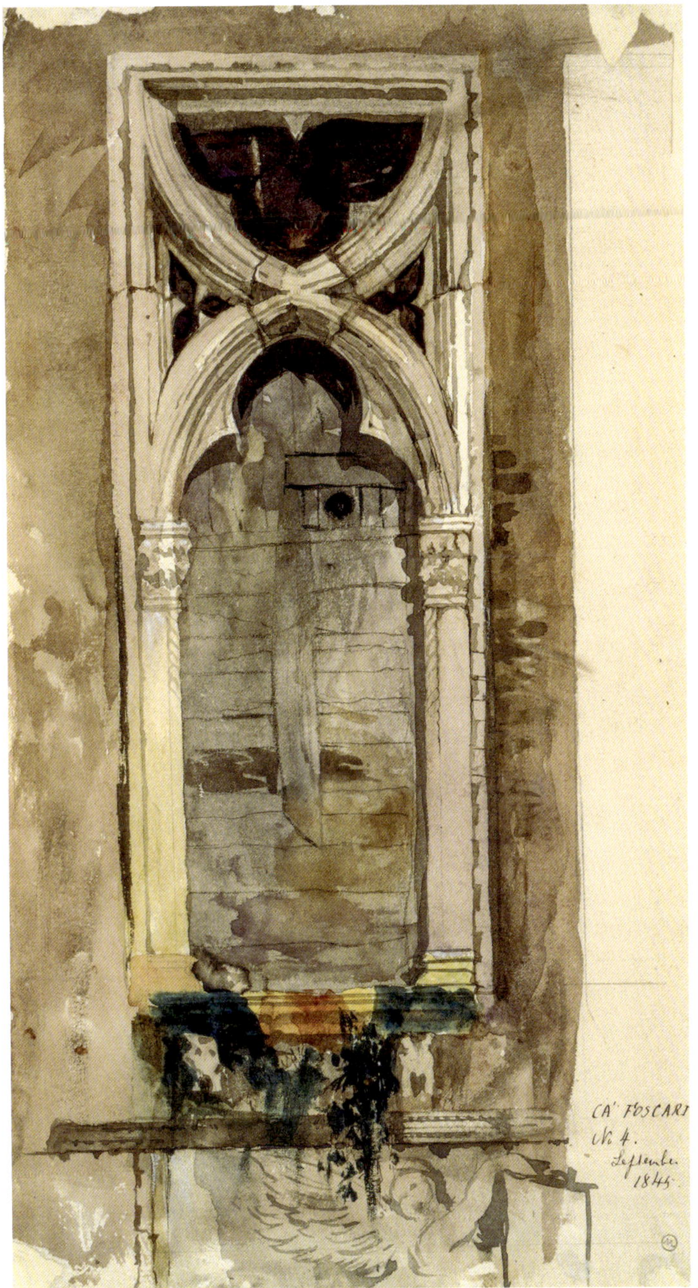

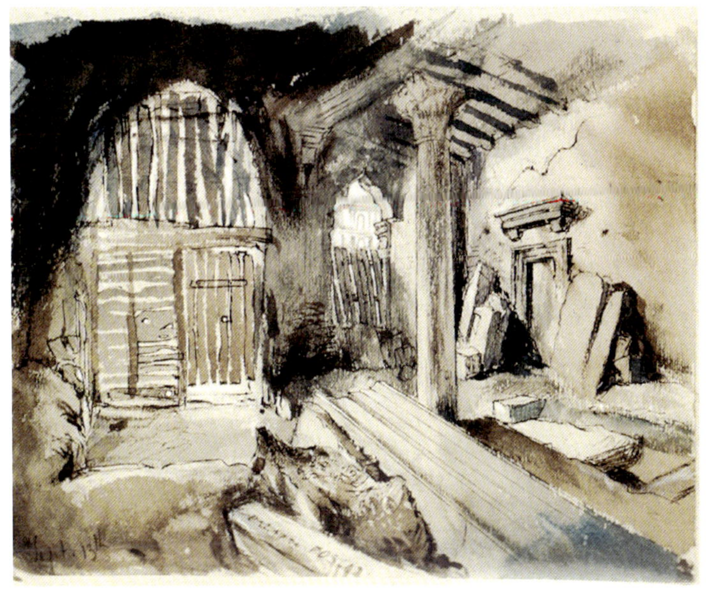

A WINDOW IN THE FOSCARI PALACE, 1845
pencil, watercolour on paper, 466 × 316 mm
inscription: "Ca' Foscari. No. 4. September 1845"
London, Victoria and Albert Museum, inv. D.1726-1908

ATRIUM OF CA' FOSCARI
FROM THE DIARY OF JOHN RUSKIN, September 13rd, 1845
pencil, ink, wash and bodycolour su carta, h. 245 mm
Lancaster, The Ruskin, Lancaster University, inv. MS 5a

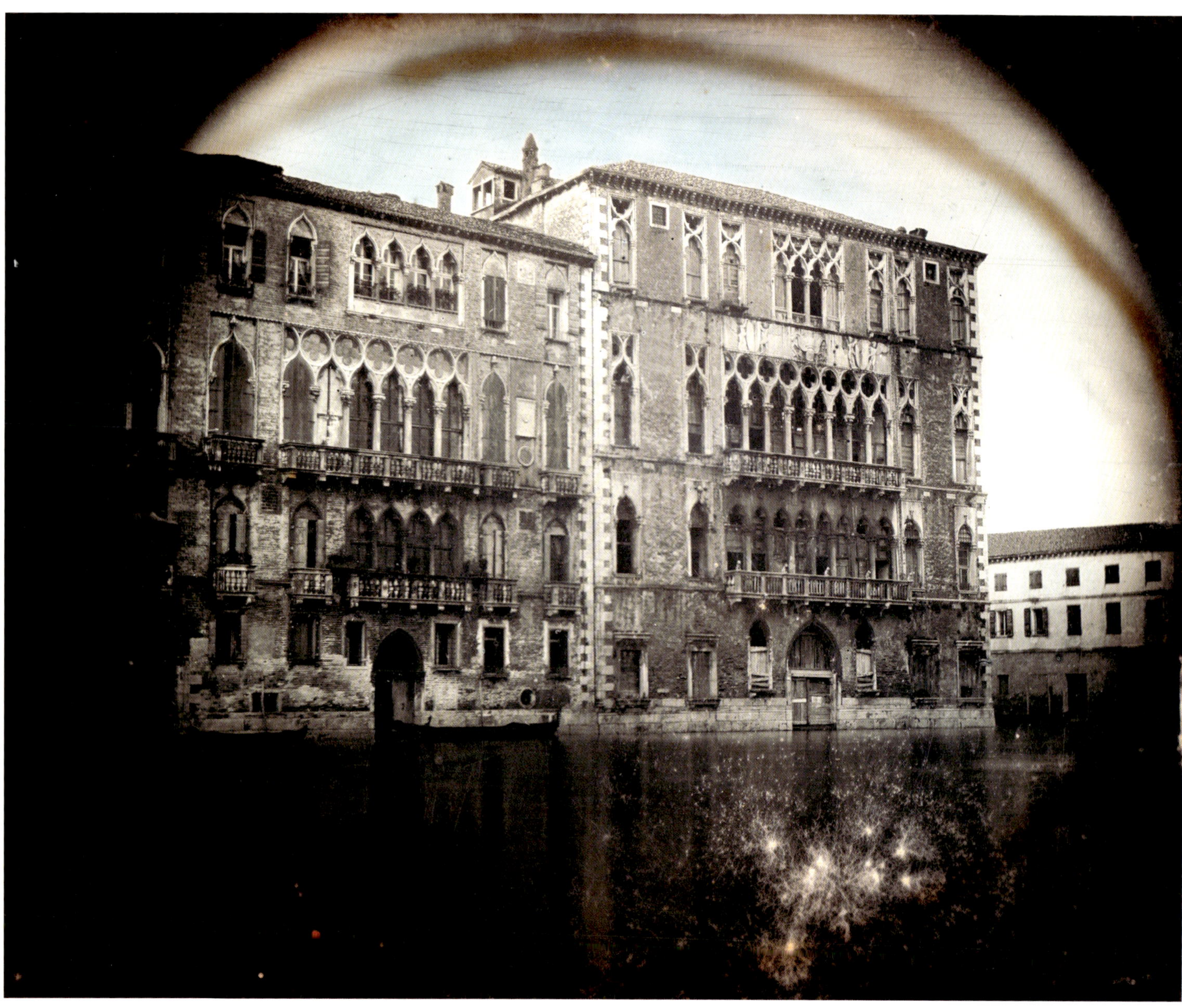

Venice, Tuesday, October 7th, 1845

My Dearest Father
... I have been lucky enough to get from a poor Frenchm[an] here, said to be in distress, some most beautiful, though small, Daguerreotypes of the palaces I have been trying to draw – and certainly Daguerreotypes taken by this glorious light are glorious things. It is very nearly the same thing as carrying off the palace itself – every chip of stone & stain is there – and of course, there is no mistake about *proportions*. I am very much delighted with these and am going to have some more made of pet bits. It is a noble invention, say what they will of it, and any one who has worked and blundered and stammered as I have for four days, and then sees the thing he has been trying to do so long in vain, *done* perfectly & faultlessly in half a minute, won't abuse it afterwards.

Harold Shapiro (ed.), *Ruskin in Italy. Letters to His Parents*, 143.

Le Cavalier Iller
THE GRAND CANAL AND CASA FOSCARI, *circa* 1845
daguerreotype, 77 × 95 mm
Courtesy of K&J Jacobson, UK

September 23rd, 1845

My Dearest Father,
You cannot imagine what an unhappy day I spent yesterday before the Casa d'Oro, vainly attempting to draw it while the workmen were hammering it down before my face. It would have put me to my hardest possible shifts at any rate, for it is intolerably difficult, & the intricacy of it as a study of colour inconceivable – if I had had the whole grand canal to myself to do it, it would have been no more than I wanted – but fancy trying to work while one s[ees] the cursed plasterers hauling up beams & dashing i[n the] old walls & shattering the mouldings, & pulling b[arge]s across your gondola bows & driving you here & there, up & down & across, and all the while with the sense that *now* one's art is not enough to be of the slightest service, but that in ten years more one might have done such glorious things. Venice has never yet been painted as she should, never, & to see the thing *just* in in one's grasp, & snatched away by these 'porci battizati'.... It is too bad, far too bad. The beauty of the fragments left is beyond all I conceived, & just as I am becoming able to appreciate it destroyed before my face. That foul son of a deal board, Canaletti – to have lived in the middle of it all & left us *nothing*.

Harold Shapiro (ed.), *Ruskin in Italy. Letters to His Parents*, 209.

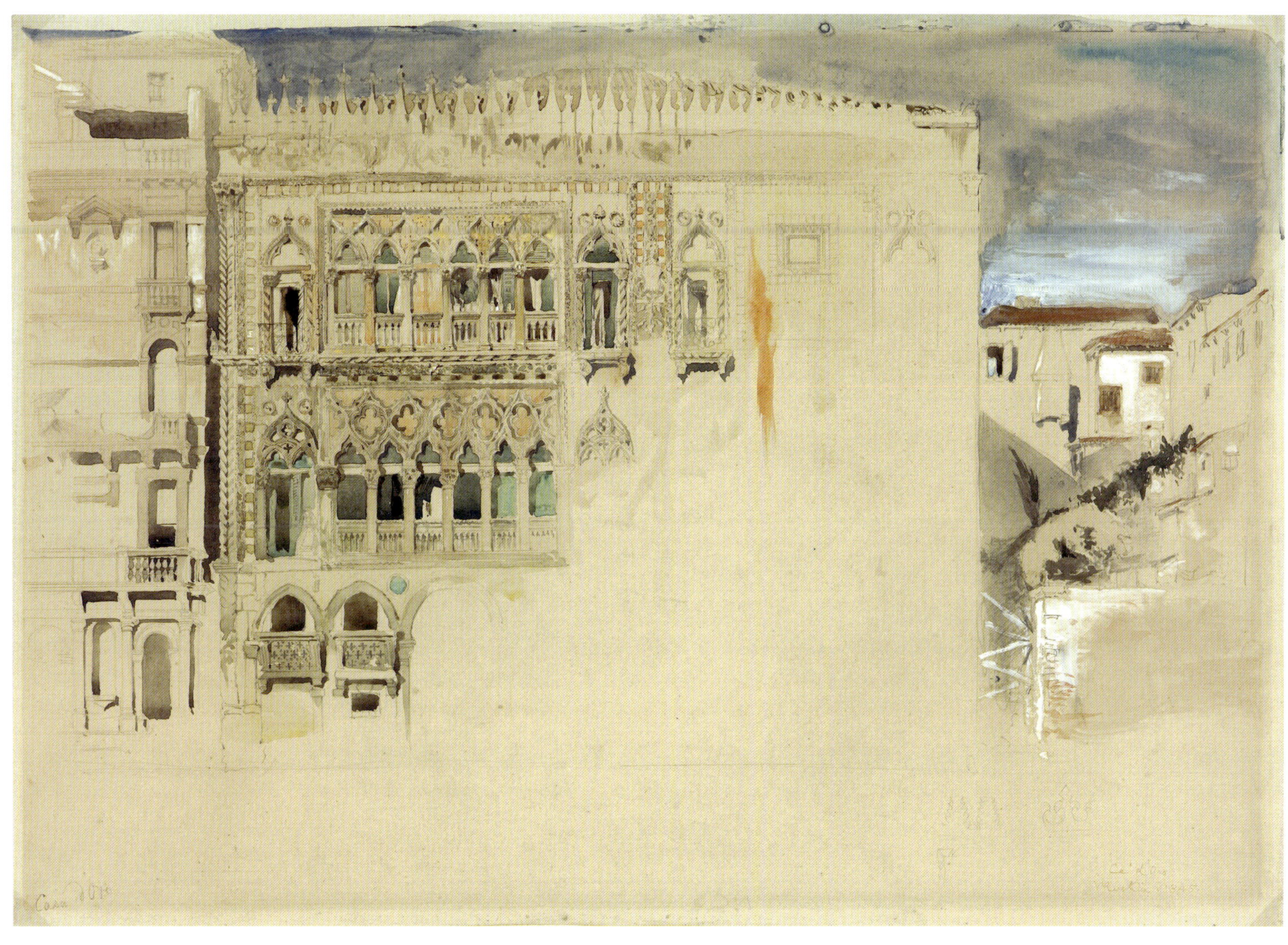

CA' D'ORO, 1845
pencil, watercolour, bodycolour on grey paper, *circa* 330 × 476 mm
inscription: "Casa d'Oro; Ca' d'Oro"
Lancaster, The Ruskin, Lancaster University, inv. 1996P1590

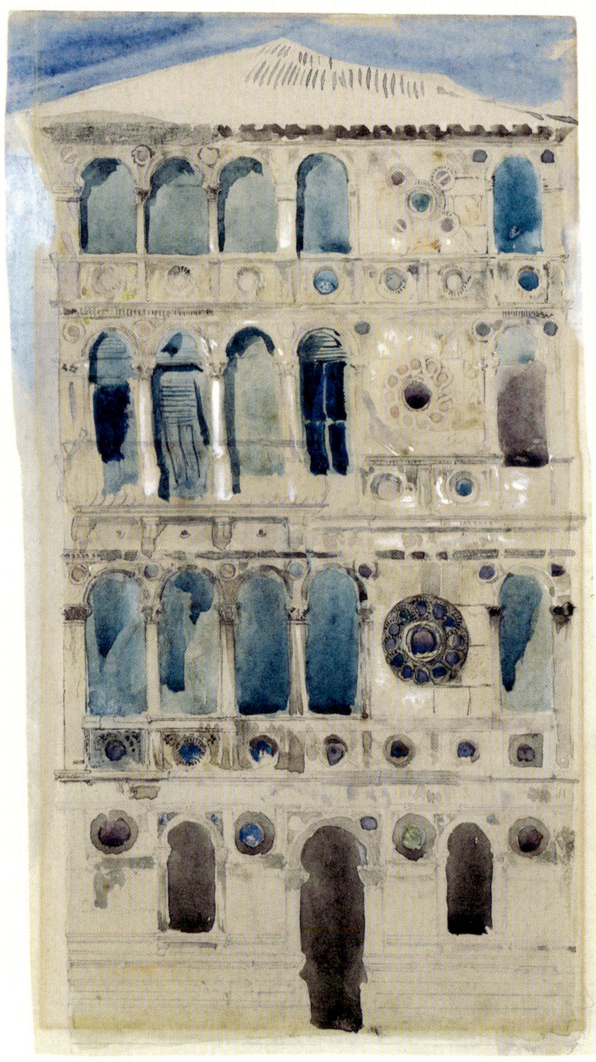

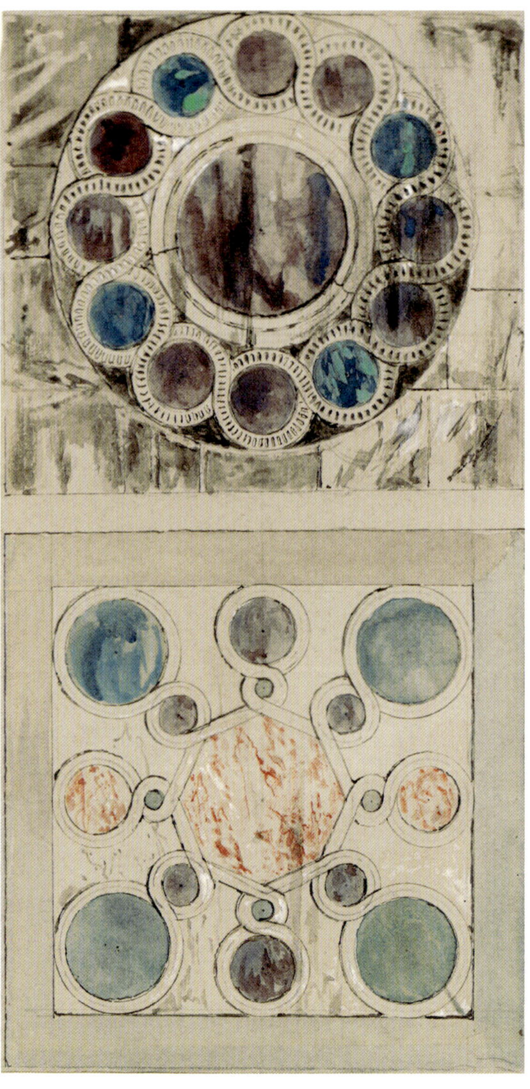

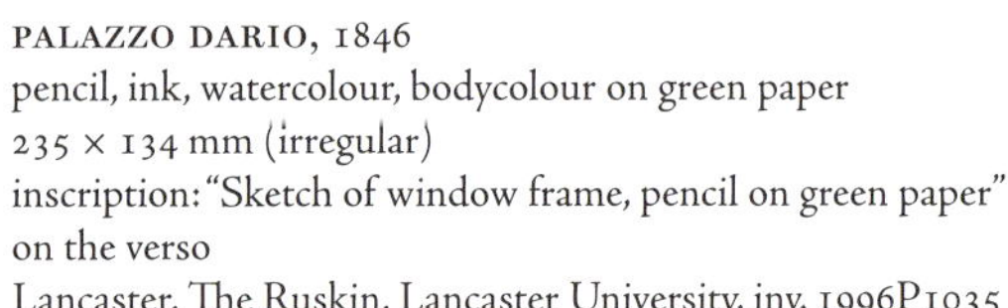

PALAZZO DARIO, 1846
pencil, ink, watercolour, bodycolour on green paper
235 × 134 mm (irregular)
inscription: "Sketch of window frame, pencil on green paper" on the verso
Lancaster, The Ruskin, Lancaster University, inv. 1996P1035

THE STONES OF VENICE: WALL VEIL DECORATION AT CASA DARIO AND CASA TREVISAN, 1849–51
ink, watercolour, bodycolour on paper, 200 × 88 mm
Lancaster, The Ruskin, Lancaster University, inv. 1996P1069

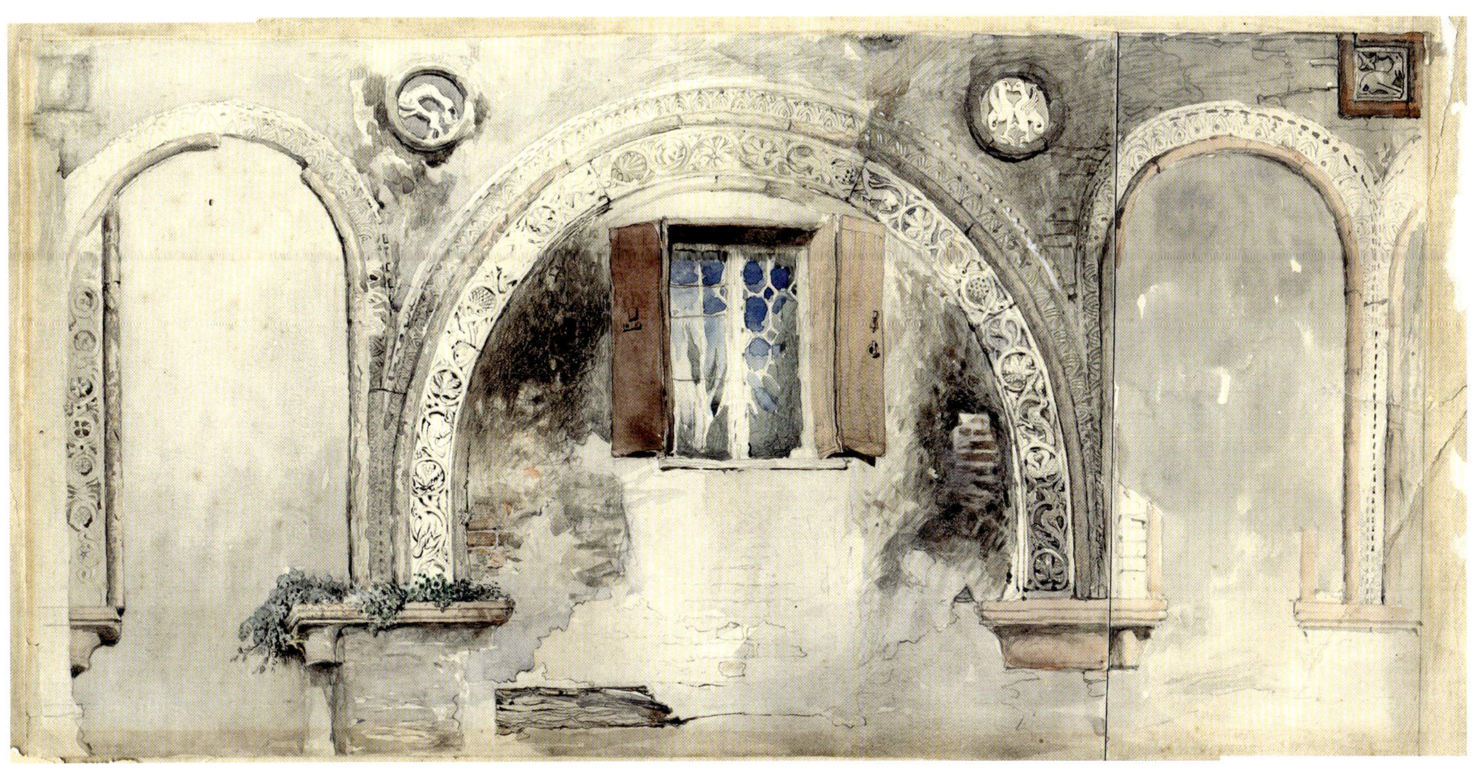

BYZANTINE RUIN, RIO DI CA' FOSCARI. STILTED ARCHIVOLTS, 1849
pencil, watercolour and bodycolour, 242 × 482 mm
Lancaster, The Ruskin, Lancaster University, inv. 1996P1583

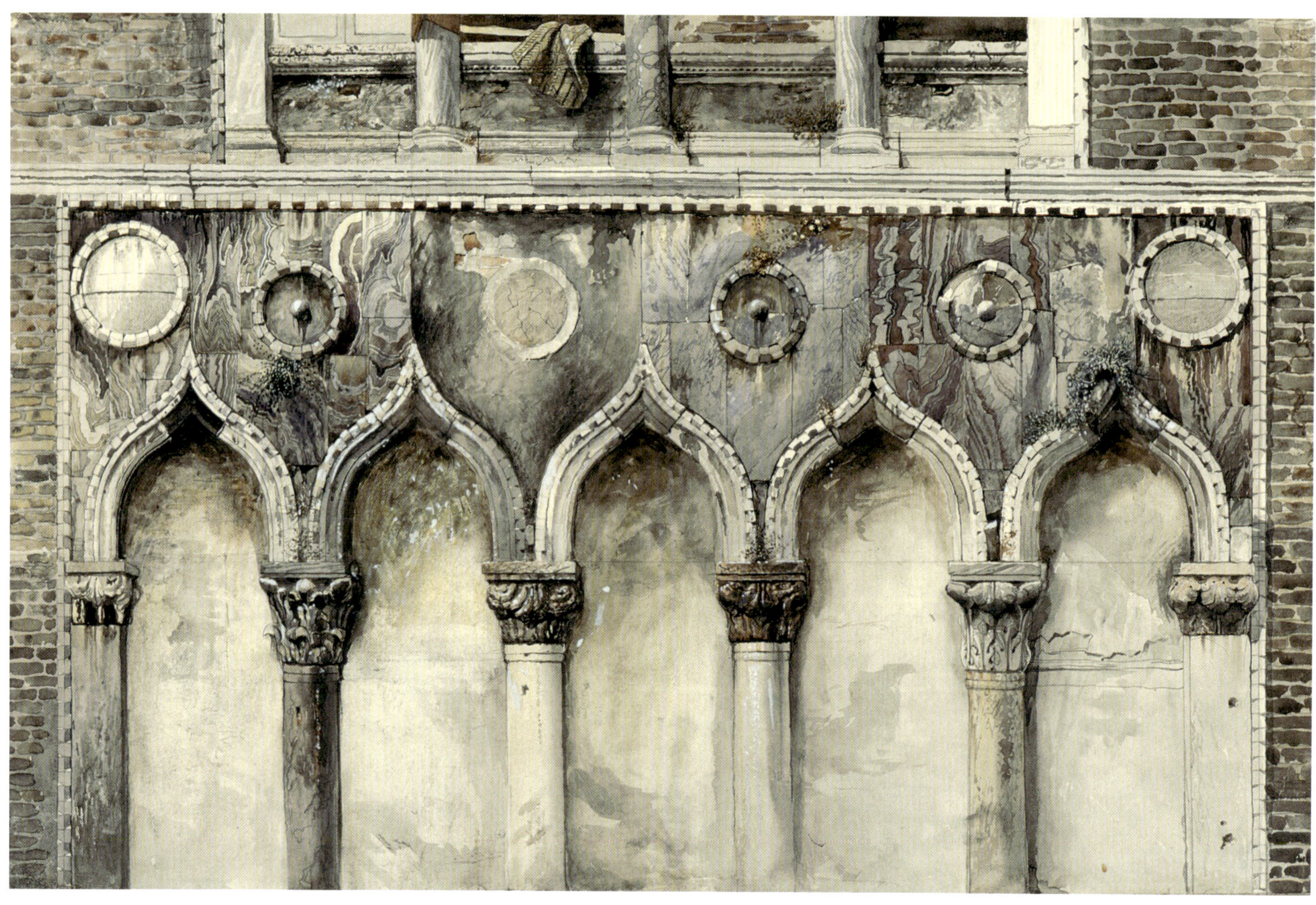

WINDOWS OF THE PALAZZO ZORZI BON
RIO DI SAN SEVERO, *circa* 1850
Watercolour, bodycolour and pencil on paper
318 × 409 mm
Private collection

PART OF THE PALAZZO PRIULI, *circa* 1852
pencil, watercolour, bodycolour on wove paper
432 × 277 mm
Oxford, Ashmolean Museum, University of Oxford, presented by John Ruskin to the Ruskin Drawing School (University of Oxford), 1875, inv. WA.RS.ED.210

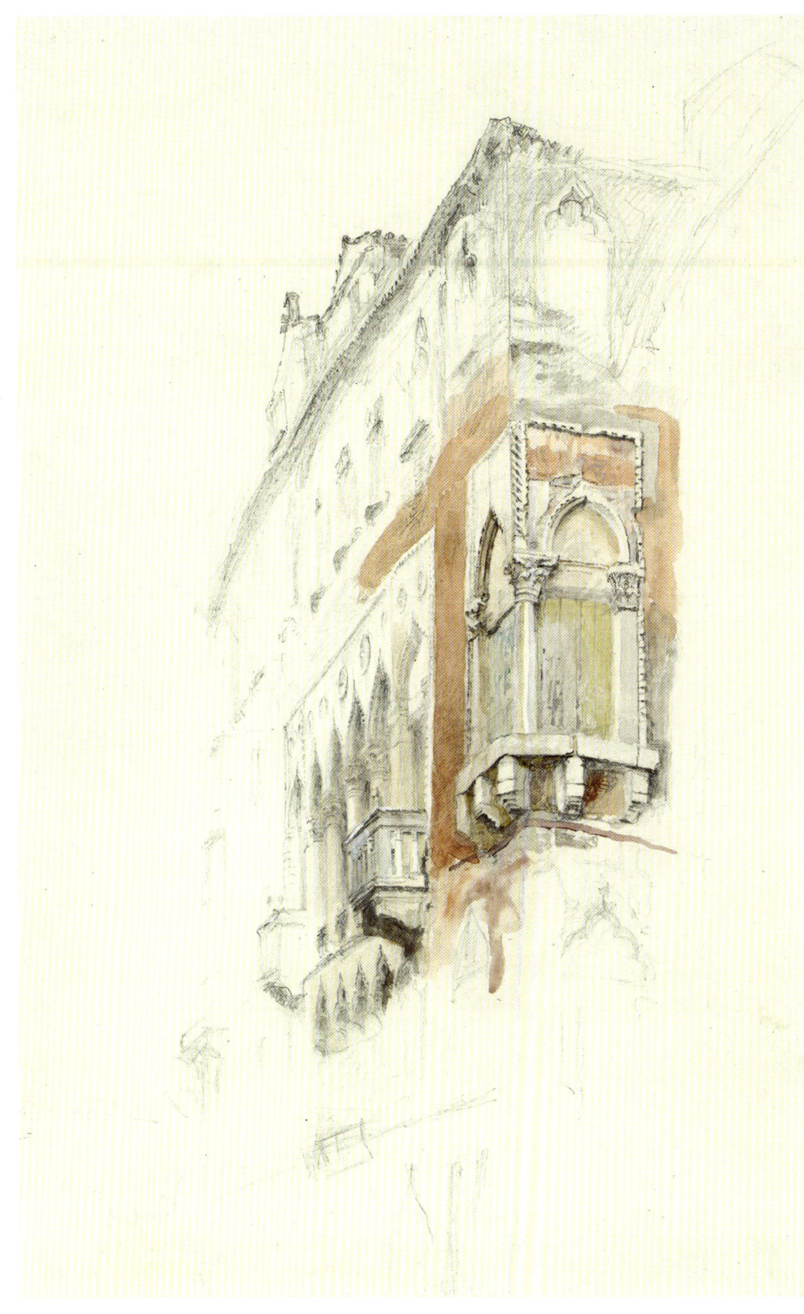

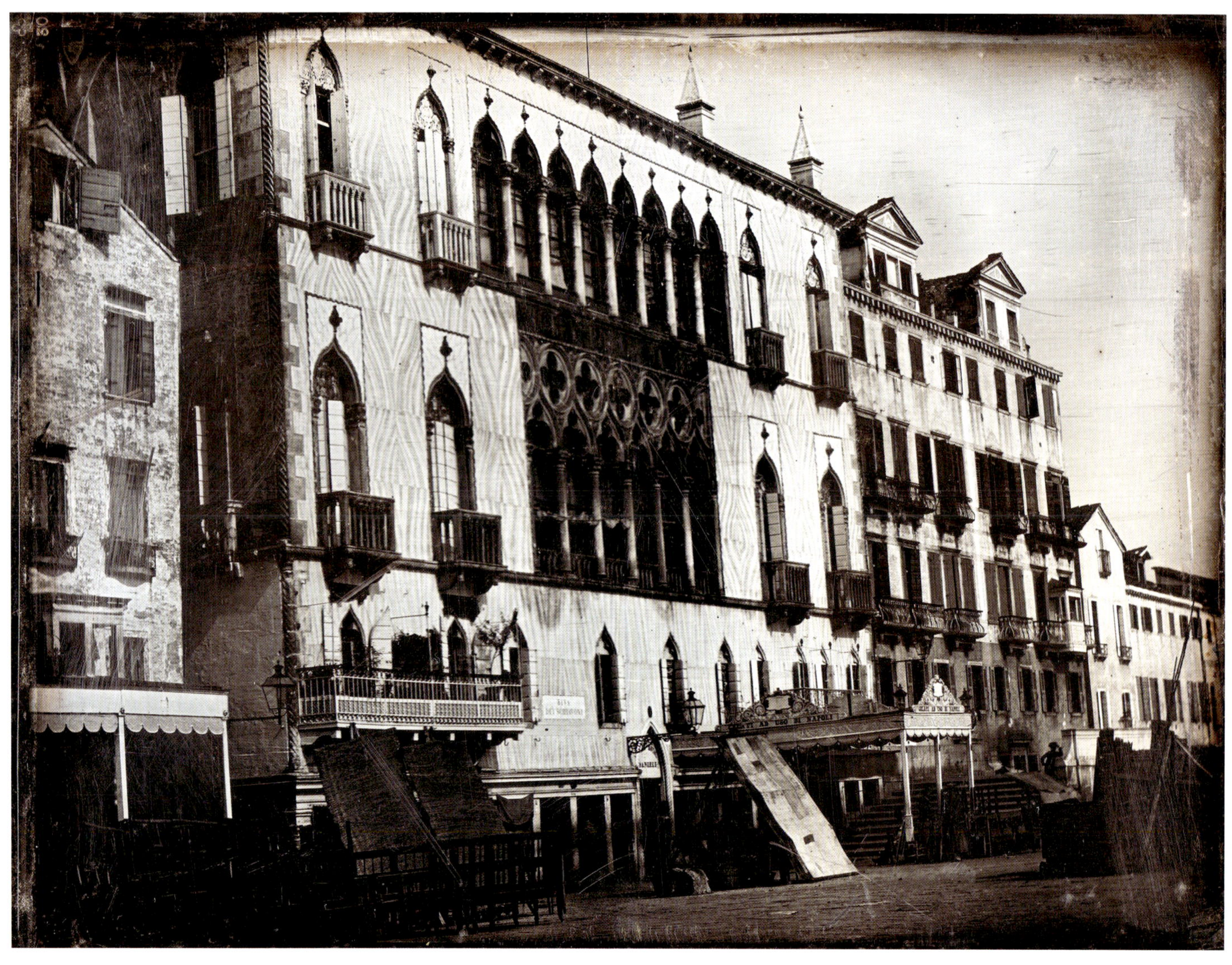

John Ruskin and Le Cavalier Iller
PALAZZO DANIELI, *circa* 1850–51
half-plate daguerreotype, 121 × 162 mm
Courtesy of K&J Jacobson, UK

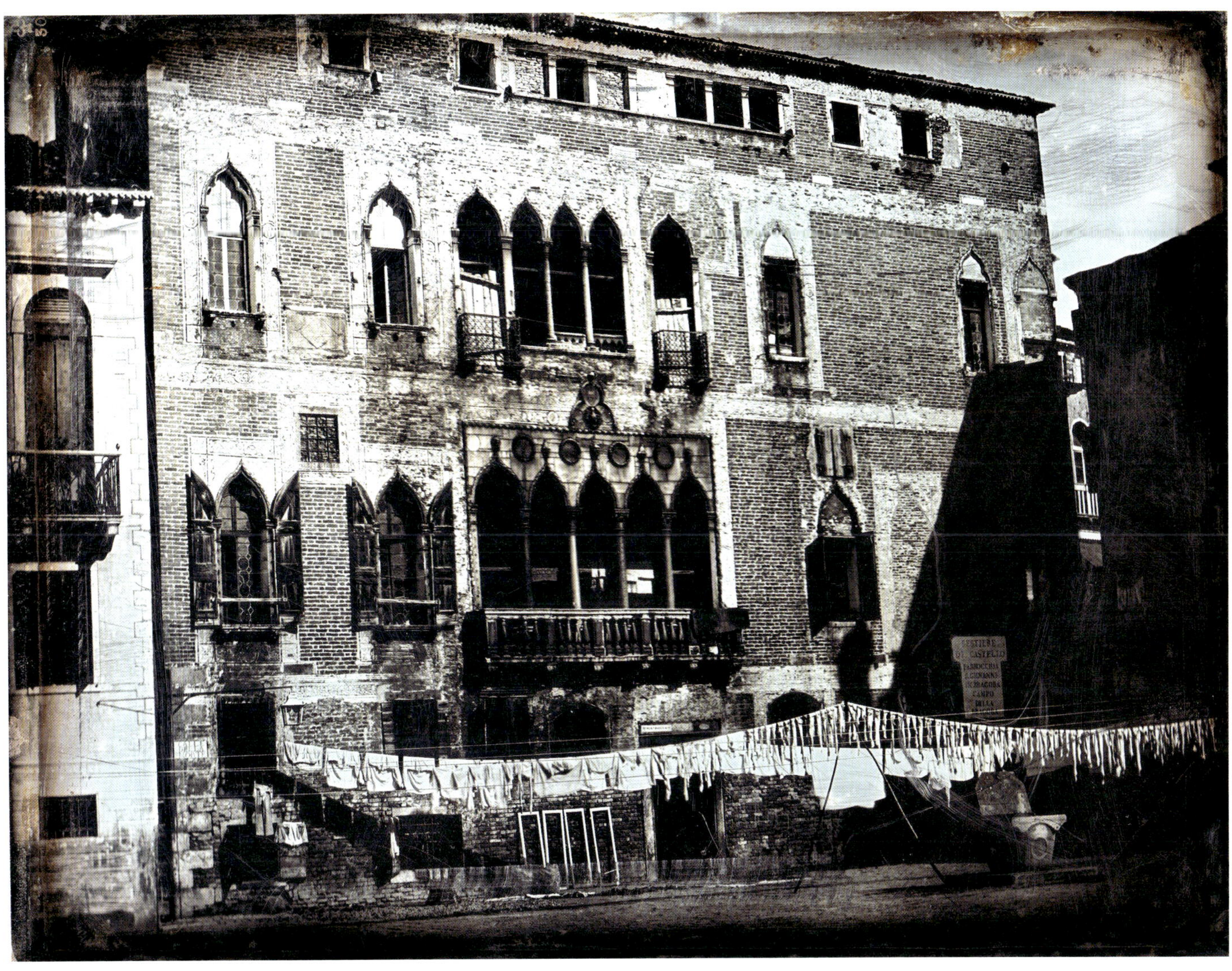

John Ruskin and Le Cavalier Iller
PALAZZO GRITTI-BADOER, 1846–52
half-plate daguerreotype, 121 × 161 mm
Courtesy of K&J Jacobson, UK

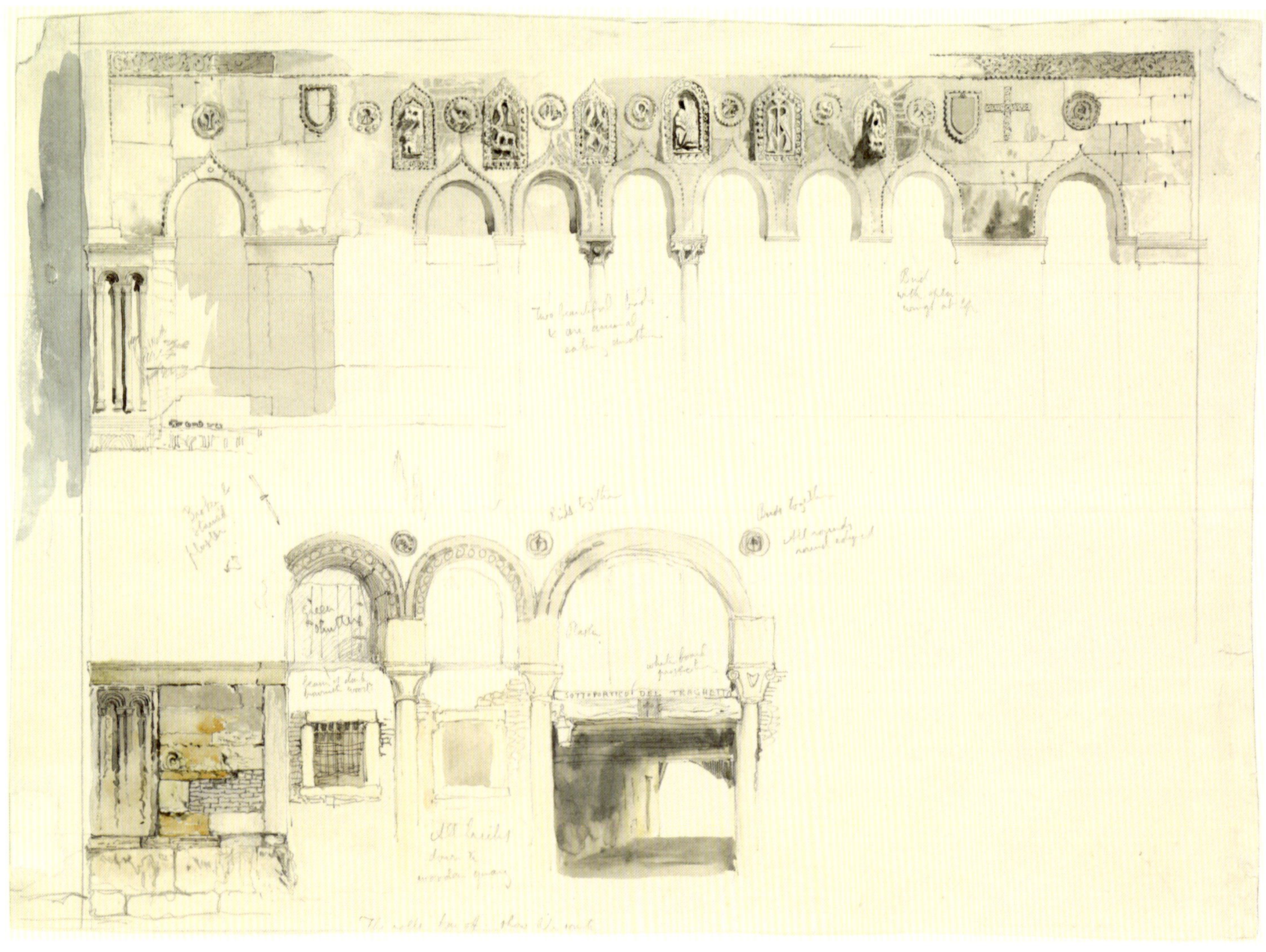

DETAILS OF FAÇADE, PALAZZO DA MOSTO, 1852
watercolour, pencil on paper, 345 × 481 mm
Birmingham, Birmingham Museums Trust / Birmingham Museum & Art Gallery, presented by Mrs Arthur Severn, 1902, inv. 1902P12

THE PALAZZO BRANDOLINI, THE CA' FOSCARI, AND THE CAMPANILE OF THE FRARI, AT THE JUNCTION OF THE GRAND CANAL, 1879
pencil, watercolour, bodycolour on cream paper, 490 × 320 mm
inscription: "Casa Foscari and Frari – Left off beaten. 1878 Fin.ed JRuskin Brant. 1879"
Private collection

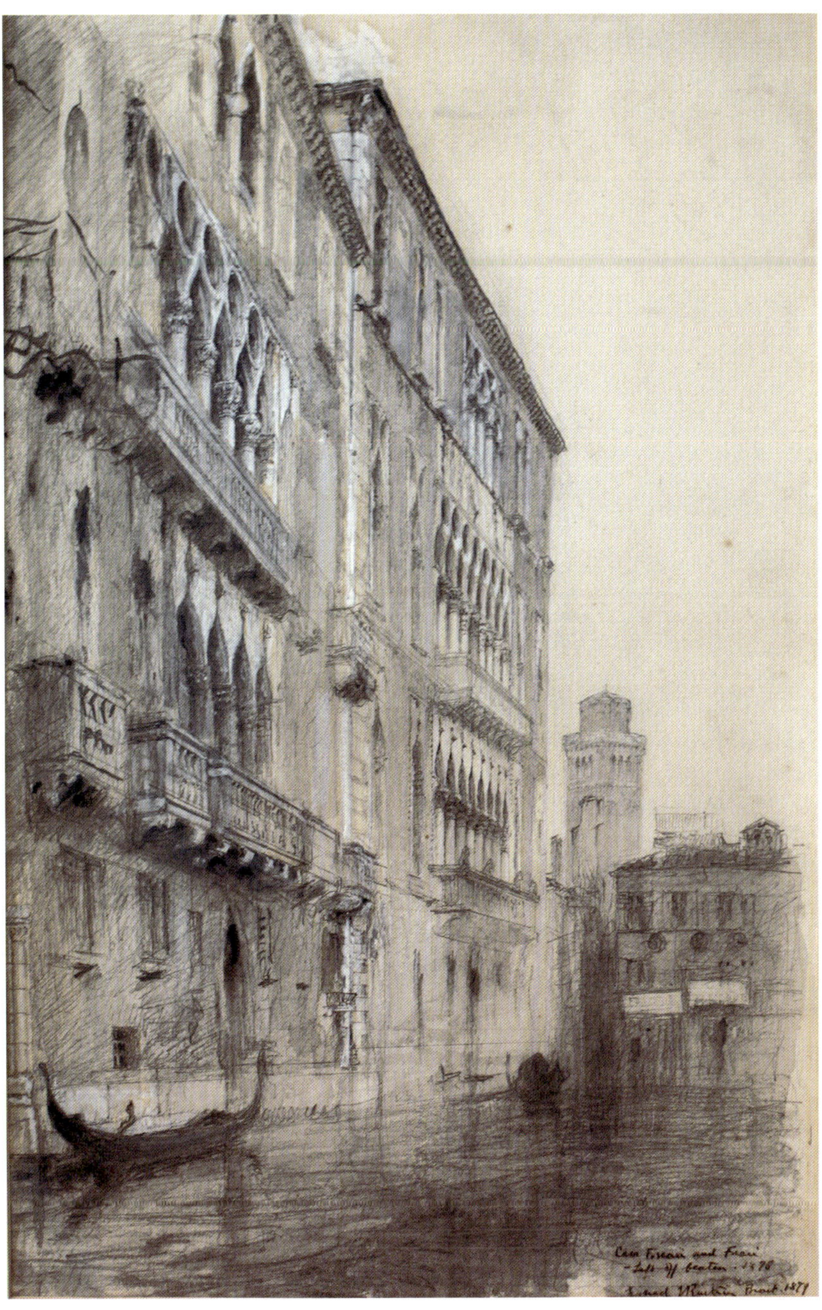

DUCAL PALACE

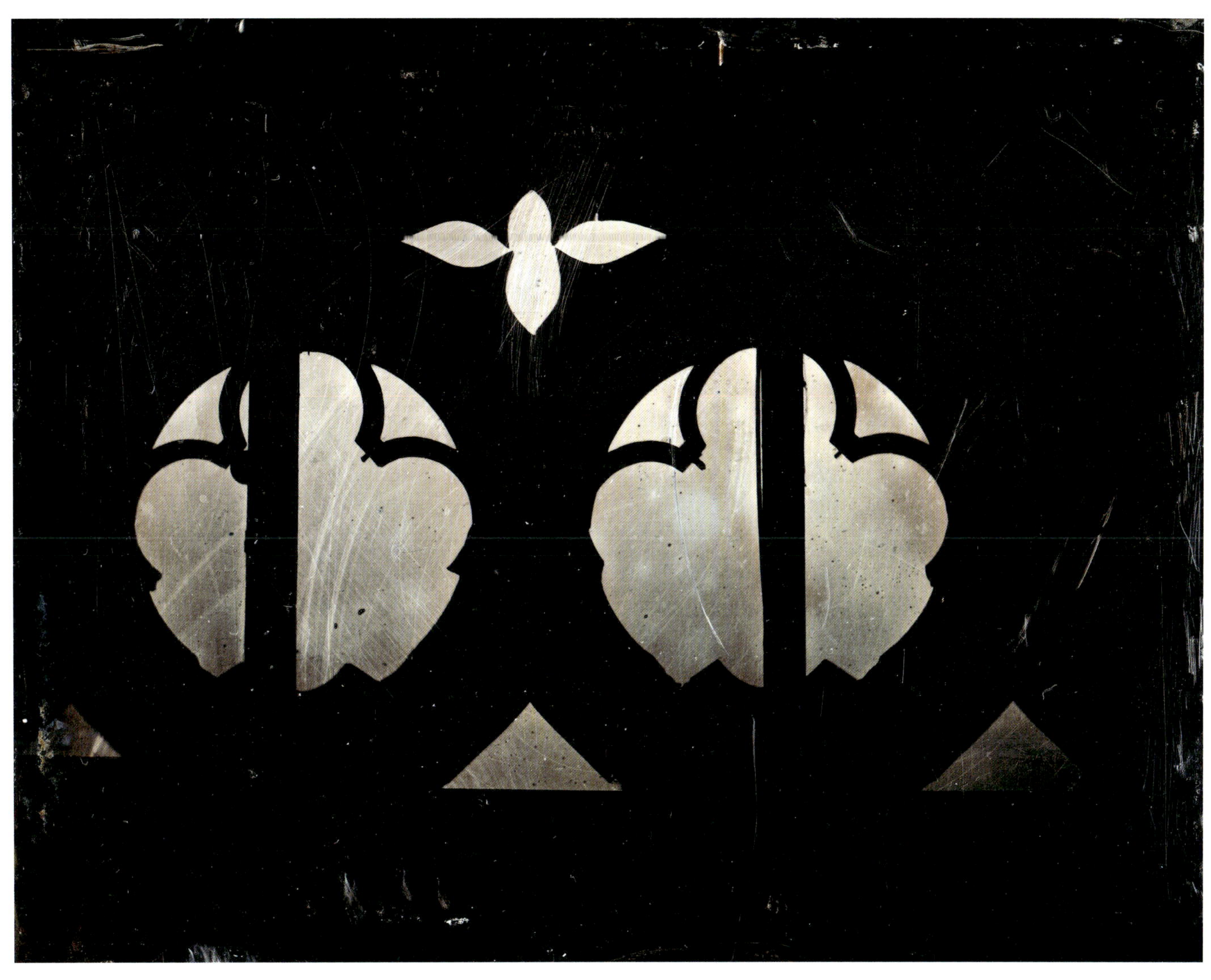

John Ruskin and John Hobbs
THE DUCAL PALACE SOUTH FACADE, "EASTERN WINDOWS" TRACERY
LOOKING OUT TOWARDS THE LAGOON, *circa* 1849
daguerreotype, 76 × 101 mm
Courtesy of K&J Jacobson, UK

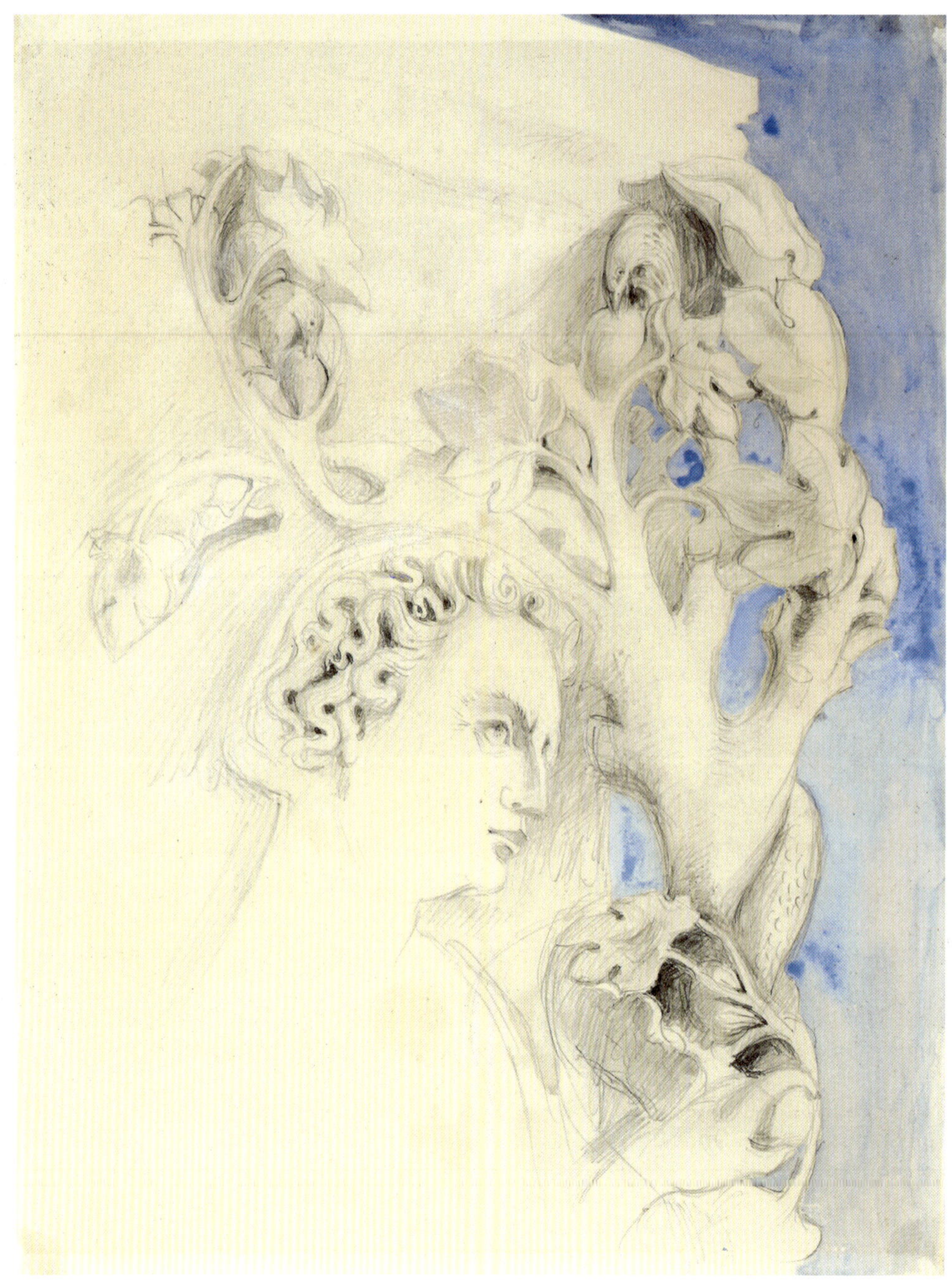

May 14th 1841

I wonder why two of the chief corner stones of the Doge's palace should be representations of human weakness? That turning from the quay into the piazzetta is Adam and Eve stealing the apple – the tree rich in the angle – that turning down the canal is Noah and his sons.

May 15th 1841

Noah pulling grapes with one hand from the vine – here also forming the angle – and upsetting his cup with the other; Shem and Ham round the corner, over the bridge of sighs canal. Japheth forming a detached decoration farther down, lifting his hands in great astonishment. The angle next to the St. Jean d'Acre columns is the judgment of Solomon – the richest group, but wanting the foliage. It is an awfully hot night and I've been working all day finishing my drawings – but there is always something or other on the way so I will try to write on.

The Diaries of John Ruskin, vol. 1, 187–88.

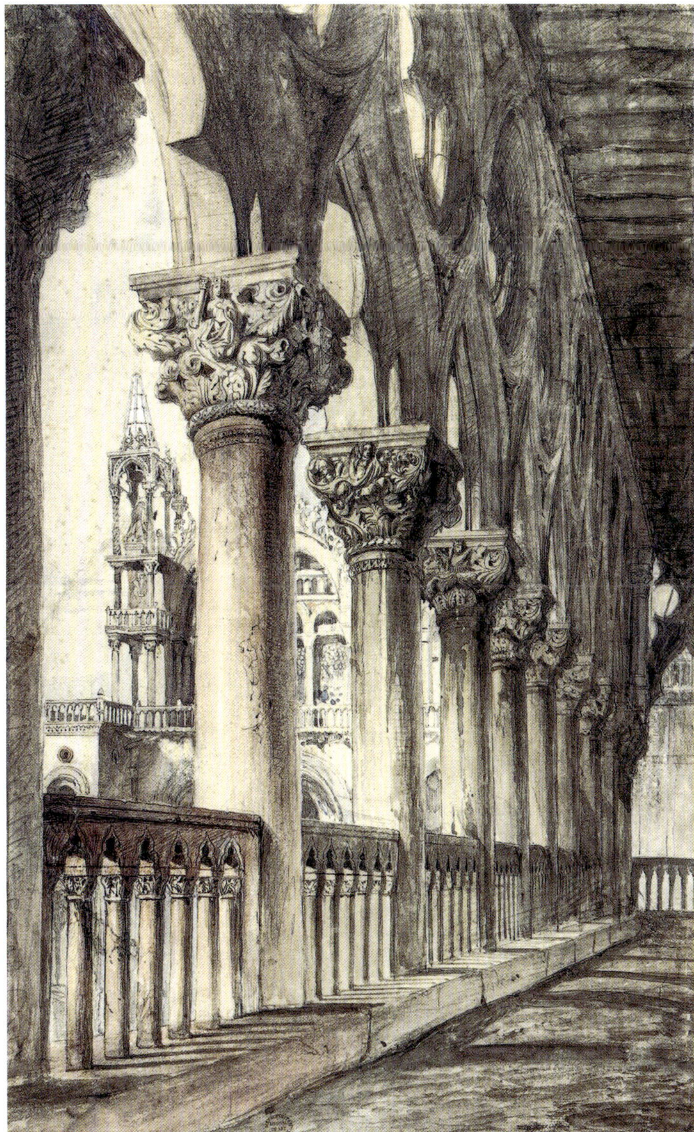

FACADE OF THE DOGE'S PALACE, HEAD OF ADAM, *circa* 1845
watercolour and pencil on paper, 344 × 265 mm
Manchester, Manchester Art Gallery, inv. 1918.475

LOGGIA OF PALAZZO DUCALE, 1849–50
watercolour over graphite, 460 × 290 mm
New York, The Metropolitan Museum of Art
inv. 08.227.39, Rogers Fund, 1908

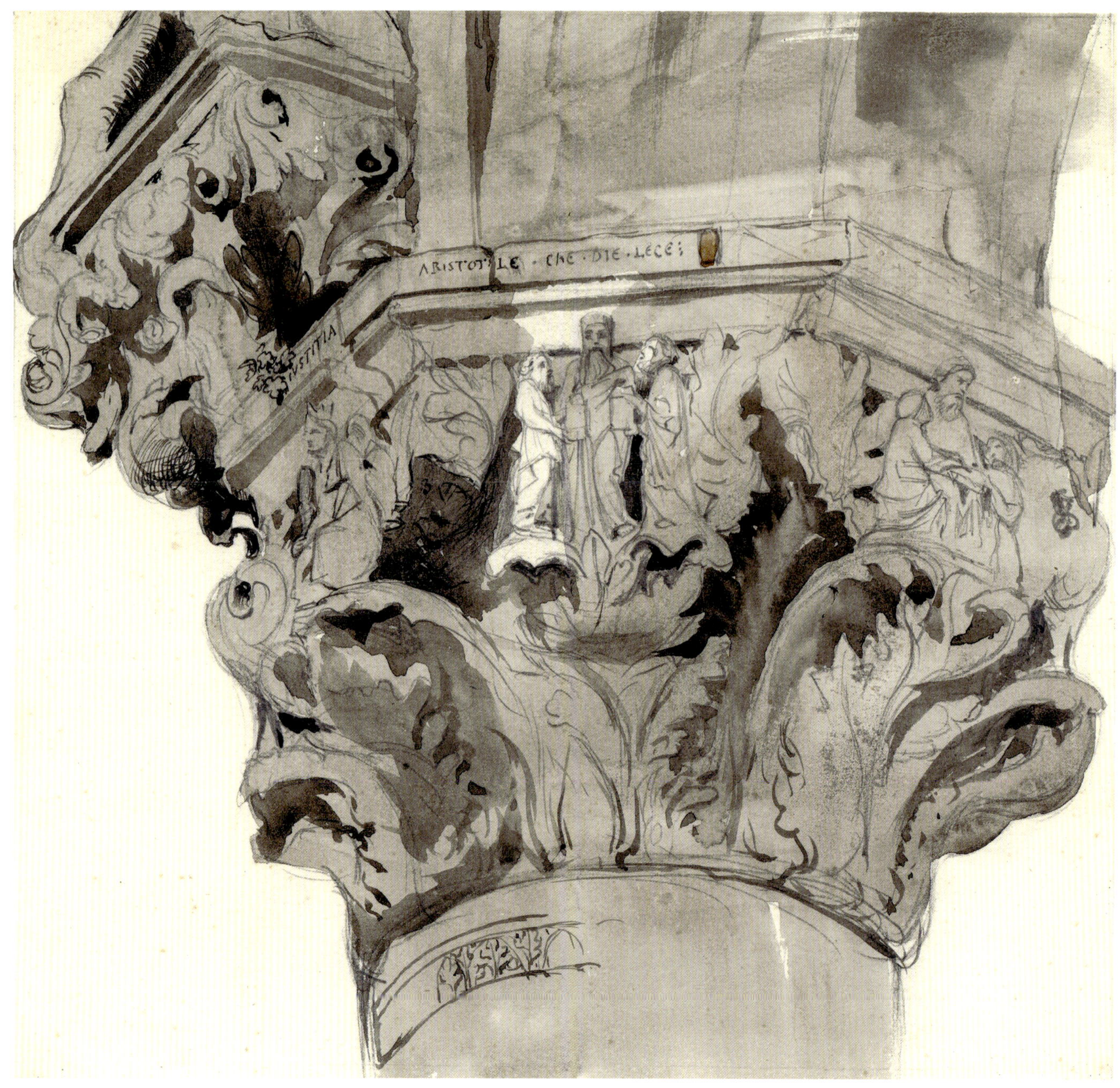
IUSTITIA
ARISTOT LE · CHE · DIE · LEGE:

DOGE'S PALACE: 36TH CAPITAL, 1849–52
pencil, ink, ink wash on paper, 223 × 235 mm
inscription: "IUSTITIA ARISTOTILE CHE DIE LEGE"
Lancaster, The Ruskin, Lancaster University, inv. 1996P1601

CAPITAL OF LOGGIA, *circa* 1850
watercolour, pencil on paper, 314 × 235 mm
inscription: "Venice, Capital of Loggia John Ruskin"
Kendal, Abbot Hall, Lakeland Arts Trust, inv. AH1954/80
bequeathed by Mr Eric Nicholson, 1980

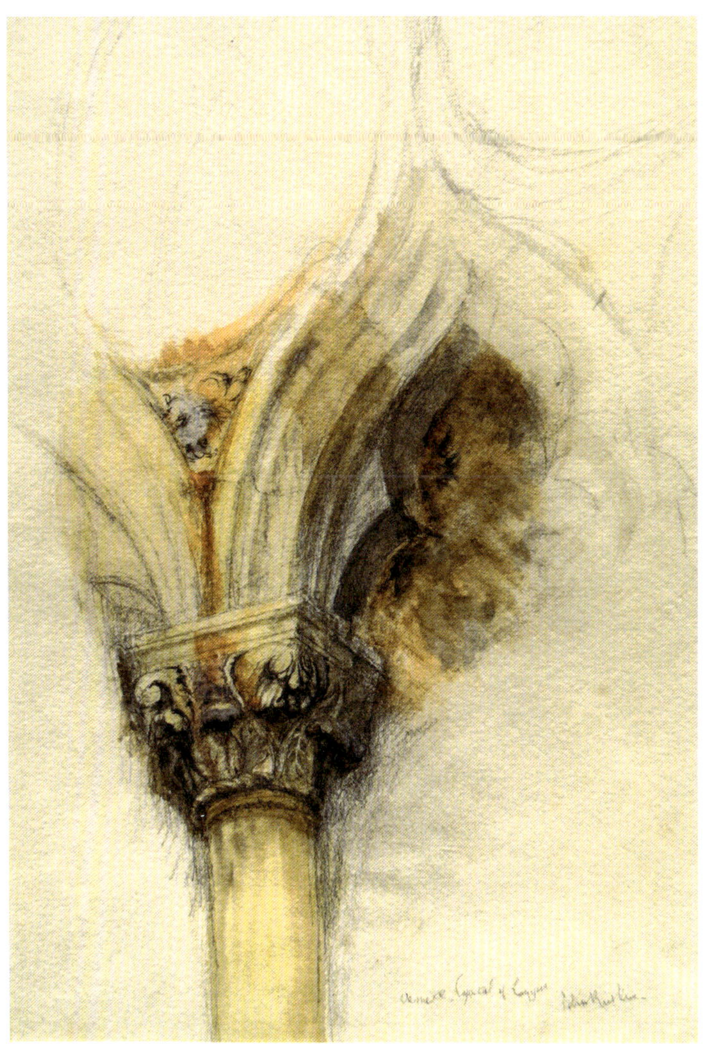

19 November 1849

Venice. DP, Lower Arcade. As a piece of carving, the vineleaves of the Noah at the angle next bridge of sighs are the most delicate work of the whole: not only have they been cut out like a net with a complete hollow between them and the pilaster; but every leaf is bent and waved like reality; and the surface so smooth that it cannot be believed it was ever chiselled – smooth almost to lustre, except one leaf thrown to the front or outer angle on purpose, which is carved with its entire reticulation: cross bars and all, in raised ribs, from its undulating surface. I never saw anything so carried in imitative sculpture. The love of surface tracery has much to do with it, for exactly the same thing is done with the veins of the figure, which are almost painfully distinct.

The Diaries of John Ruskin, vol. II, 449.

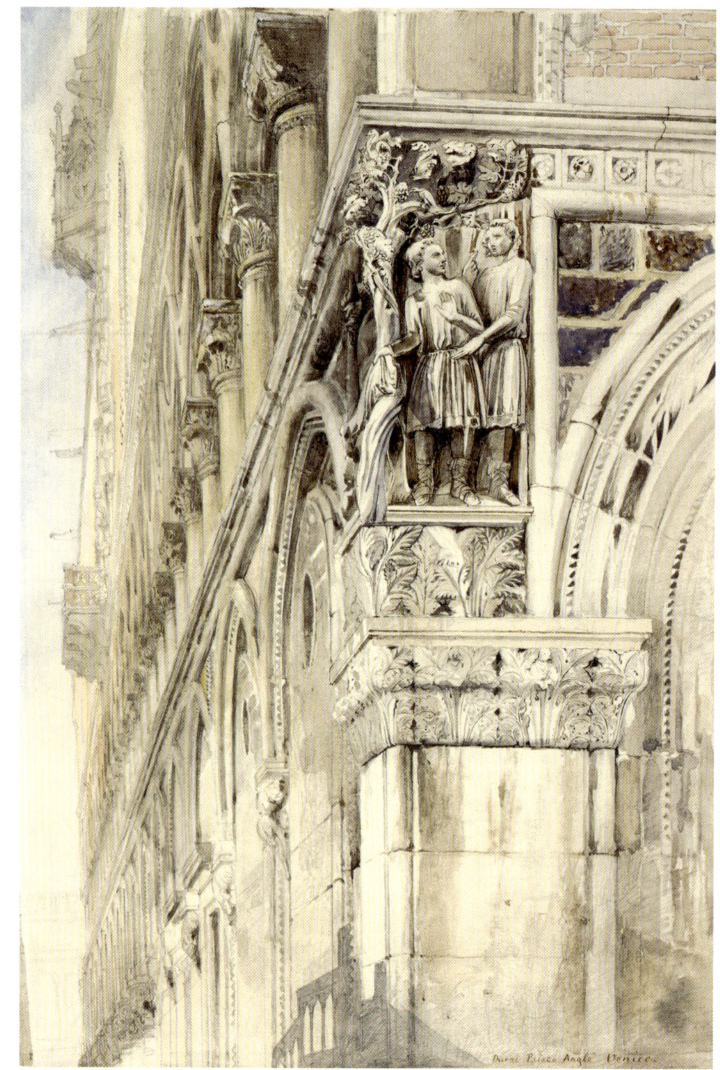

FACADE OF THE DOGE'S PALACE.
THE VINE ANGLE, *circa* 1870
watercolour, ink and pencil on paper, 496 × 337 mm
Manchester, Manchester Art Gallery, inv. 1907.5

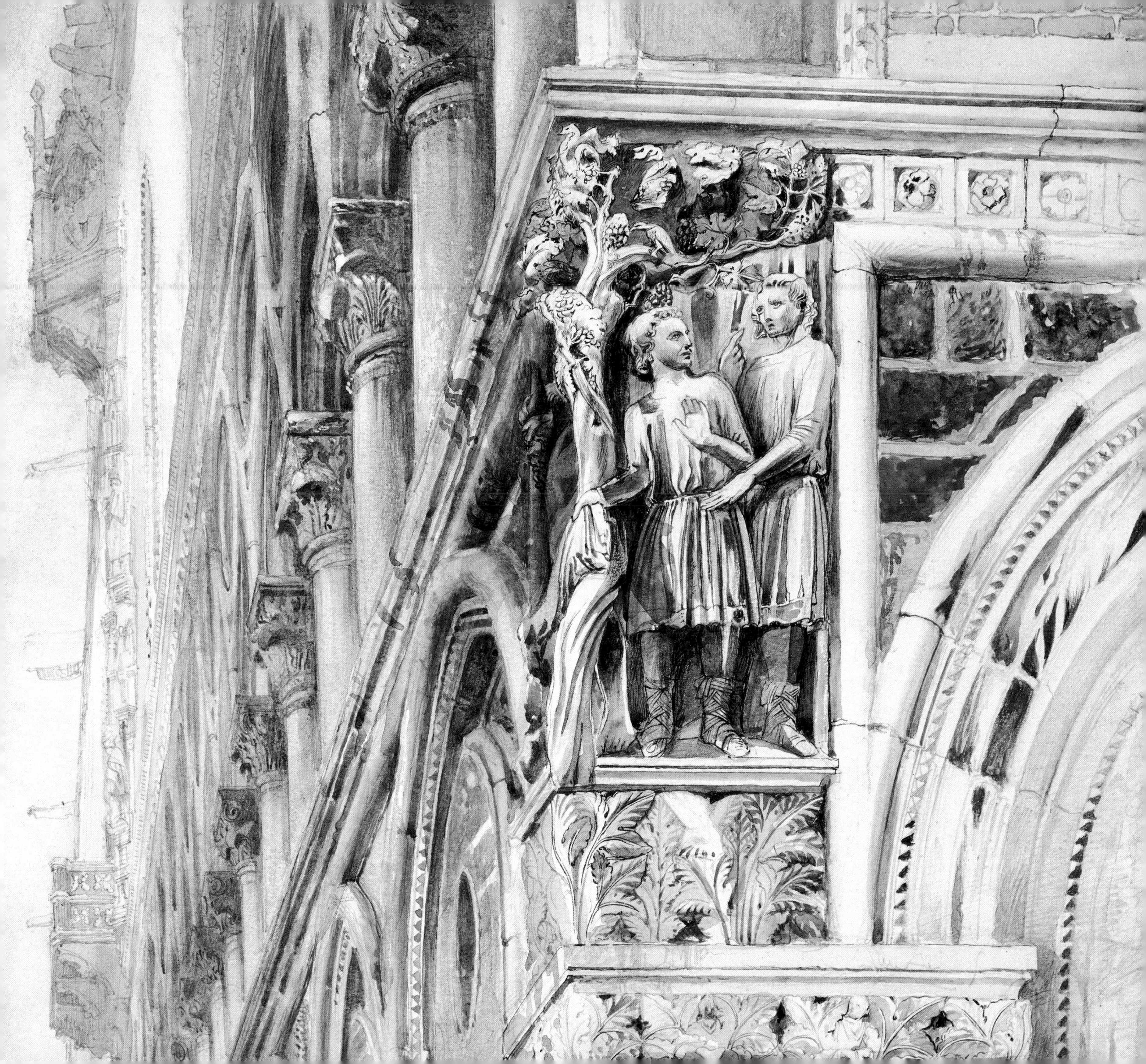

FONDACO DEI TURCHI

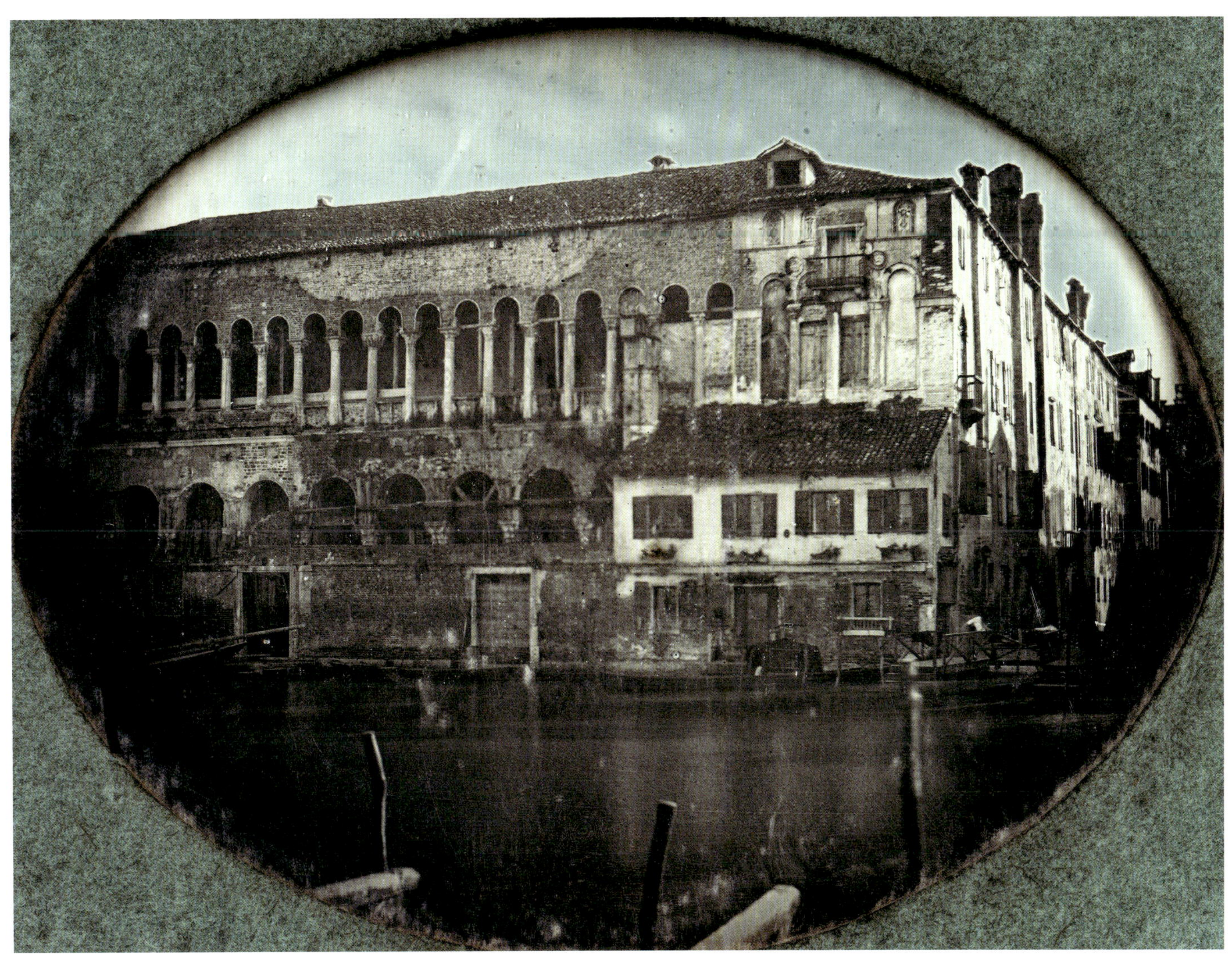

John Ruskin and Le Cavalier Iller (?)
FONDACO DEI TURCHI, *circa* 1845–46
daguerreotype, 70 × 95 mm
Courtesy of K&J Jacobson, UK

November 23rd, 1849

School I A. Example ist. Fondaco de' Turchi. It would be difficult to find anything, in slender proportion, more exquisite than the three terminal arches of the lower arcade of the Fondaco de' Turchi. [...] The brickwork of the arches has been so much defaced that it is impossible to say which of it is ancient; some large bricks seem to have composed a very finished facing after the marble has been broken off: but it appears that a common brick arch has carried the main weight, and this is faced on the soffit with curved, on the stilt, with plain, slabs of alabaster, whose projecting edges were simply touched alternately with the chisel; thus in the most natural and easy way, forming the Venetian dentil. The second, or outermost line of dentils has been inserted to about its own depth; or it would seem so by fissure which in a few places marks its former place. The circles are traced in the same manner; and then the whole wall face is covered with irregular slabs of marble; and the spaces between the dentils carefully fitted with long apparent voussoirs.

The Diaries of John Ruskin, vol. II, 452.

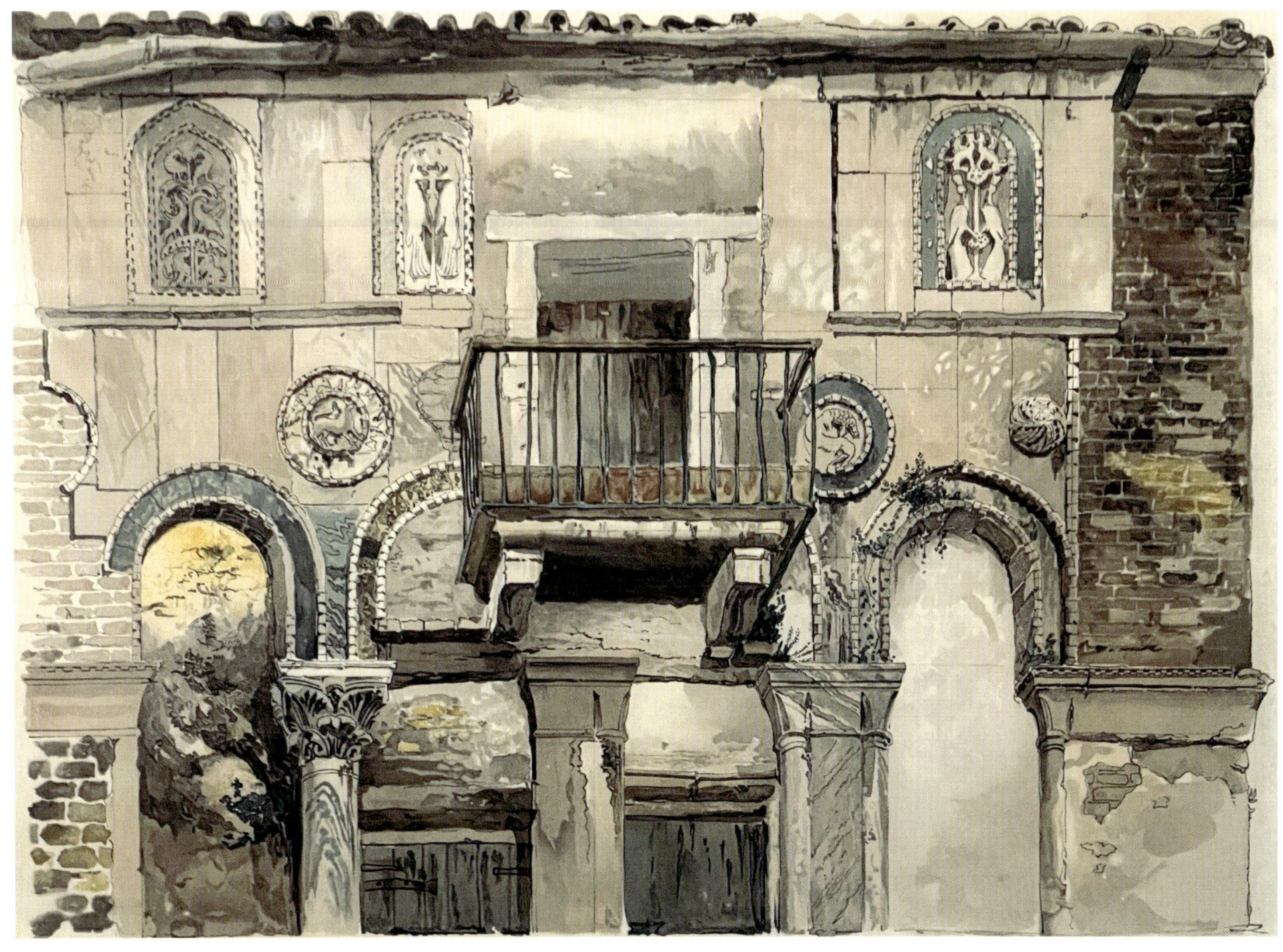

FONDACO DEI TURCHI
GENERAL VIEW OF UPPER RIGHT FRONT, 1849–50
drawing reproduced in colour, 250 × 180 mm
Coniston, The Ruskin Museum, inv. ConRM 1989.654

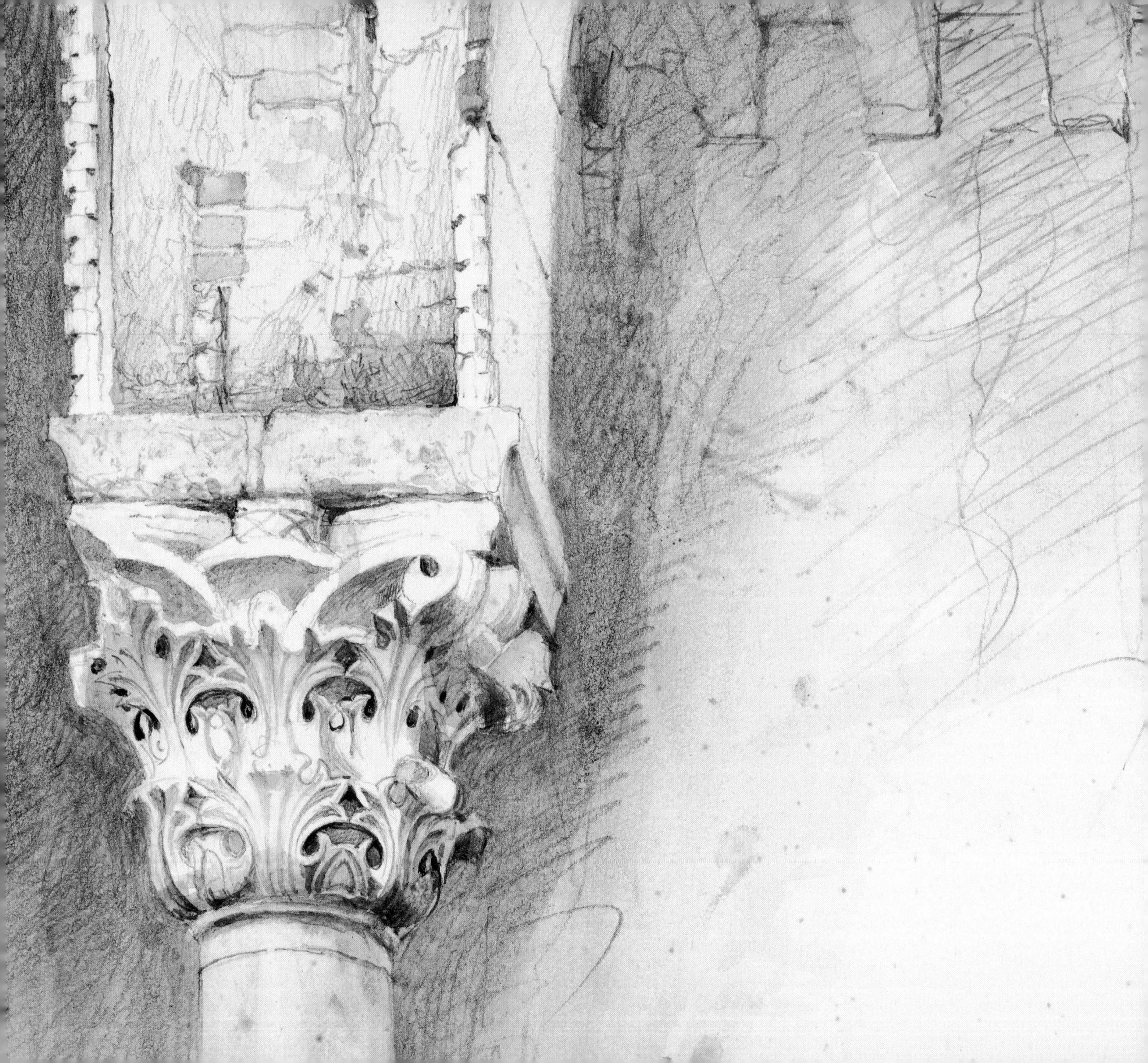

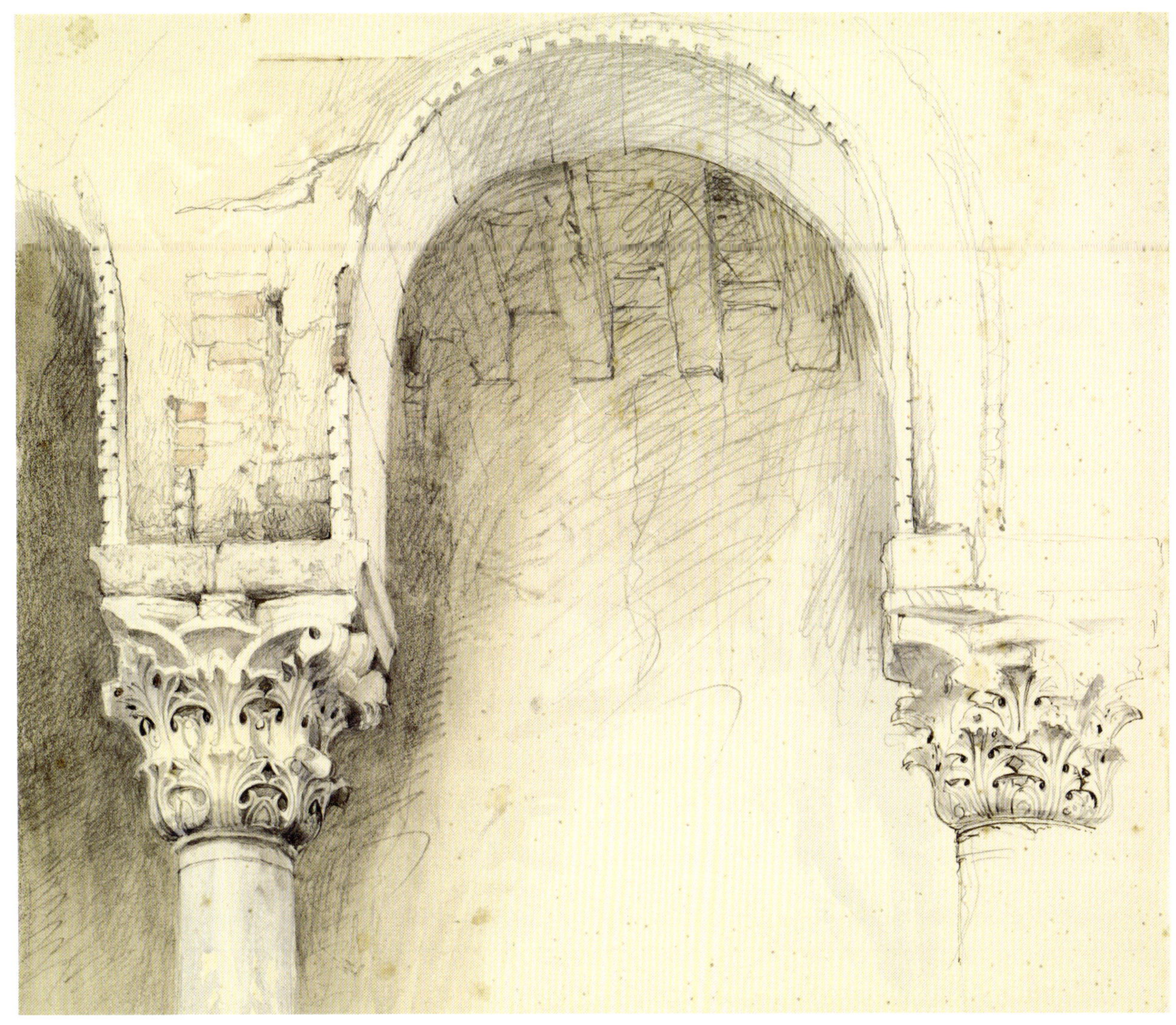

ARCHES AND CAPITALS, 1849–52
pencil and watercolour on paper, 221 × 260 mm
Birmingham, Birmingham Museums Trust /
Birmingham Museum & Art Gallery, inv. 1907P149
presented by Trustee of the Public Picture Gallery Fund, 1907

GRAND CANAL AND RIALTO

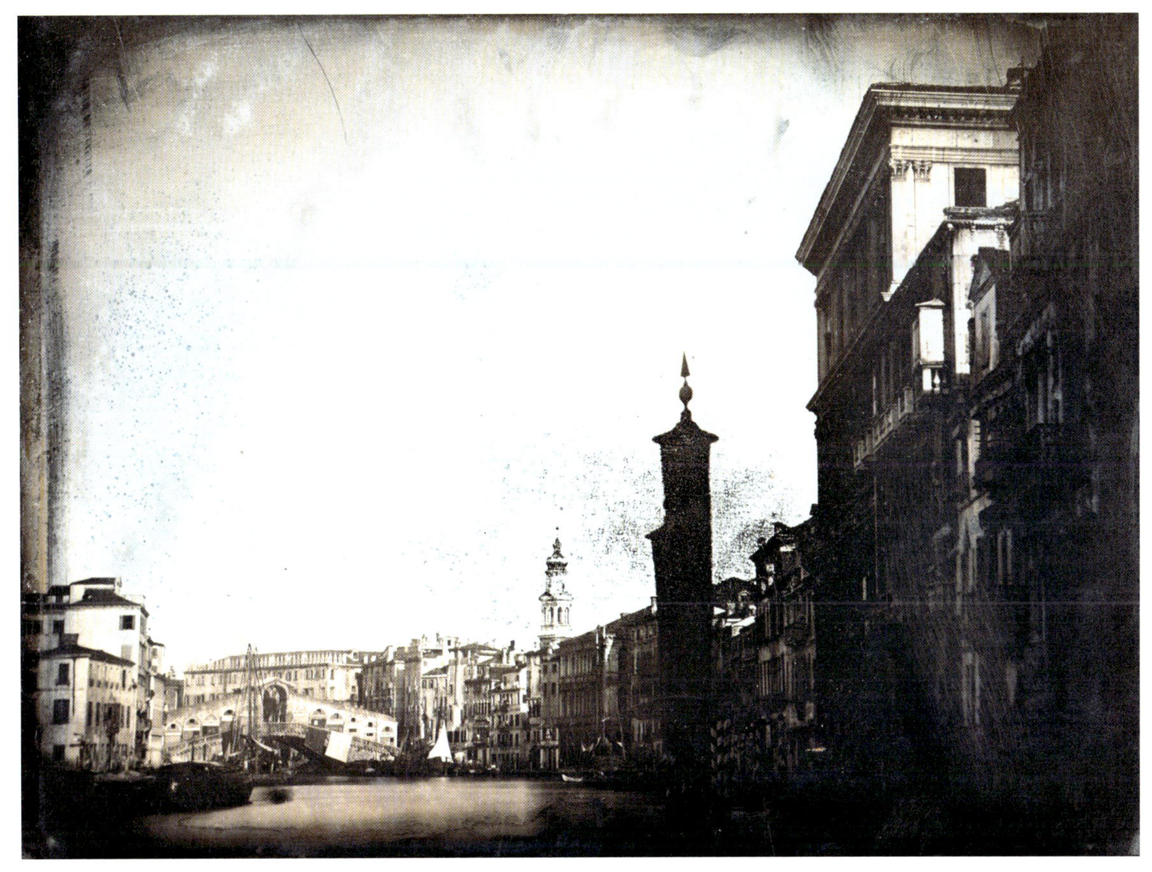

John Ruskin and John Hobbs (?)
THE GRAND CANAL FROM PALAZZO GRIMANI TO THE RIALTO BRIDGE (TURNER'S VIEW)
circa 1850–52
half-plate daguerreotype, 121 × 163 mm
Courtesy of K&J Jacobson, UK

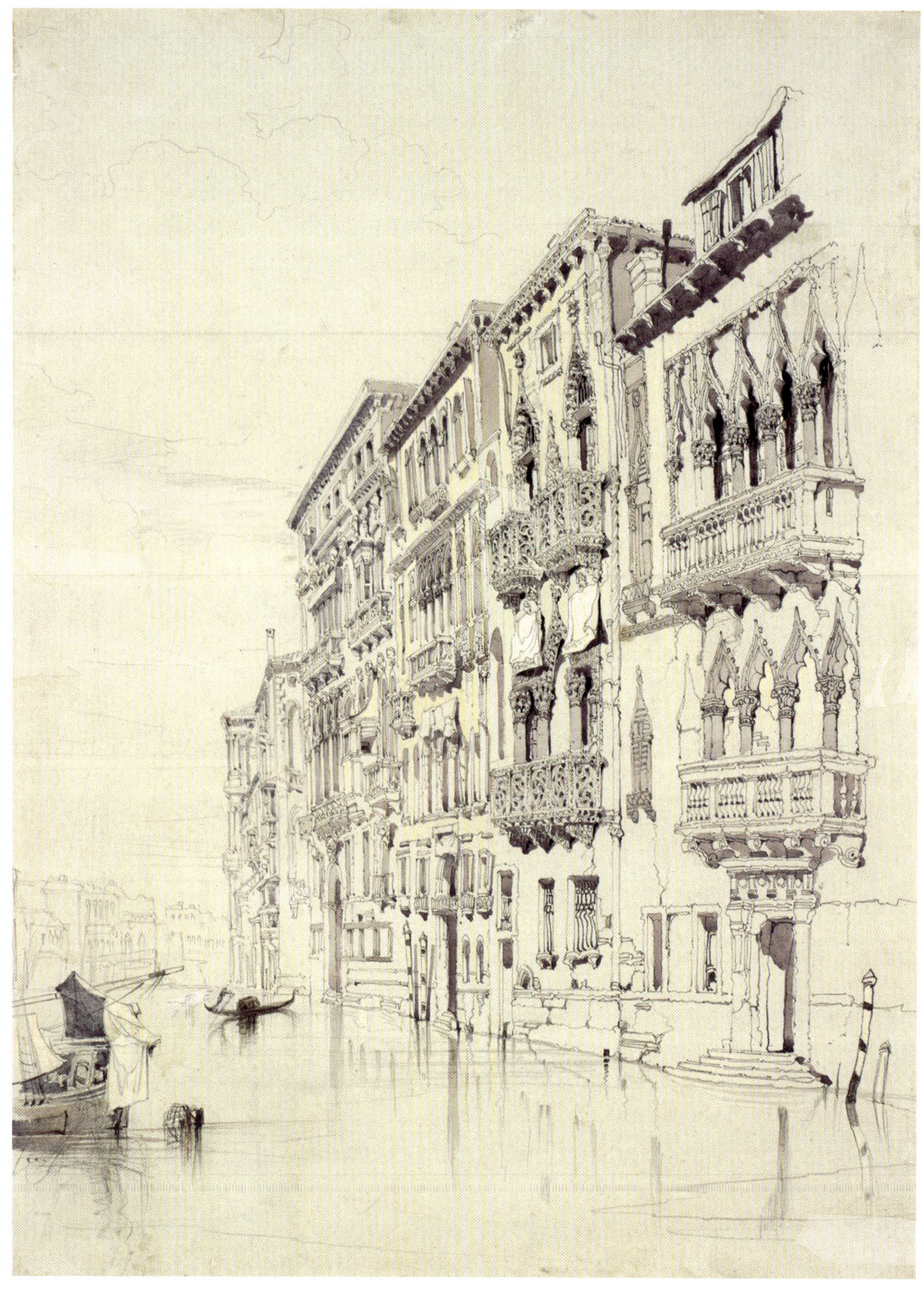

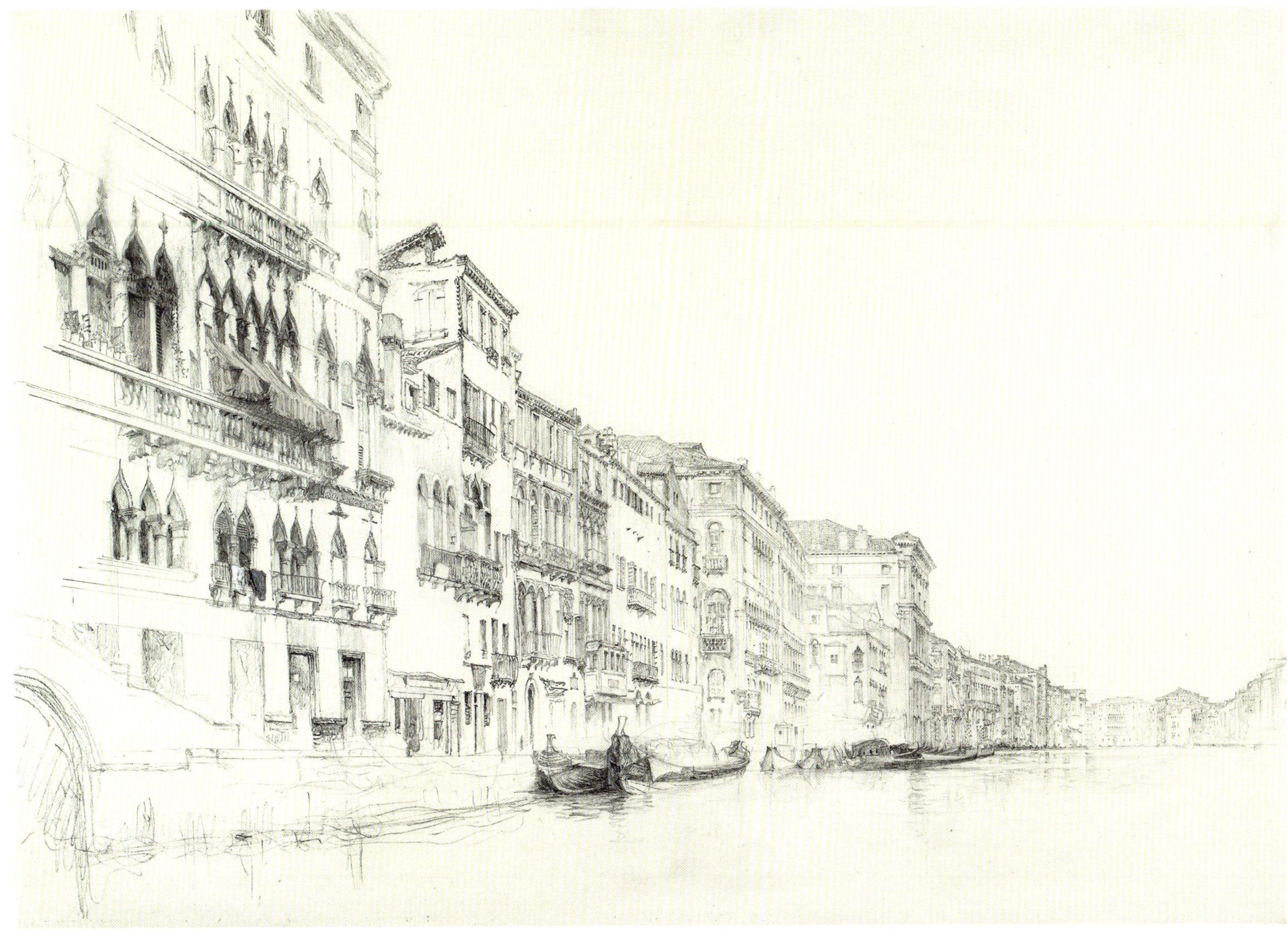

THE PALAZZO CONTARINI-FASAN, 1841
pencil, watercolour, bodycolour on grey paper, 428 × 315 mm
Oxford, Ashmolean Museum, University of Oxford, inv. WA.RS.REF.065
presented by John Ruskin to the Ruskin Drawing School (University of Oxford)
1875

VIEW FROM THE PALAZZO BEMBO TO THE PALAZZO GRIMANI, 1870
pencil, watercolour on paper, 353 × 508 mm
Oxford, Ashmolean Museum, University of Oxford. inv. WA.RS.REF.066
presented by John Ruskin to the Ruskin Drawing School (University of Oxford)
1875

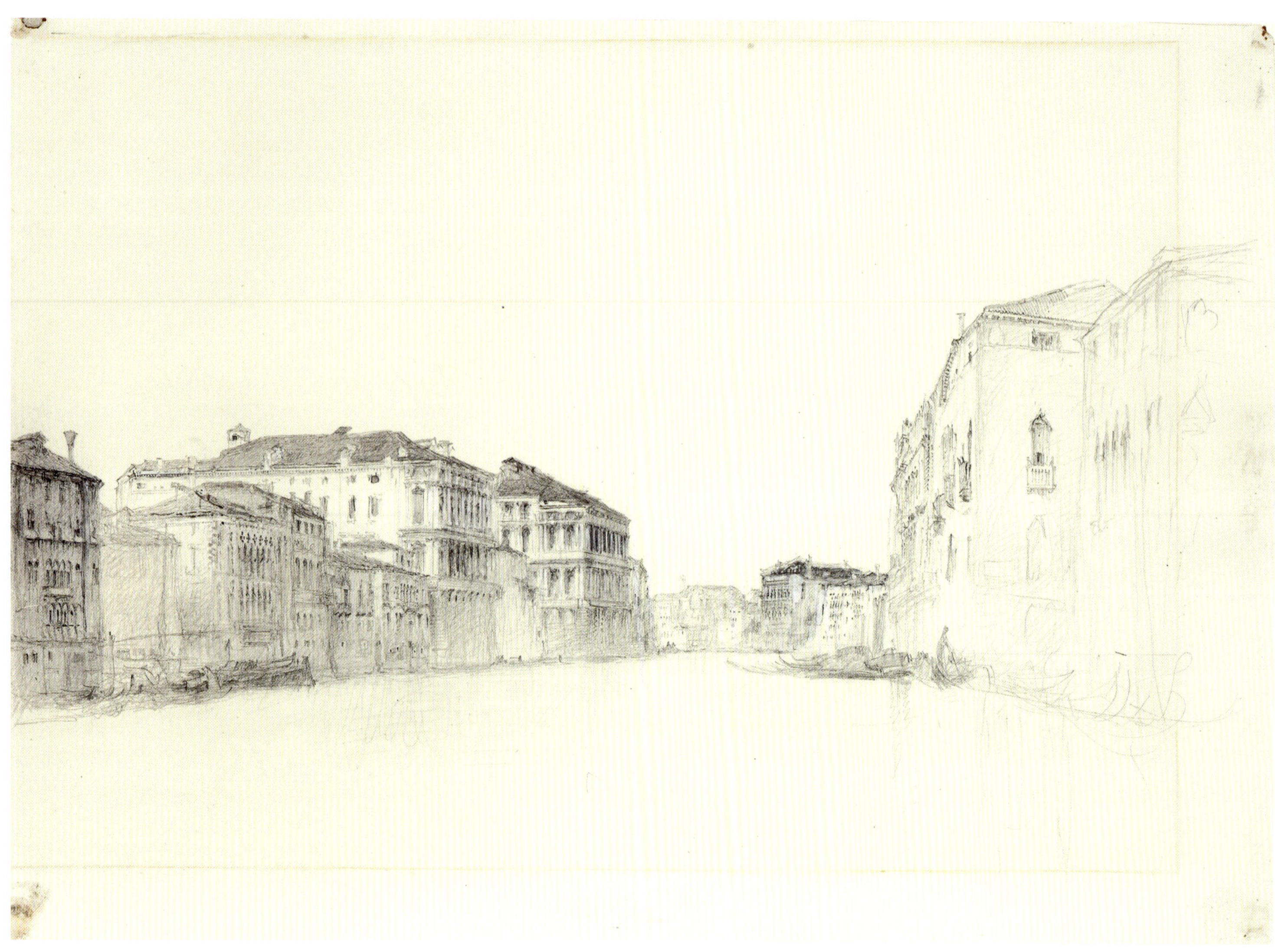

VIEW ON THE UPPER REACH OF THE GRAND CANAL
WITH THE PALAZZI CORNER AND PESARO, 1876
pencil, bodycolour on paper, 362 × 521 mm
Lancaster, The Ruskin, Lancaster University, inv. 1996P1612

VIEW OF THE UPPER REACH OF THE GRAND CANAL
WITH THE PALAZZI TRON AND DUODO, 1876
pencil on paper, 358 × 511 mm
inscription: "Pal. Capovilla"
Lancaster, The Ruskin, Lancaster University, inv. 1996P1622

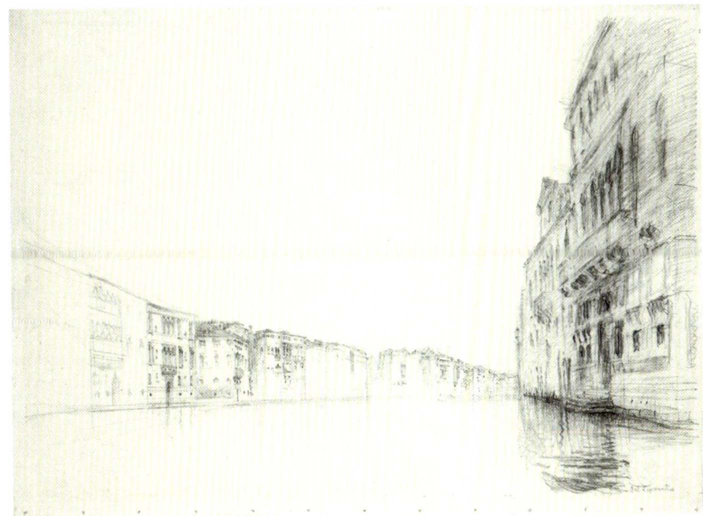

Saturday September 9th, 1876

A week since I drove down the Simplon. It is too terrible, the little I get done! But here, yesterday, a really wonderful number of things found in safety that I never expected to have seen more, and intense crimson stormy sunset in Giudecca, and moonlight and starlight evening. Oh me, if I could conquer the shadow of death which harries me at work and saddens me at rest! This morning, entirely glorious scarlet dawn. I out on balcony in my nightgown, with bare feet; air quite delicious. I. Grand Canal sketch begun.

The Diaries of John Ruskin, vol. III, 906

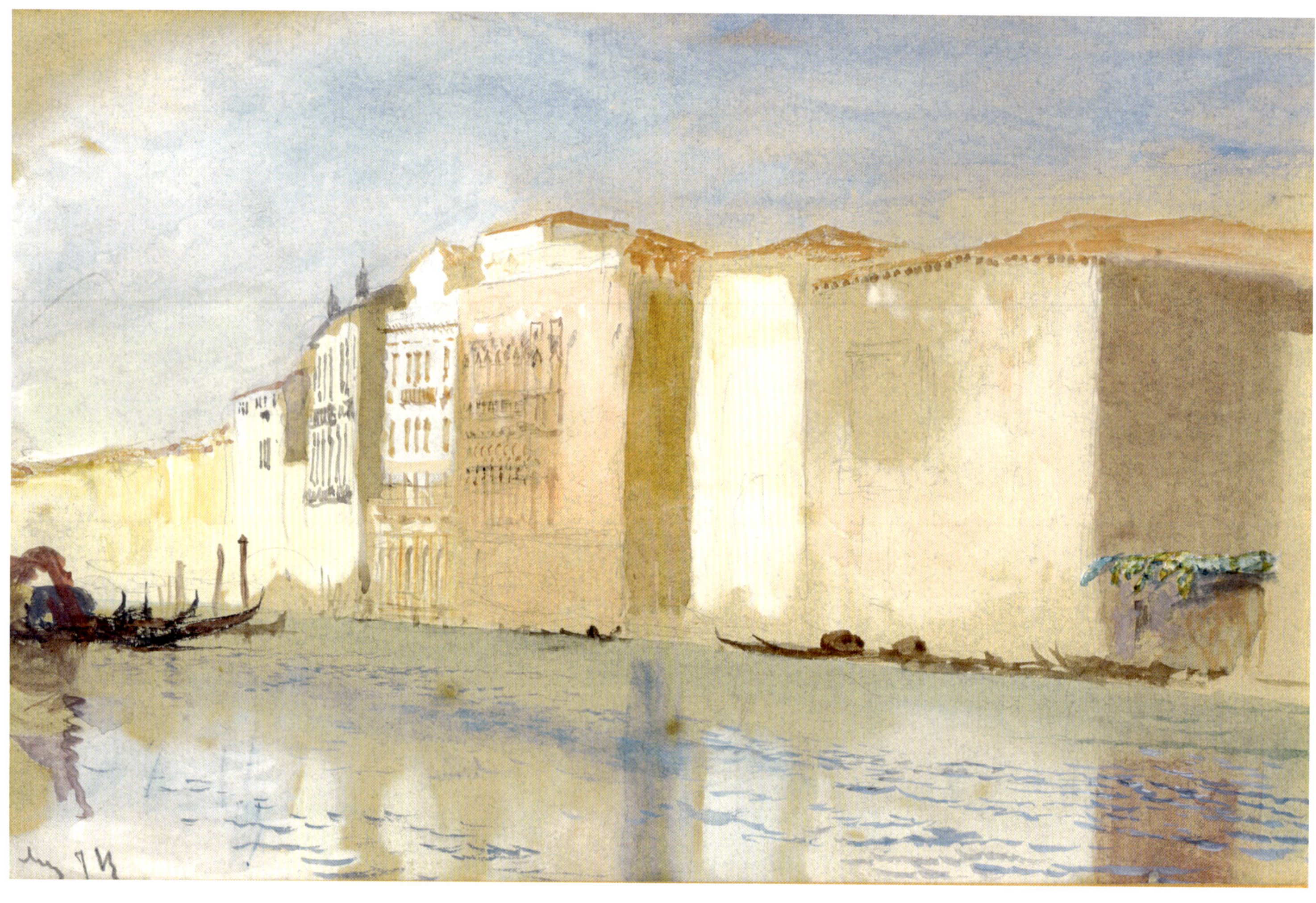

VIEW ON THE GRAND CANAL, 1876–77
pencil, watercolour, bodycolour on paper, *circa* 171 × 260 mm
inscription: "by JR" by Joan Severn
Lancaster, The Ruskin, Lancaster University, inv. 1996P1067

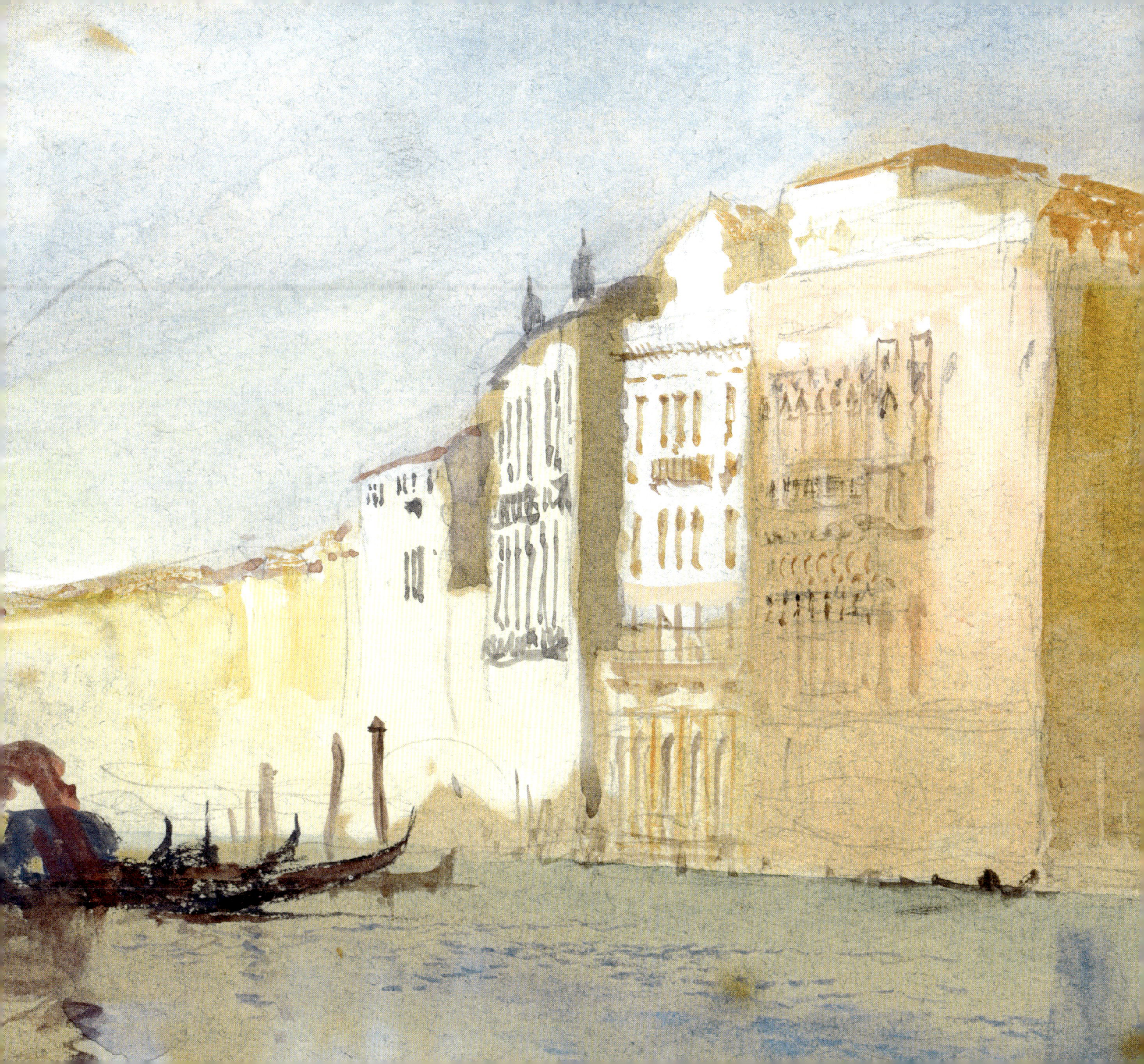

ST. MARK'S
AND OTHER
RELIGIOUS BUILDINGS

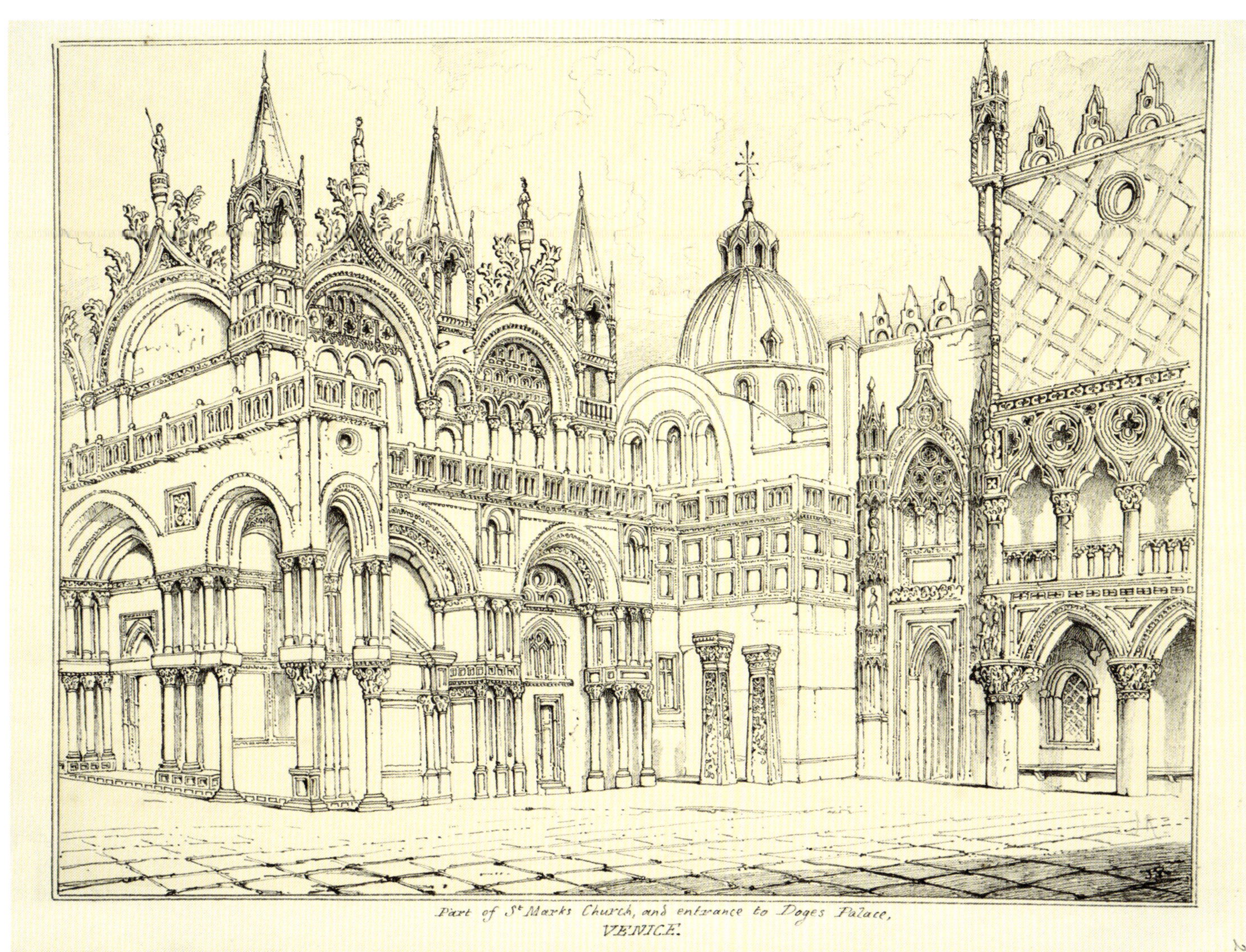

THE PIAZZETTA, ST. MARK'S AND THE ENTRANCE TO THE DUCAL PALACE, 1835
pencil, pen, black ink, 267 × 364 mm
Lancaster, The Ruskin, Lancaster University, inv. 1996P1055

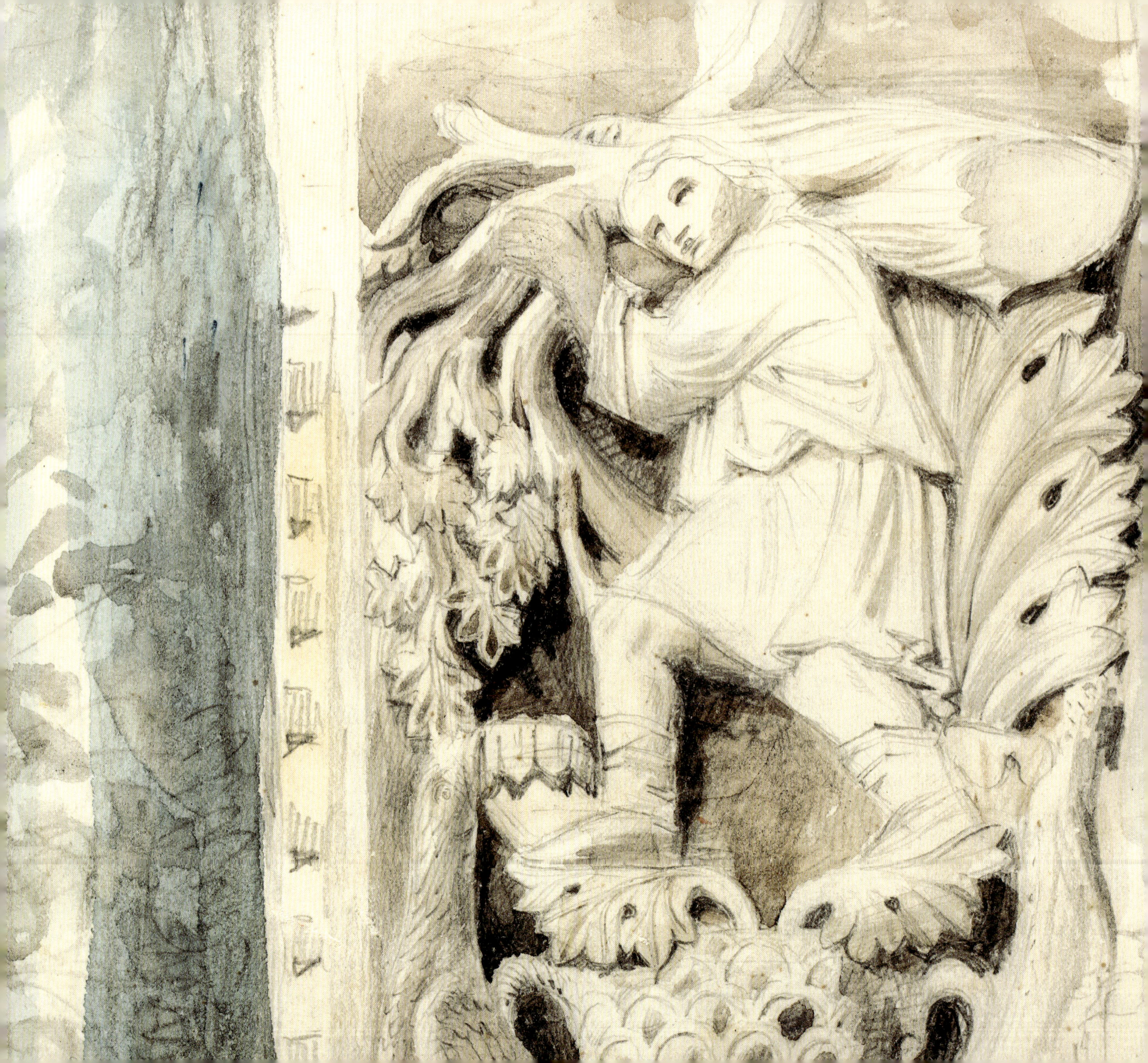

Venice, May 6th, 1841

Thank God I am here! It is the Paradise of cities and there is a moon enough to make half the sanities of earth lunatic, striking its pure flashes of light against the grey water before the window; and I am happier than I have been these five years – so happy – happier than in all probability I ever shall be again in my life, I feel fresh and young when my foot is on these pavements, and the outline of St. Mark's thrill me as if they had been traced by A[dèle']s hand. This and Chamouni are my two bournes of earth; there might have been another, but that has become all pain. Thank God I am here!

The Diaries of John Ruskin, vol. 1, p. 183

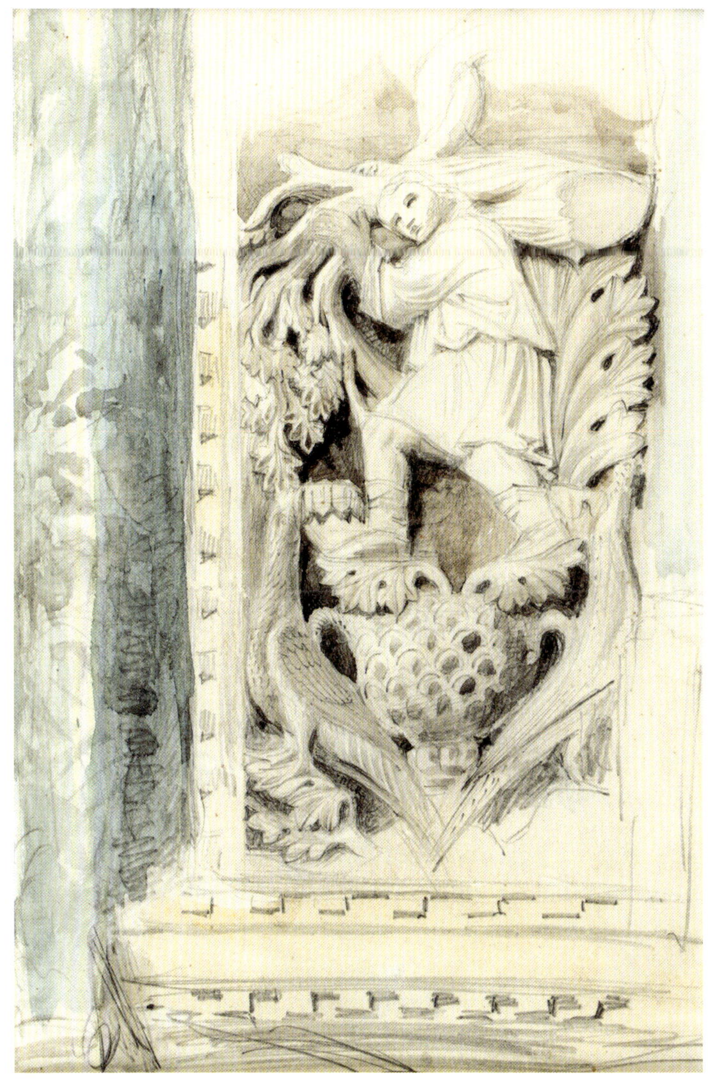

FIRST OF THE MONTH'S SCULPTURES
ST. MARK'S, 1840
pencil and watercolour on card, 222 × 154 mm
Oldham, Gallery Oldham, inv. 3.55/8

May 12th [1841]

What a delicious afternoon I spent yesterday in St. Mark's – trying to get the local colour of the church. It was such a pleasure to have one's eye kept on those beautiful and strange details with the quiet sketching attention, and to be able to lie back in one's chair every now and then and look around on the vast square and bright evening sky, and red relief of St. Giorgio, and blue sea, with the bright-eyed people moving through it all. I never took so luxurious a drawing in my life. I have sat now and then in such places, but always idly, seldom with my pencil in my hand, touching now and then, feeling I was doing something, and that with no picturesque ugliness, but with an object which it is delight to have one's eyes drawn to. Then when I left the square, before the sunset – at it, rather – there was a light such as Turner in his maddest moments never came up to; it turned the masts of the guard frigade into absolute pointed fire, and the woods of the botanic garden took it in the same way – not as if it were light *on* them, but in them. It was impossible to believe it was not autumn; and the brick buildings, far over the lagoon, blazing in pure crimson. When it left the earth, and got into the sky it turned it, as usual, into the purple grey with red touches; but one effect, new to me, was a stray ray which caught vertically on a misty undefined cloud, and turned it into a perpendicular pillar of crimson haze, like the column that led the Israelites.

The Diaries of John Ruskin, vol. 1, 185–86.

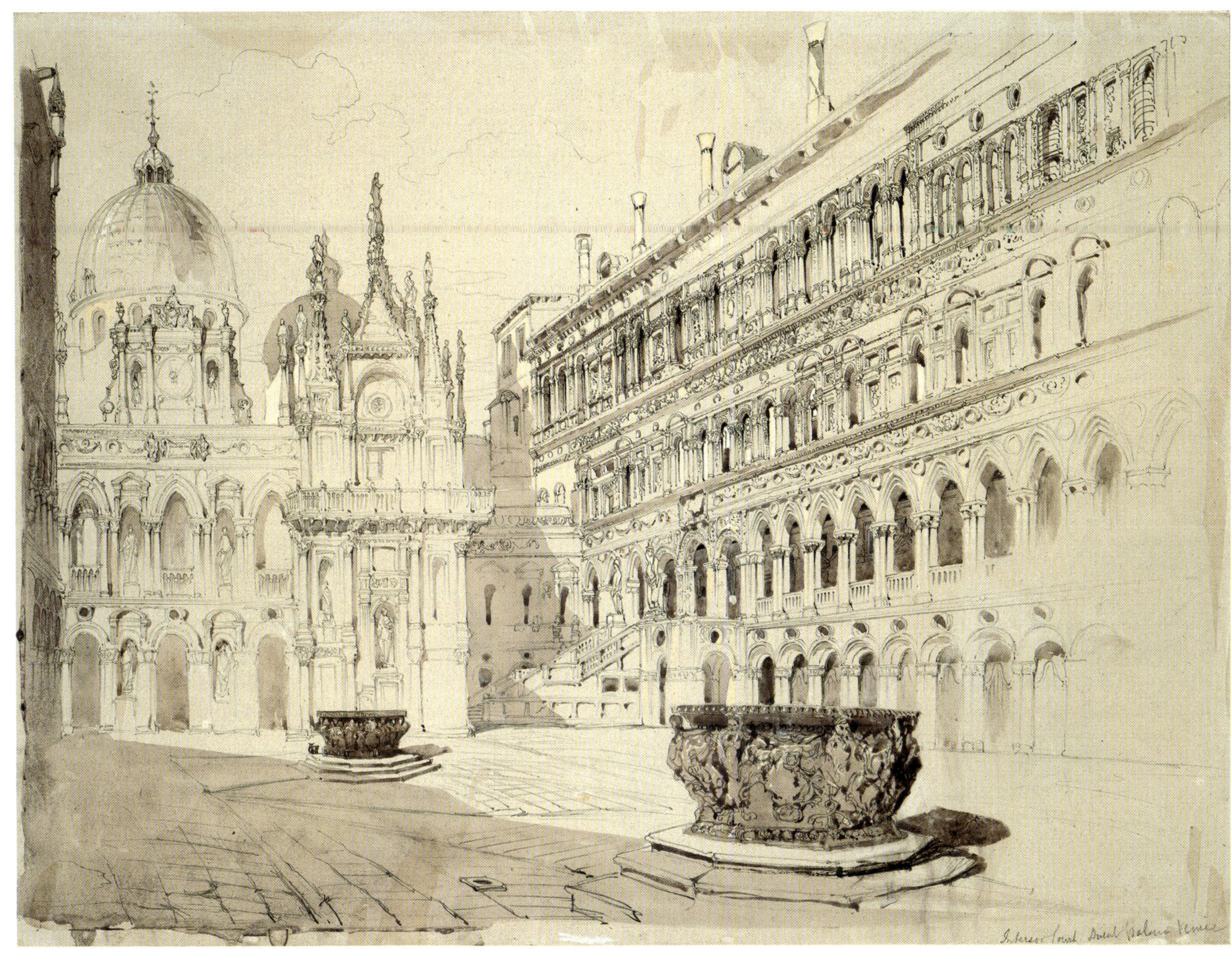

THE COURT OF THE DUCAL PALACE, May 1841
graphite, watercolour, bodycolour and pen and ink on pale grey wove paper, 344 × 465 mm
Oxford, Ashmolean Museum, University of Oxford, inv. WA.RS.REF.064
presented by John Ruskin to the Ruskin Drawing School (University of Oxford), 1875

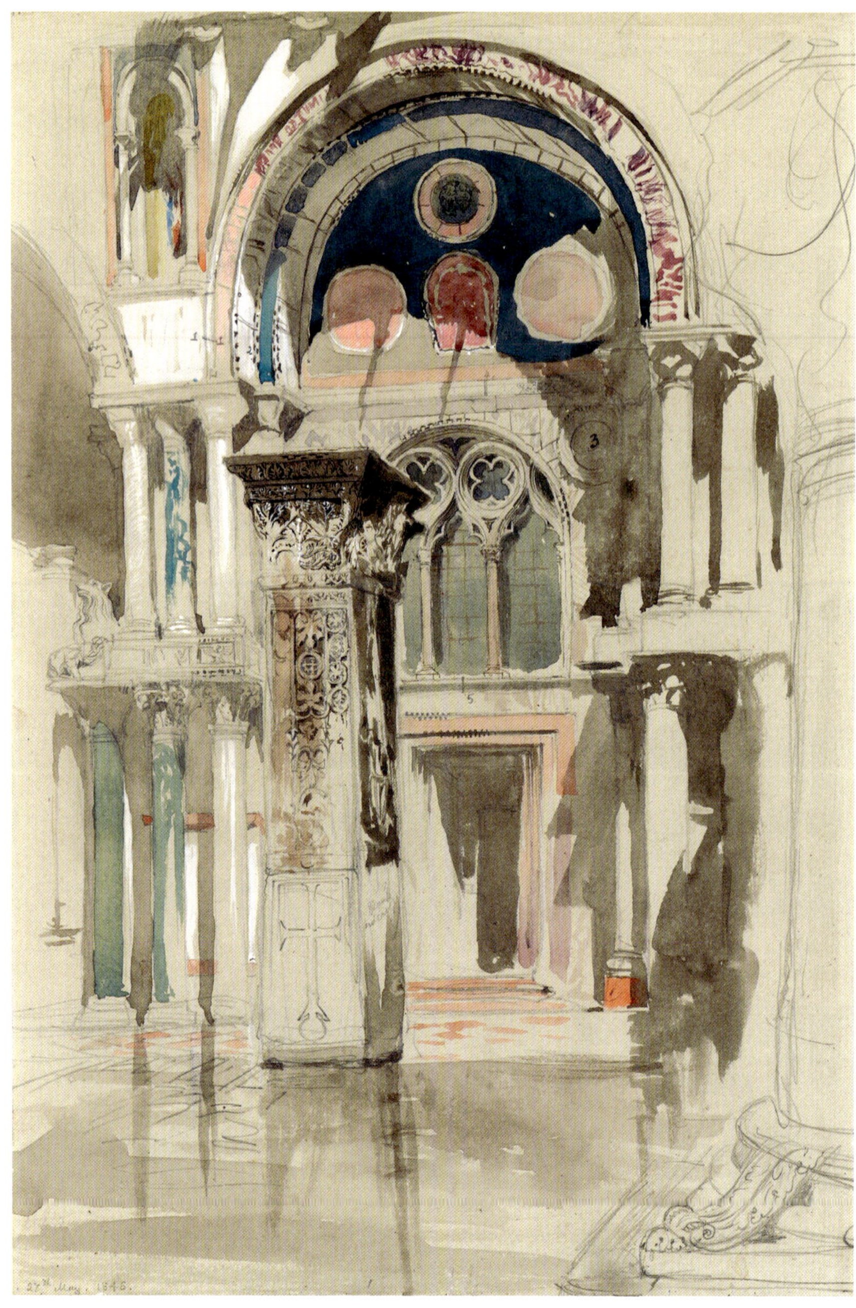

May 23rd 1846

In the porch of St. Mark's, the mosaics of the Deluge are peculiarly interesting, especially that of the ark seen through the rain; the rain is in close blue and white stripes, but through the blue the form of the ark is shown in brown; and because this, from its darkness, would escape notice, the square window of the ark is given in bright gold, which shows in vivid light with black and white border, between the stripes, having exactly the effect of a window lighted by reflected sunshine. The ponderousness of the rain, and the real existence of the object, though thus slightly hinted, are thus more impressively suggested than in any other instance I know. The raven, as usual, stays to feed on a dead body.

The Diaries of John Ruskin, vol. 1, 339.

ST. MARK'S BASILICA SOUTH SIDE, AFTER THE RAIN, 1846
watercolour, bodycolour, ink, pencil on wove paper, 421 × 286 mm
inscription: "27th May. 1846" on the verso
Oxford, Ashmolean Museum, University of Oxford, inv. WA.RS.ED.209

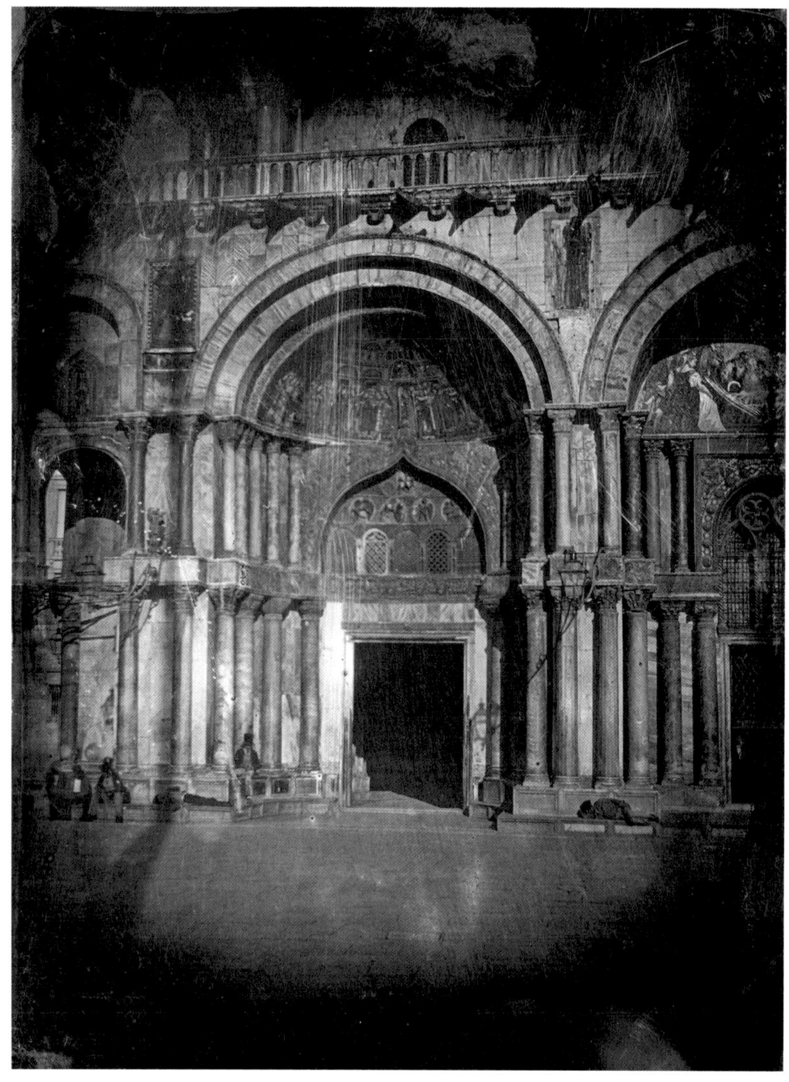

John Ruskin and Le Cavalier Iller
THE ST. MARK'S PRINCIPAL FACADE
FIRST PORCH, *circa* 1845–46
daguerreotype, 108 × 81 mm
Courtesy of K&J Jacobson, UK

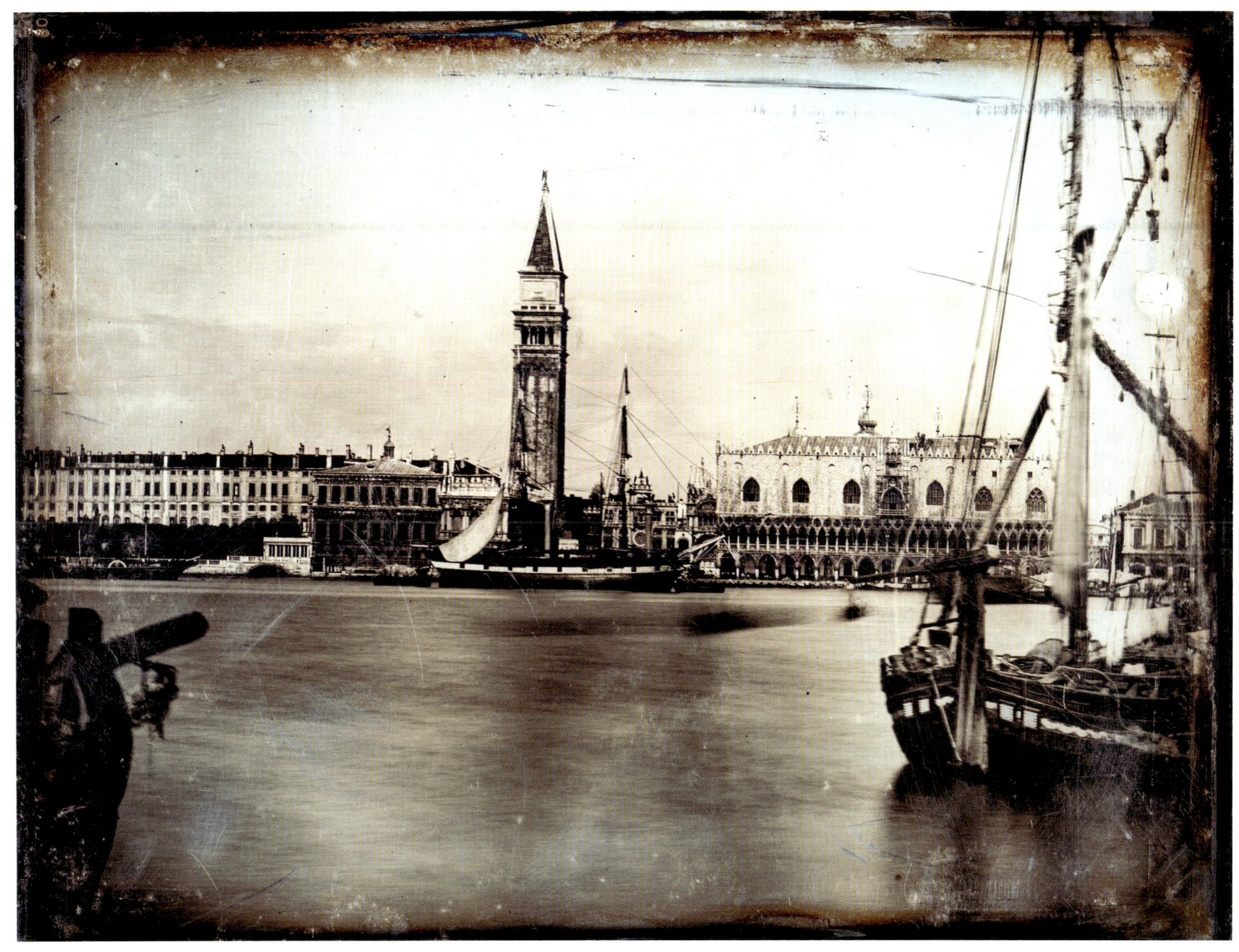

John Ruskin and Le Cavalier Iller
THE DUCAL PALACE, THE ZECCA AND THE CAMPANILE
WITH MOORED SHIPS IN FOREGROUND
circa 1851
half-plate daguerreotype, 121 × 162 mm
Courtesy of K&J Jacobson, UK

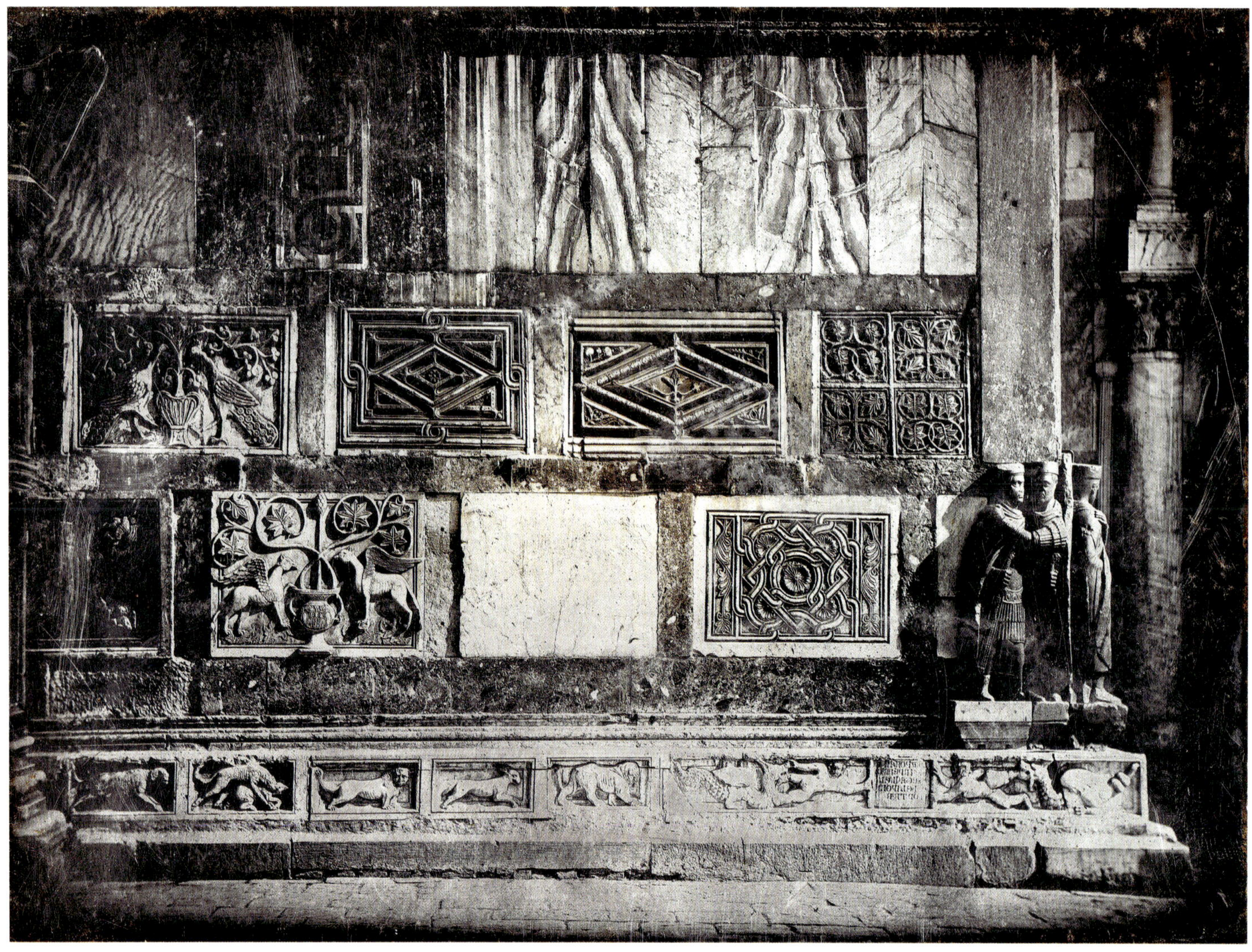

John Ruskin and John Hobbs
ST. MARK'S: SOUTH FACADE DETAIL AND THE TETRARCHS SCULPTURE, 1850
daguerreotype, 122 × 163 × 3 mm
Lancaster, The Ruskin, Lancaster University, inv. 1996D0021

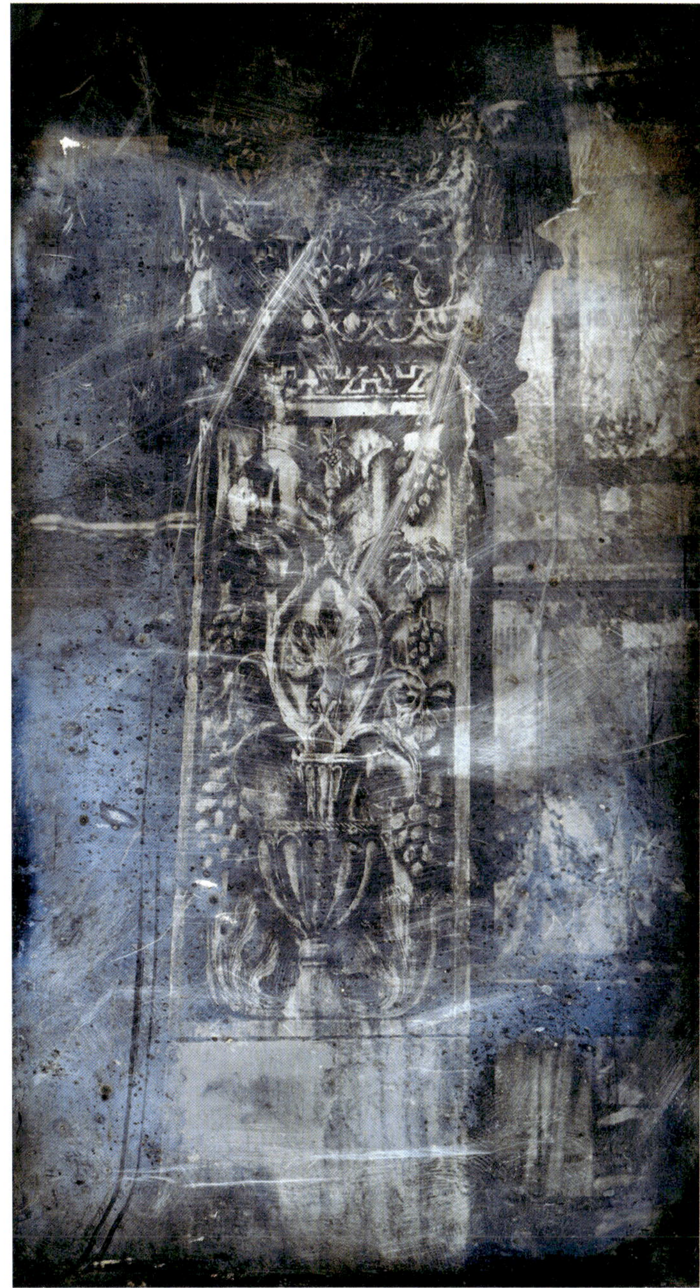

John Ruskin and John Hobbs
THE VINE PILLAR, 1850–52
daguerreotype, 156 × 93 mm (laterally reversed)
Courtesy of K&J Jacobson, UK

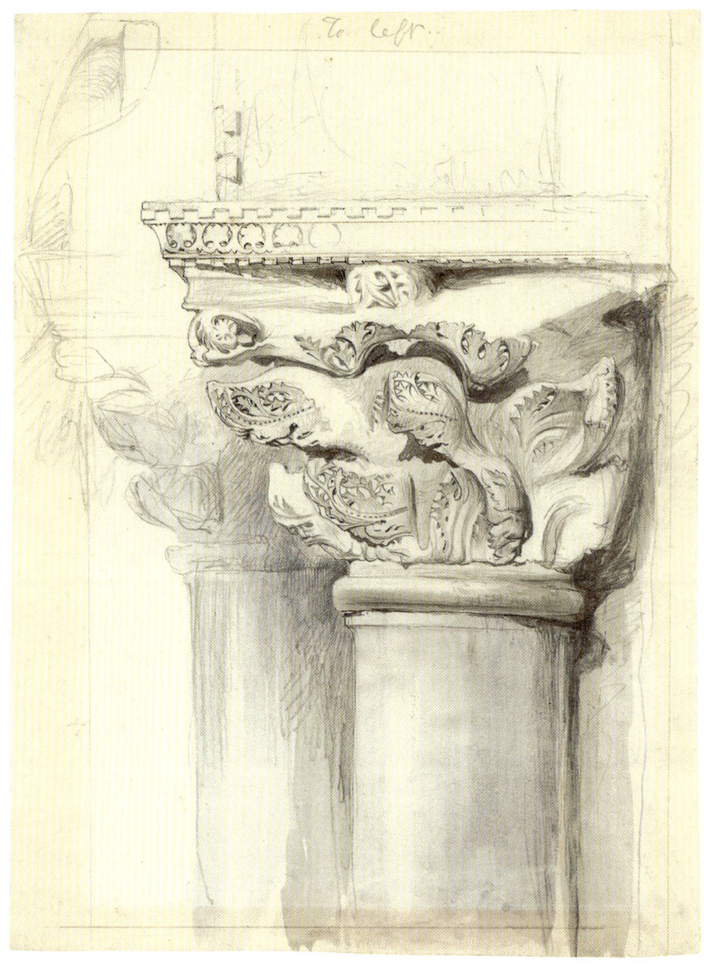

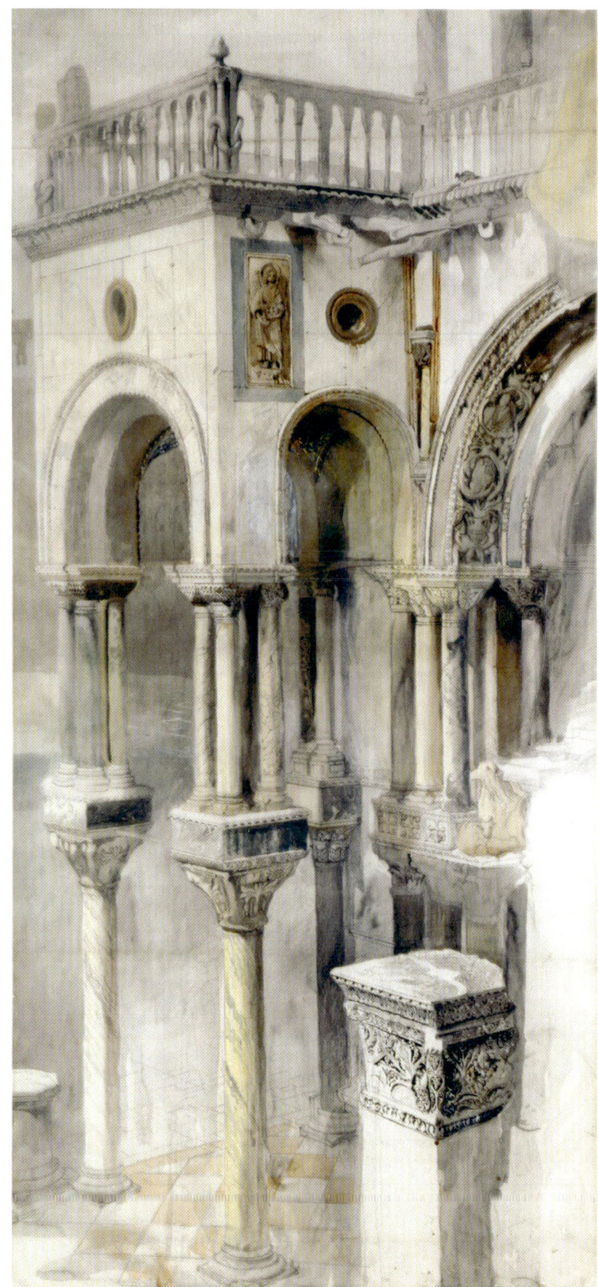

ST. MARK'S: CAPITAL OF SHAFT OF CENTRAL PORCH, *circa* 1851
pencil, watercolour on paper, *circa* 273 × 187 mm
Lancaster, The Ruskin, Lancaster University, inv. 1996P1057

THE SOUTH SIDE OF ST. MARK'S
FROM THE LOGGIA OF THE DUCALE PALACE, 1851
watercolour, tempera, bodycolour on paper, 959 × 454 mm
Private collection (courtesy of Sotheby's, Inc.)

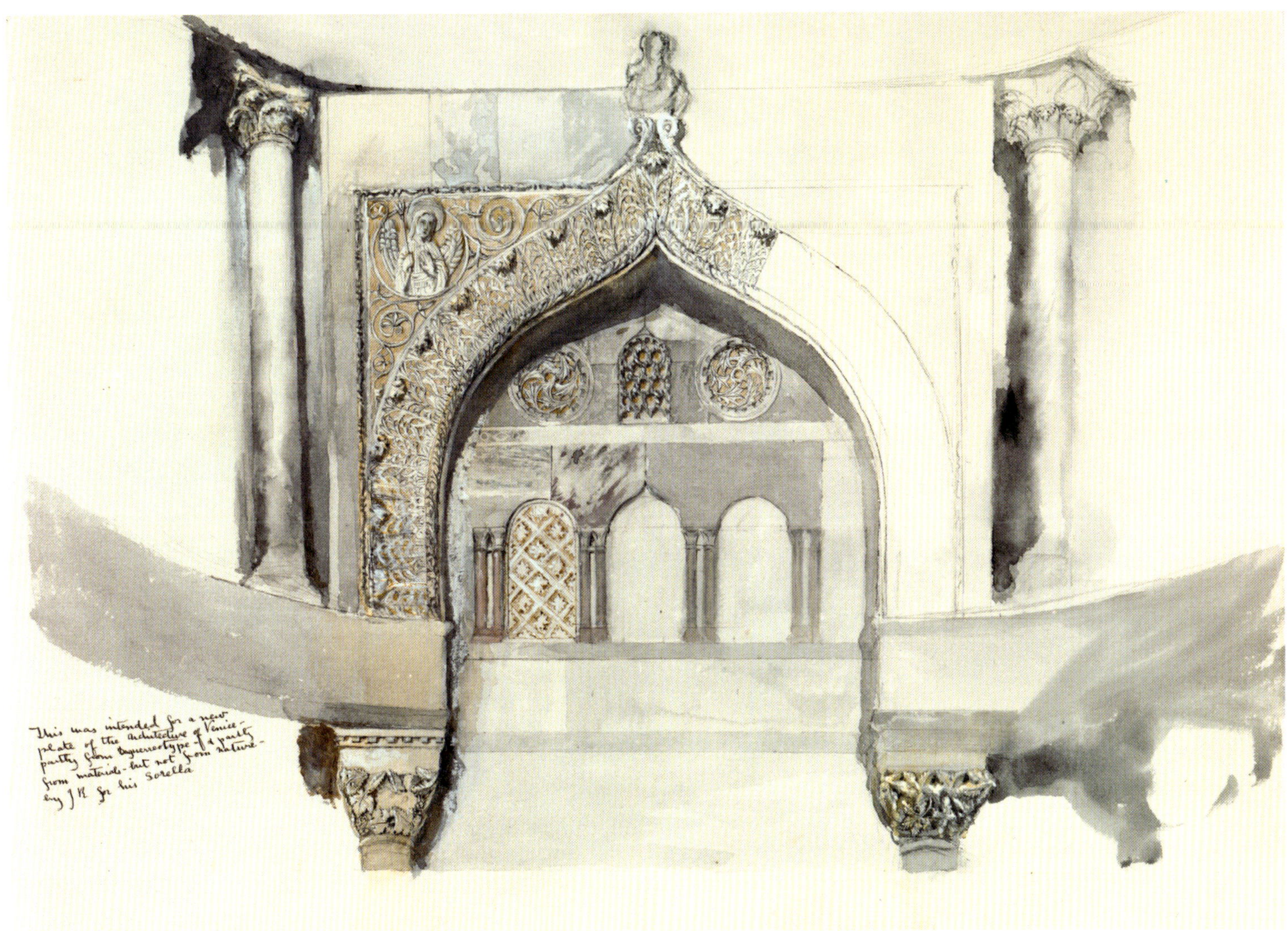

STUDY OF AN ARCHIVOLT IN ST. MARK'S, 1852
watercolour, white gouache, graphite, black ink, and gold paint on off-white wove paper
391 × 559 mm
Harvard, Harvard Art Museums / Fogg Museum, gift of Edward W. Forbes, inv. 1953.206

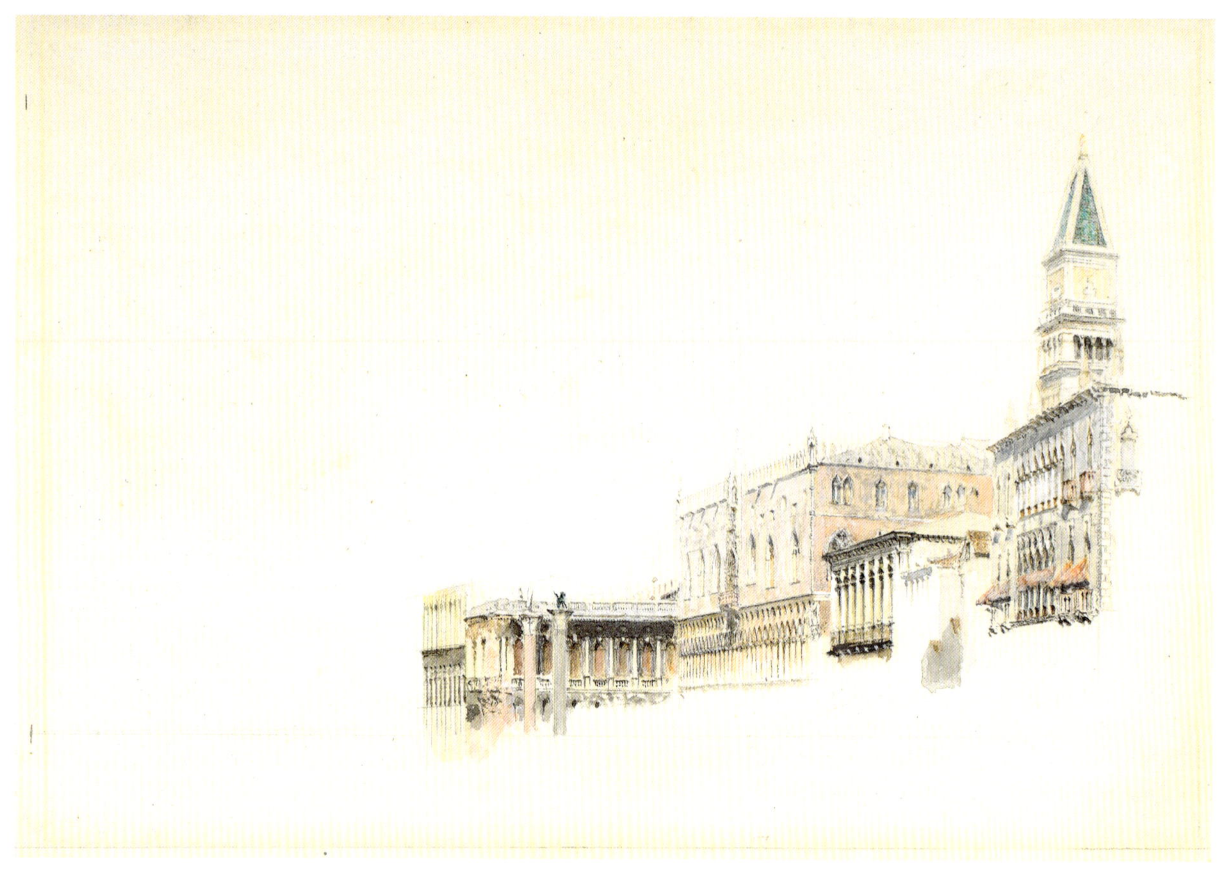

RIVA DEGLI SCHIAVONI, THE DUCAL PALACE AND THE CAMPANILE OF ST. MARK'S, *circa* 1870?
watercolour and graphite on paper, 248 × 370 mm
Cambridge, The Fitzwilliam Museum, inv. 1154

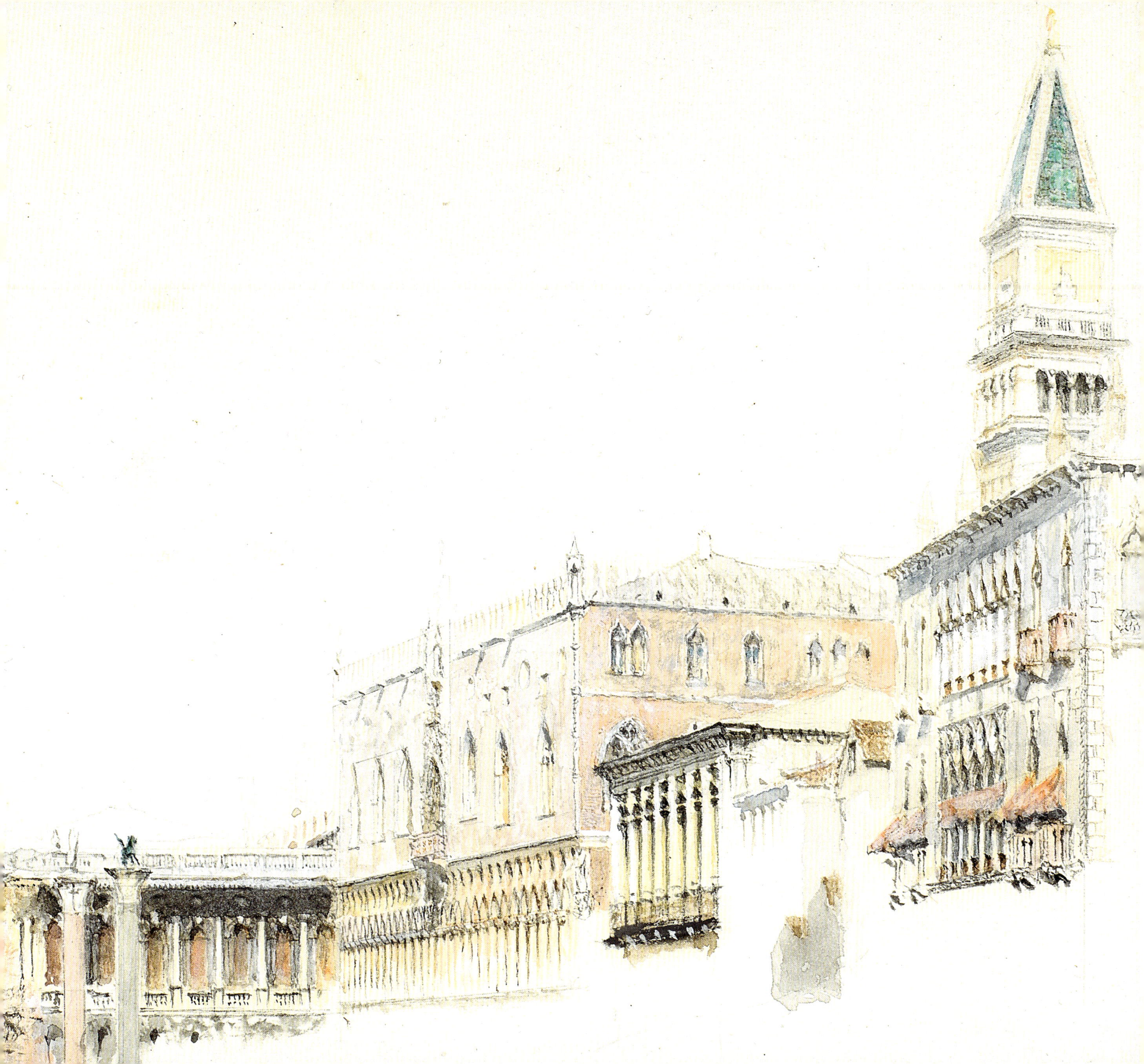

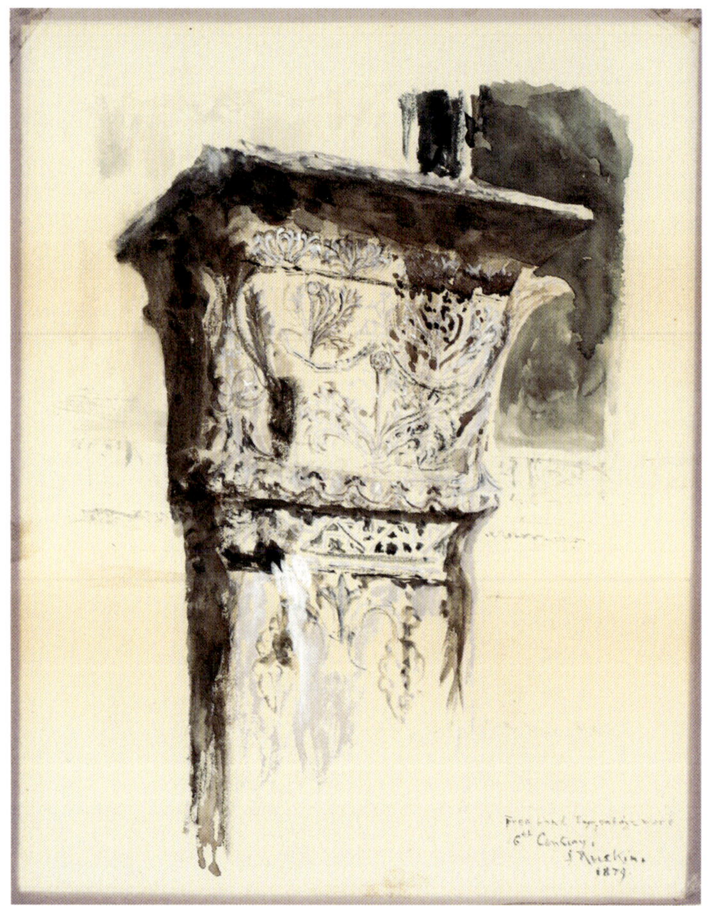

EARLY BYZANTINE CARVING, 1877–78
blue-black, brown and purplish washes, and white gouache
on faded blue-purple paper, 280 × 220 mm
Harvard, Harvard Art Museums / Fogg Museum, transfer from
the Fine Arts Department, Harvard University, inv. 1924.49

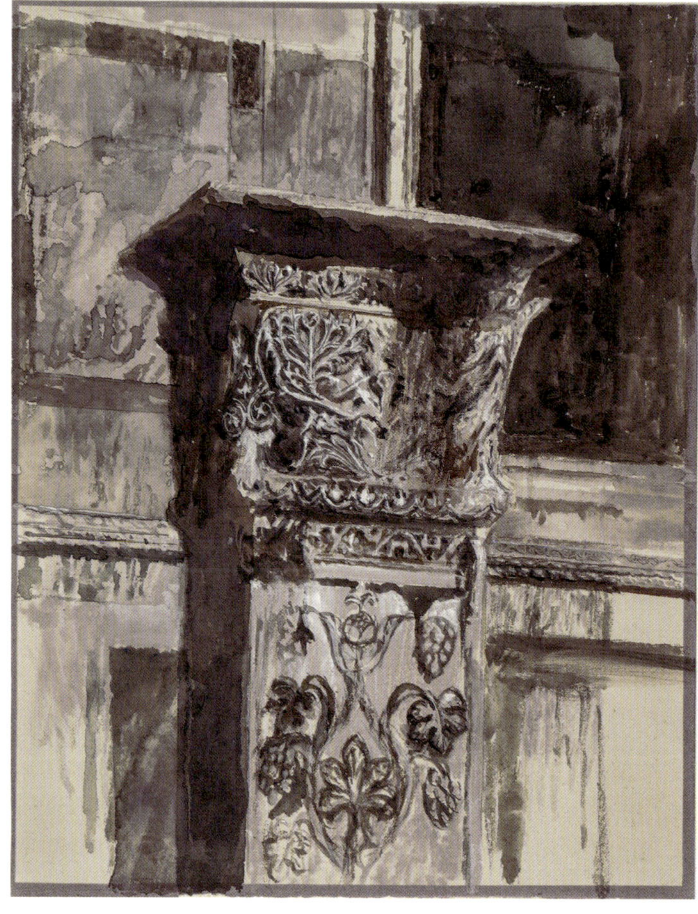

ONE OF THE SAINT JEAN D'ACRE COLUMNS, ON THE SOUTH SIDE
OF ST MARK'S; ISOLATED PILLAR WITH DECORATION
IN RELIEF, WALL AND WINDOW BEYOND, 1879
watercolour, touched with white, on purple paper, 280 × 222 mm
London, The British Museum, inv. 1967,1014.141

THE SAINT JEAN D'ACRE COLUMNS
WITH THE SOUTH SIDE OF ST. MARK'S, 1879
watercolour, white lead on purple paper, 150 × 90 mm
London, The British Museum, inv. 1901,0516.2

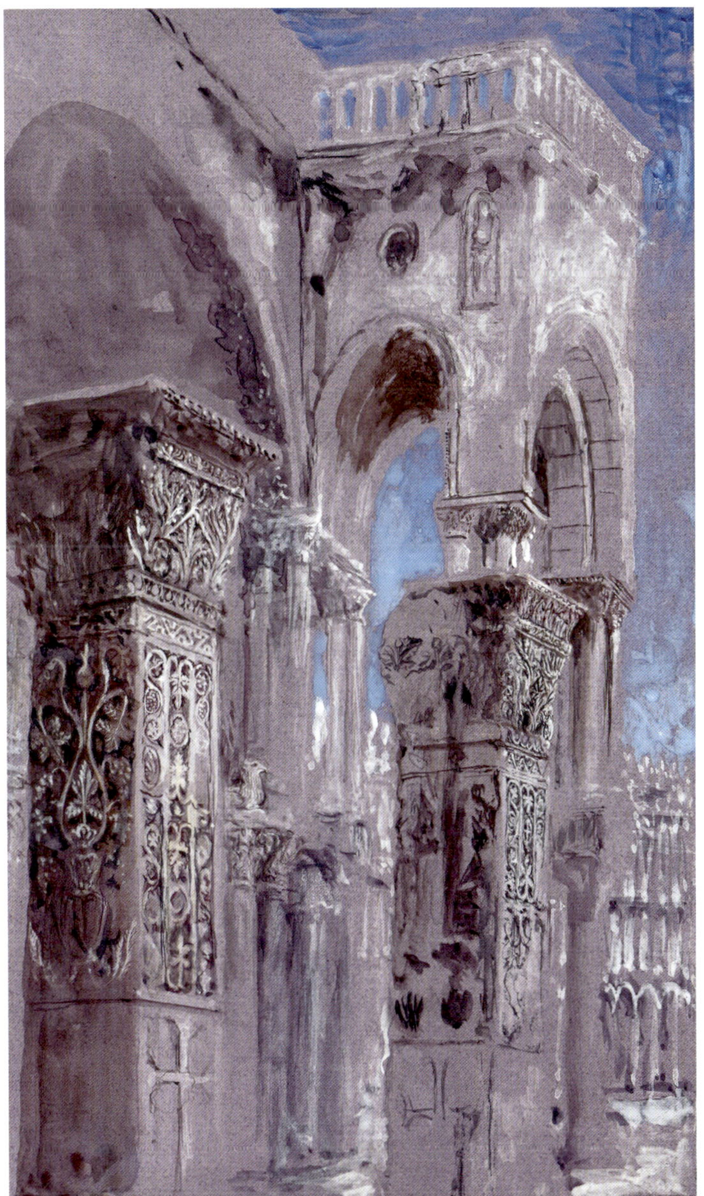

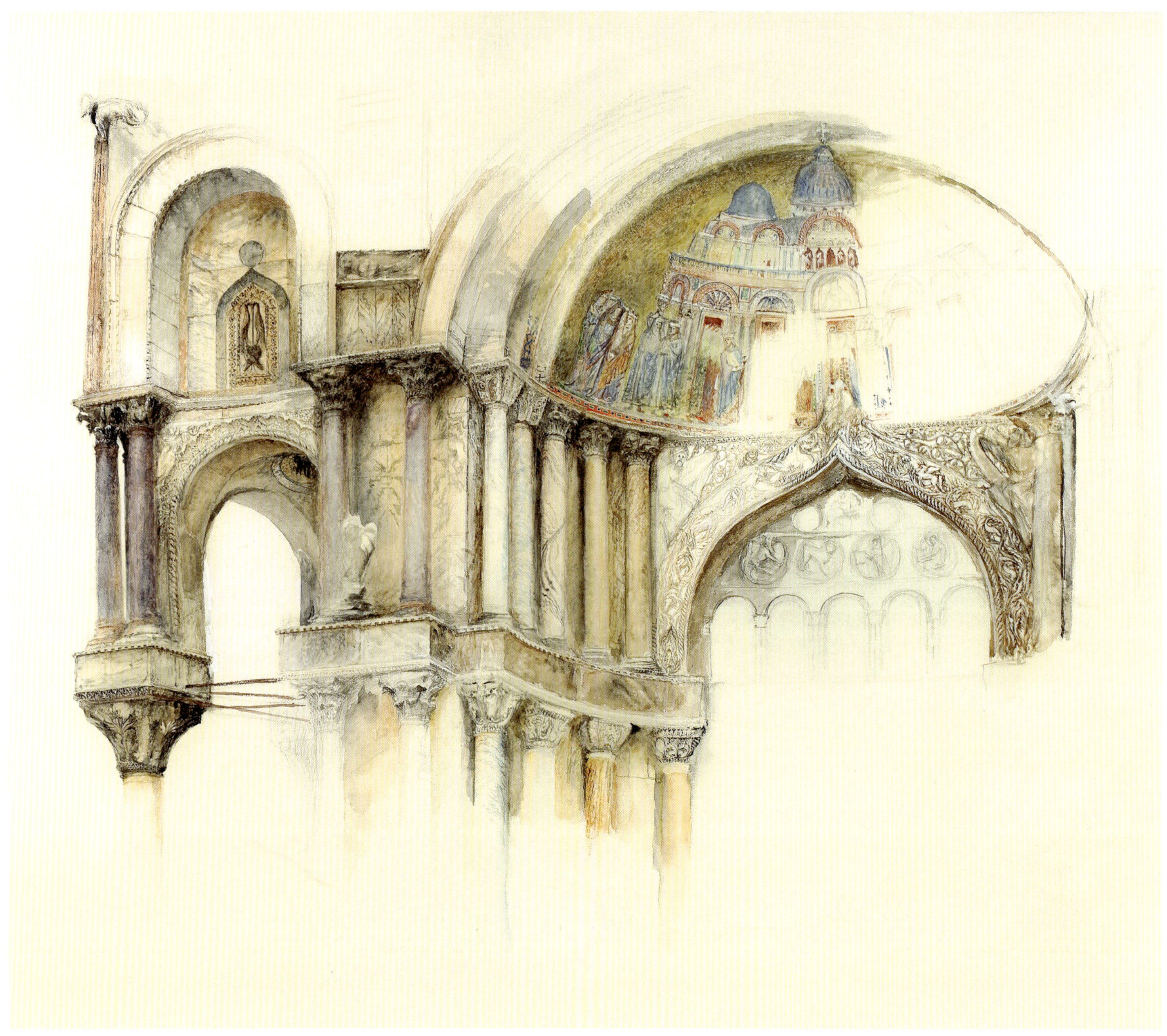

NORTH-WEST PORCH OF ST. MARK'S, 1877
pencil, watercolour, bodycolour on paper, 648 × 770 mm
Lancaster, The Ruskin, Lancaster University, inv. 1996P1633

PART OF A SKETCH OF THE NORTH-WEST PORCH OF ST. MARK'S, 1879
watercolour, white gouache, brown and black ink, and graphite on cream wove paper, 512 × 381 mm
Harvard, Harvard Art Museums / Fogg Museum
gift of Samuel Sachs, inv. 1919.259

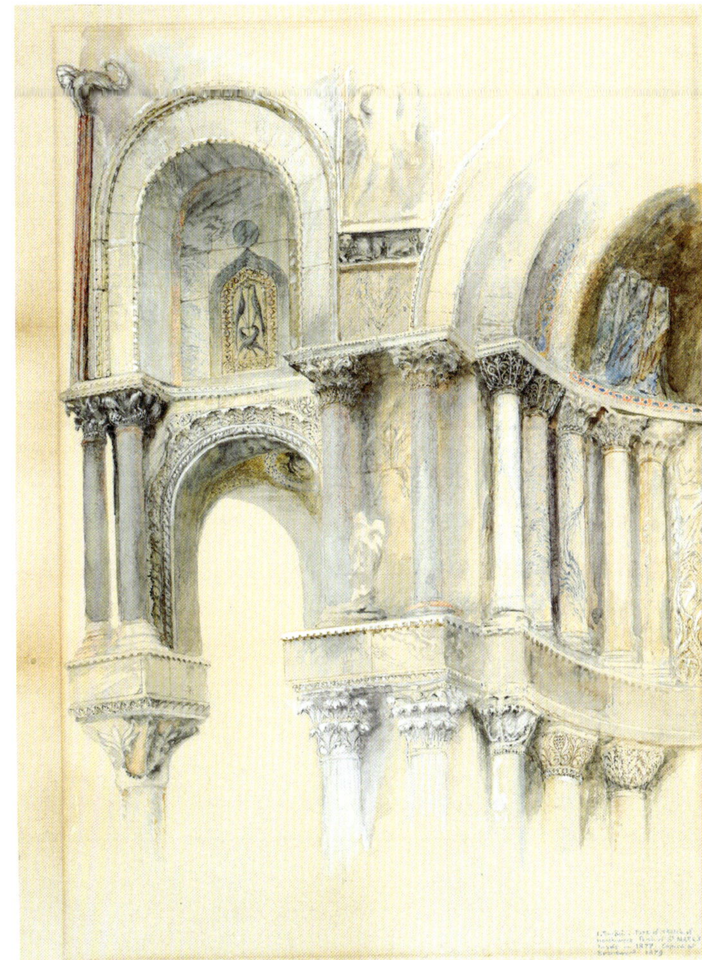

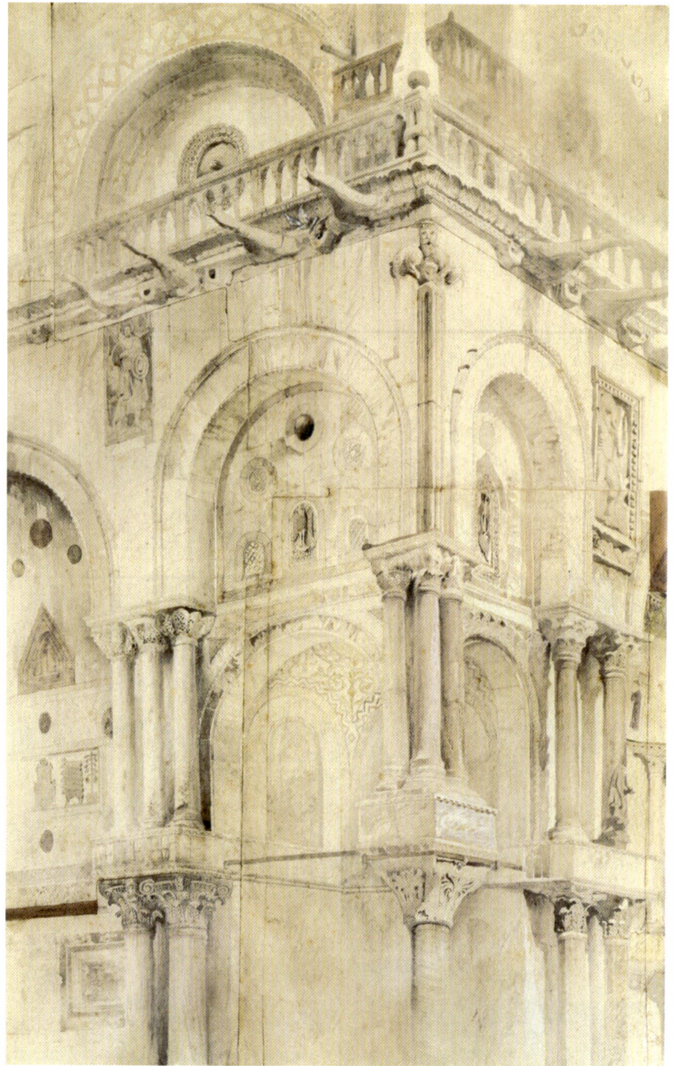

THE NORTH-WEST ANGLE
OF THE FACADE OF ST. MARK'S, undated
watercolour and graphite on paper, 940 × 610 mm
London, Tate, inv. N02972, presented by Art Fund, 1914

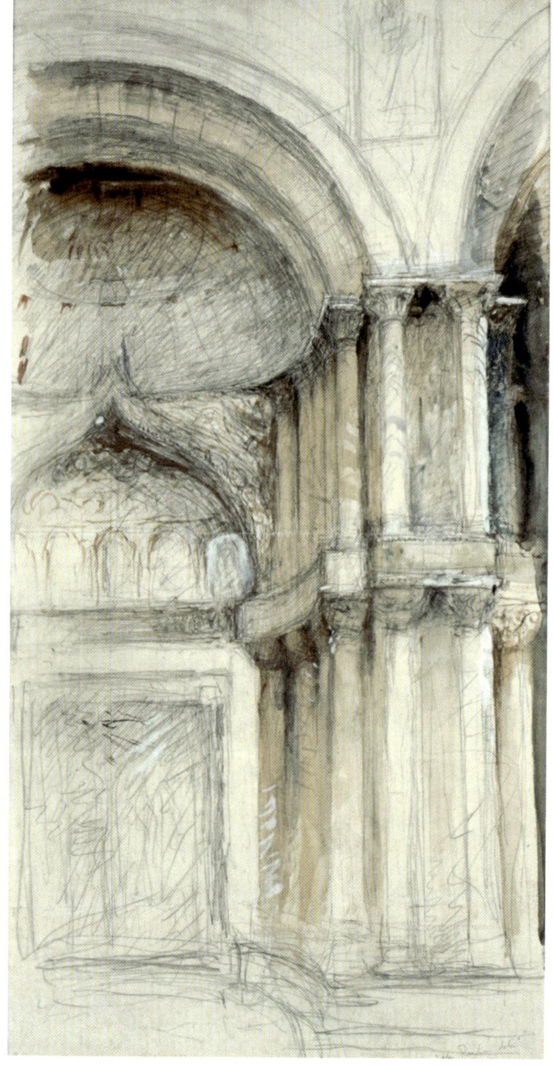

NORTH-WEST PORTICO OF ST. MARK'S, *circa* 1877
watercolour, bodycolour and pencil on paper, 630 × 330 mm
Private collection

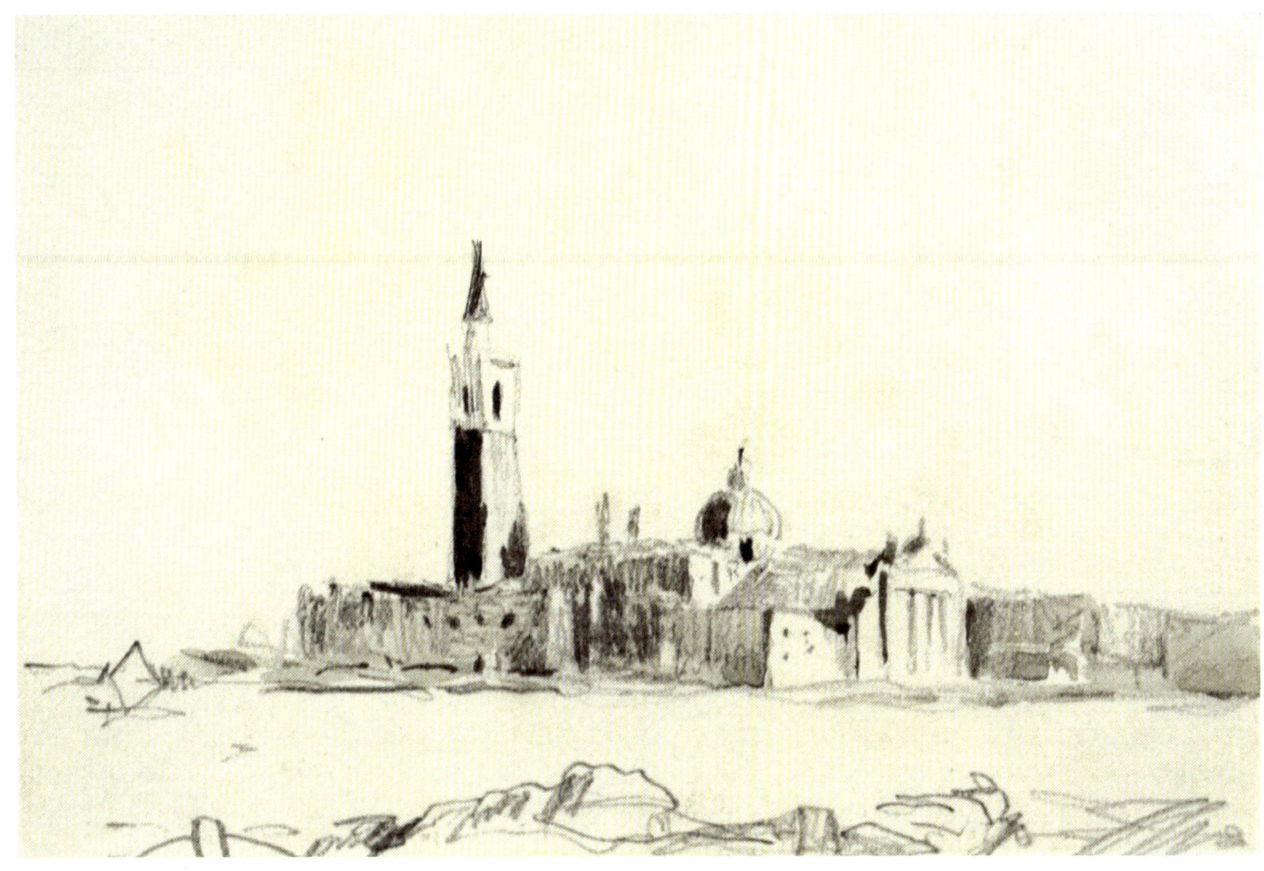

SAN GIORGIO MAGGIORE, *circa* 1850
watercolour and pencil on paper, 89 × 128 mm
Kendal, Abbot Hall, Lakeland Arts Trust, inv. AH2622/84
the Banner Bequest, given by Mrs Josephine Banner, 1984

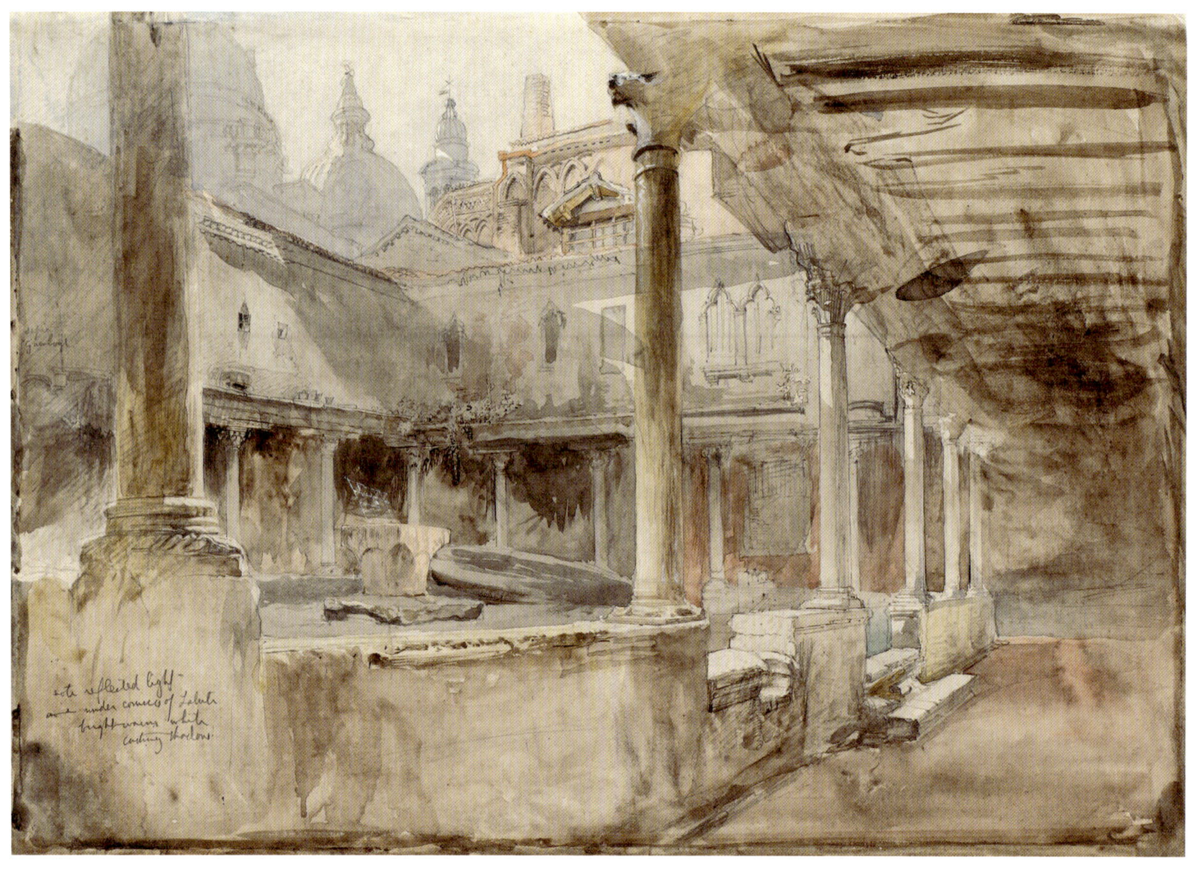

THE CLOISTER OF SAN GREGORIO, 1846
pencil, watercolour with touches of gouache, 343 × 493 mm
inscription: by Ruskin, left centre "sepia gamboge"; lower left "note reflected light / under cornice of Salute / bright warm white / casting shadows"; on the verso in another hand "Miss Tovey, 29 Paddington Street, Portman Square"
Private collection (courtesy of Lowell Libson & Jonny Yarker Ltd)

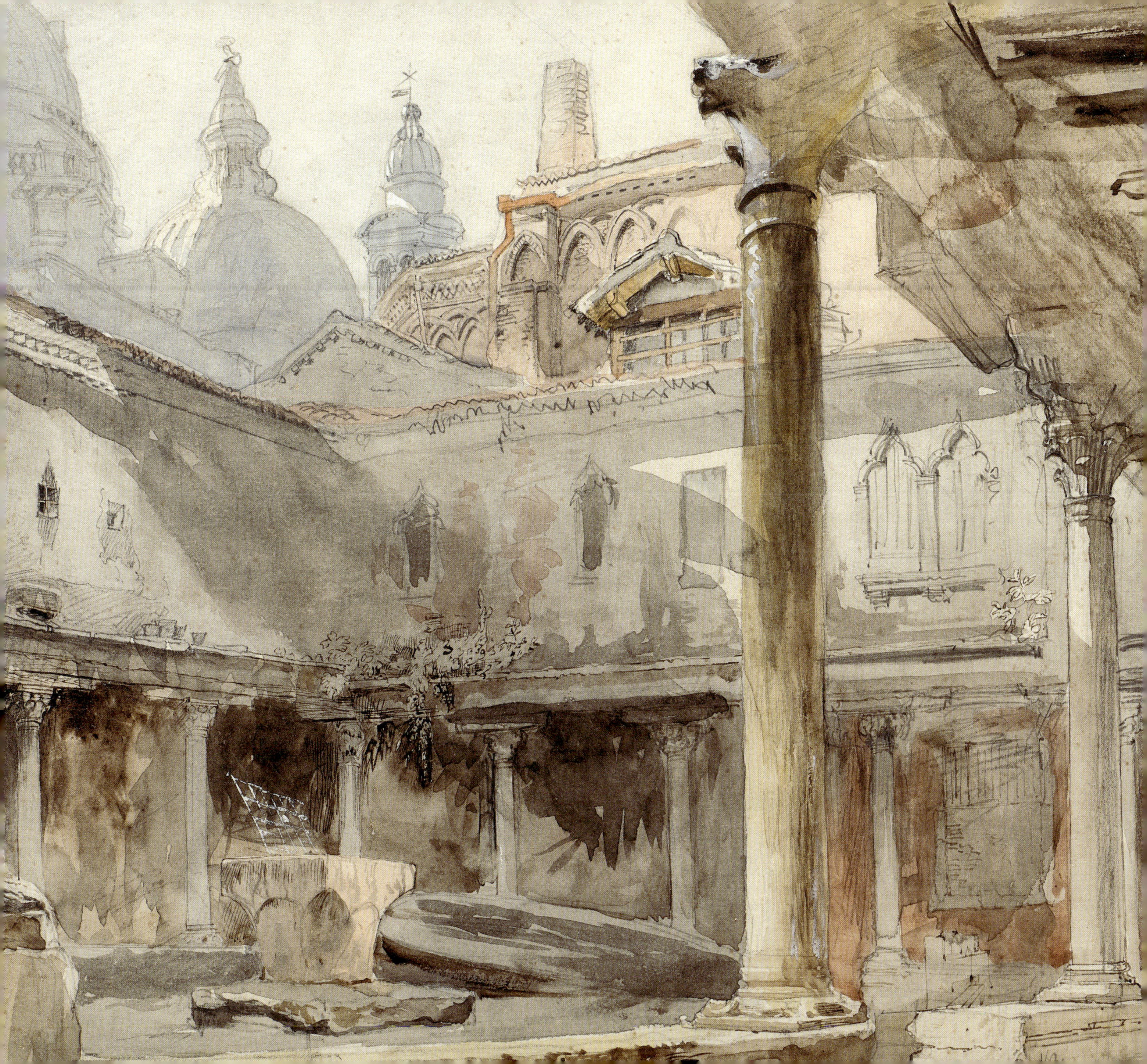

THE STONES OF VENICE

WORKSHEET/DETAILS

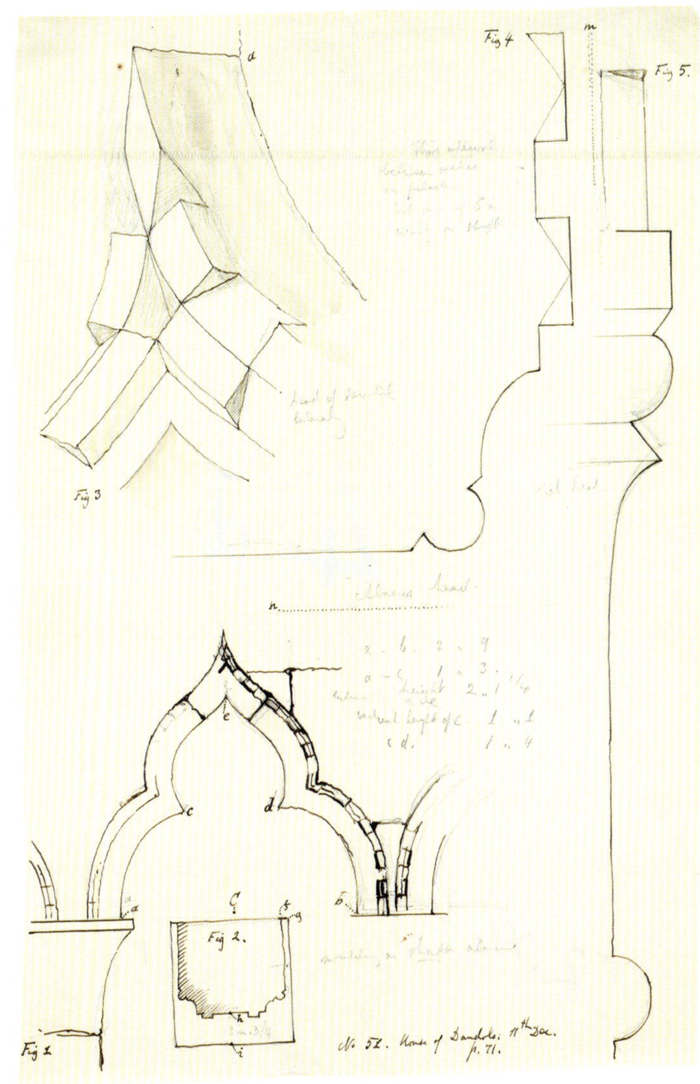

ARCHITECTURAL STUDIES: LINTELS, ABACUS HEADS, ARCHES, ETC. (HOUSE OF DANDOLO), 1849
brown ink, brown wash, and graphite on thin cream wove paper, 359 × 240 mm
Harvard, Harvard Art Museums / Fogg Museum, transfer from the Fine Arts Department, Harvard University, inv. 1926.33.125

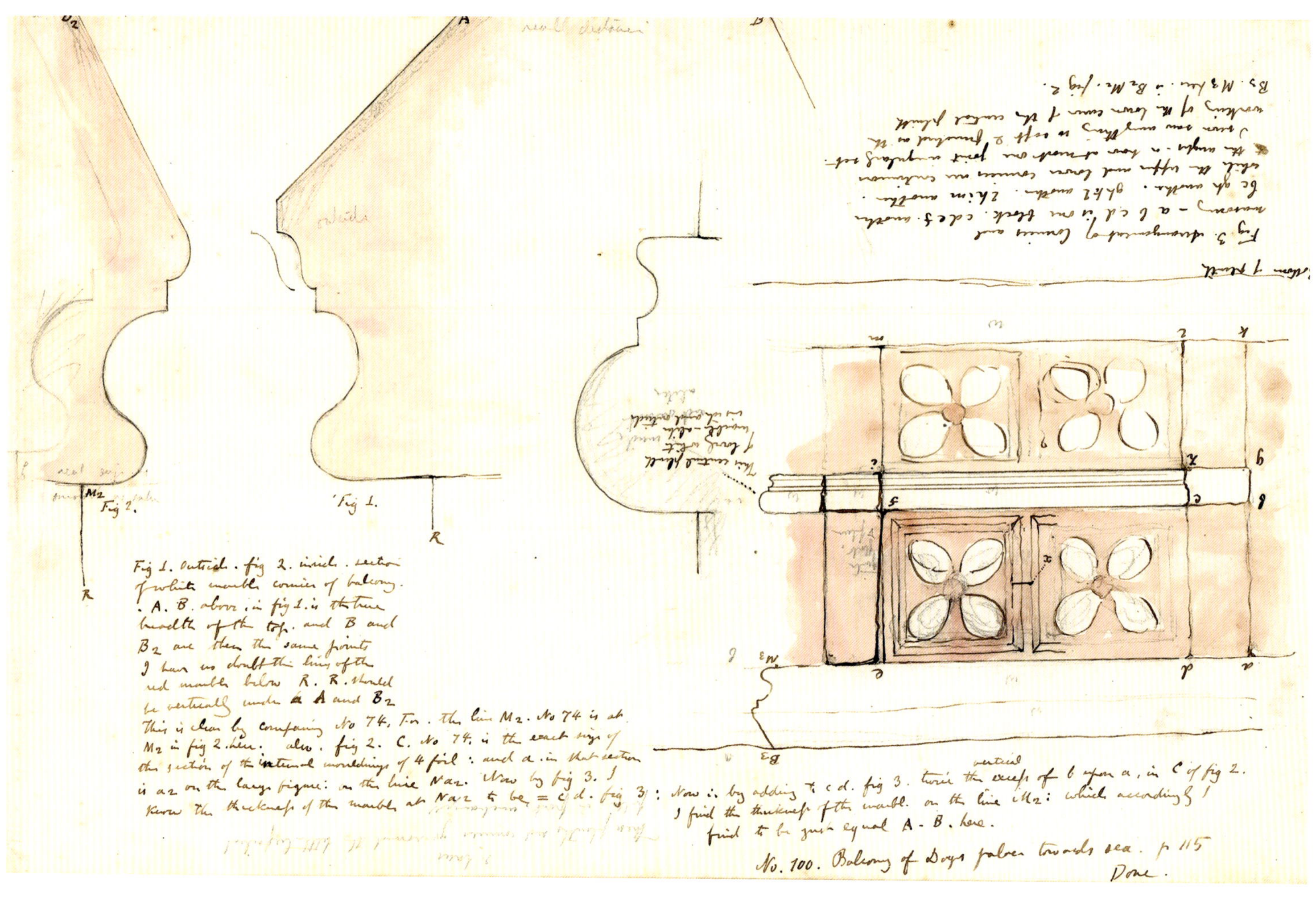

THE STONES OF VENICE WORKSHEET: BALCONY OF DOGE'S PALACE, 1849
pencil, black ink, watercolour on paper, *circa* 278 × 429 mm
inscription: "No. 100. Balcony of Doges palace towards sea. P. 115 / Done"
Lancaster, The Ruskin, Lancaster University, inv. 1996P1597

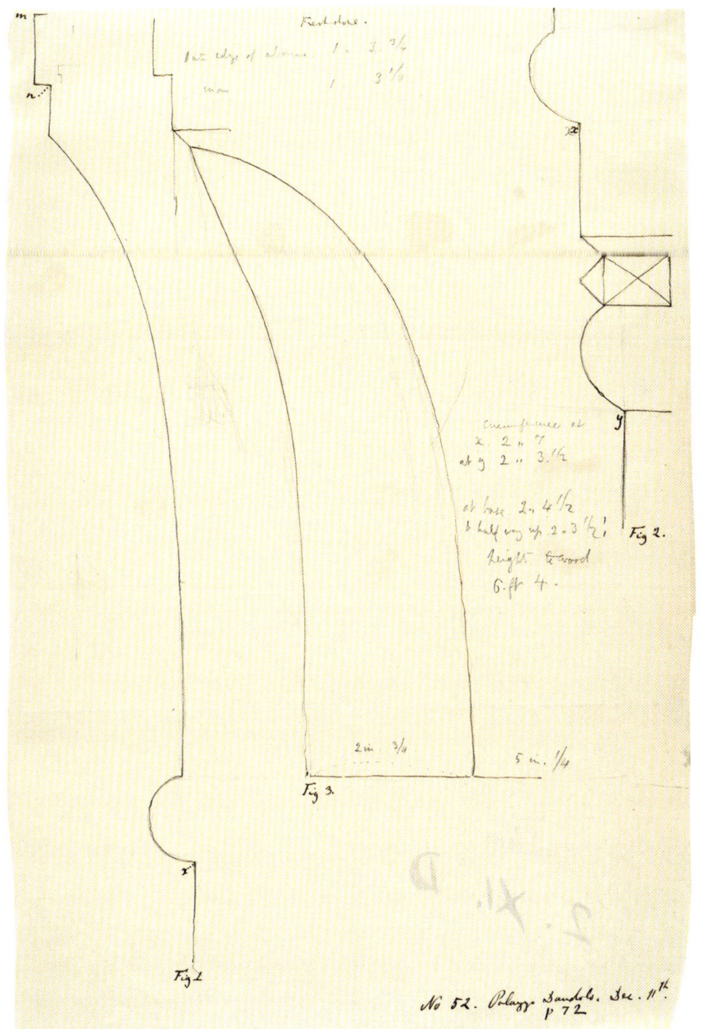

ARCHITECTURAL STUDY: PALAZZO DANDOLO, 1849
brown ink and graphite on thin cream wove paper, 355 × 240 mm
Harvard, Harvard Art Museums / Fogg Museum, transfer from
the Fine Arts Department, Harvard University, inv. 1926.33.123

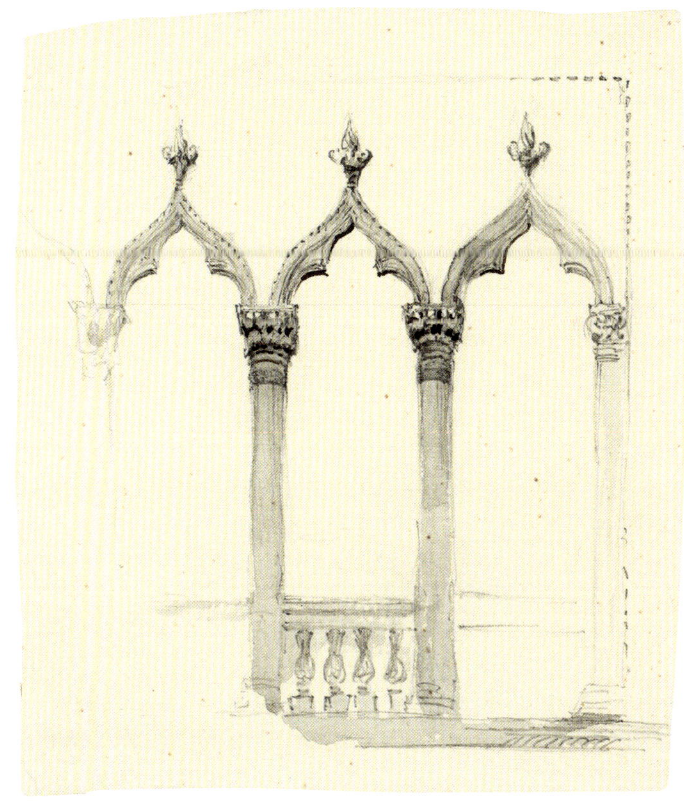

ARCHITECTURAL STUDY: THREE SECTIONS OF A VENETIAN ARCADE, undated
brown and black ink, grey wash, and graphite on cream card, 125 × 110 mm (irregular)
Harvard, Harvard Art Museums / Fogg Museum, transfer from
the Fine Arts Department, Harvard University, inv. 1926.33.124

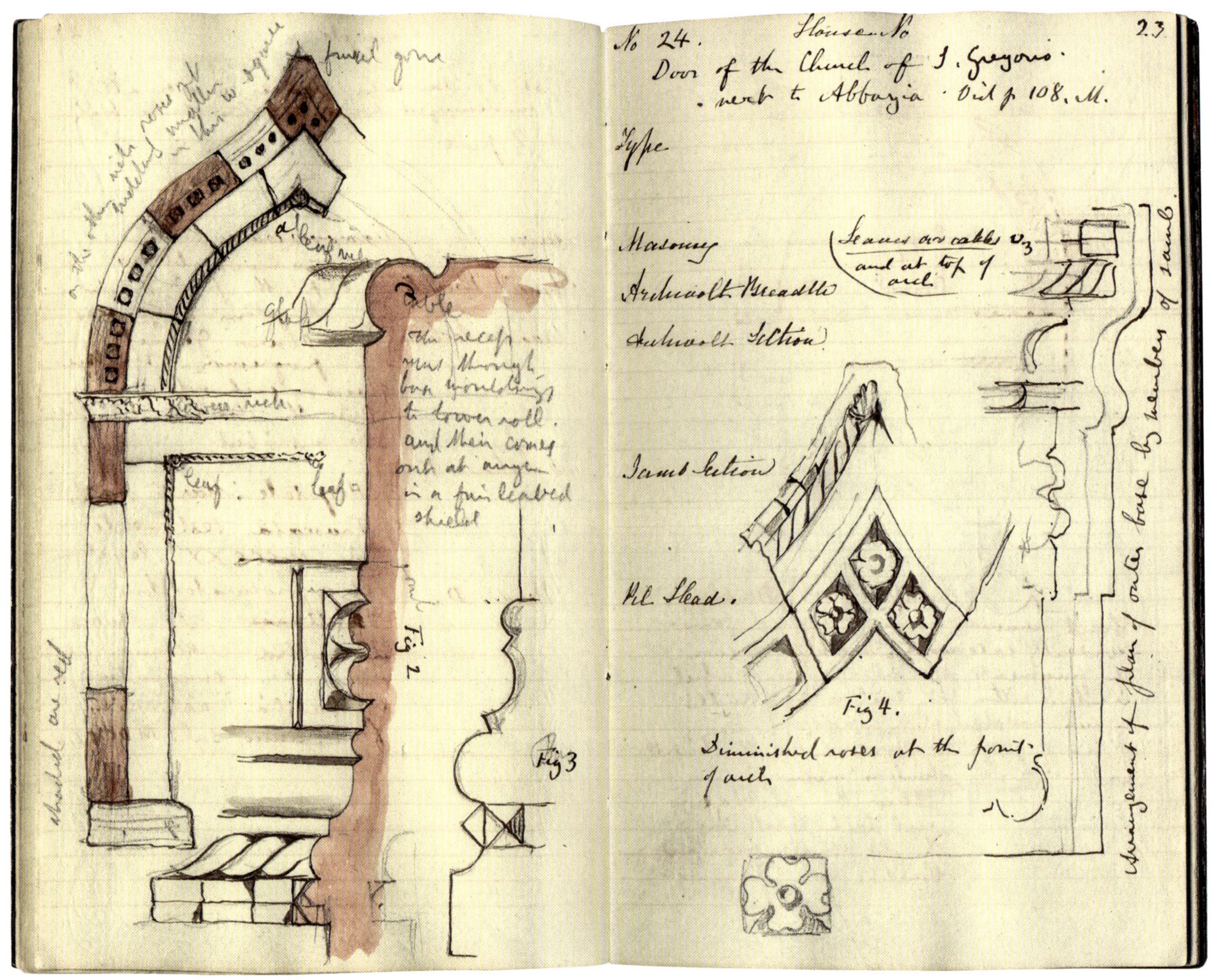

DOOR OF THE CHURCH OF SAN GREGORIO
SHEET 22V FROM DOOR BOOK, 1849–50
manuscript notebook, green/red marbled binding, 195 × 123 × 9 mm
inscription: on the cover, on label "Door Book"; on the back cover "Door"
Lancaster, The Ruskin, Lancaster University, inv. 1996P1615

SHEET FROM RUSKIN'S *STONES OF VENICE* MANUSCRIPT
WATERCOLOUR DRAWING OF AN ARCHWAY WITH STEPS, 1851–53
pencil, ink, watercolour on paper, drops of sealing wax, 342 × 251 mm
New York, The Morgan Library & Museum, inv. MA 398#2

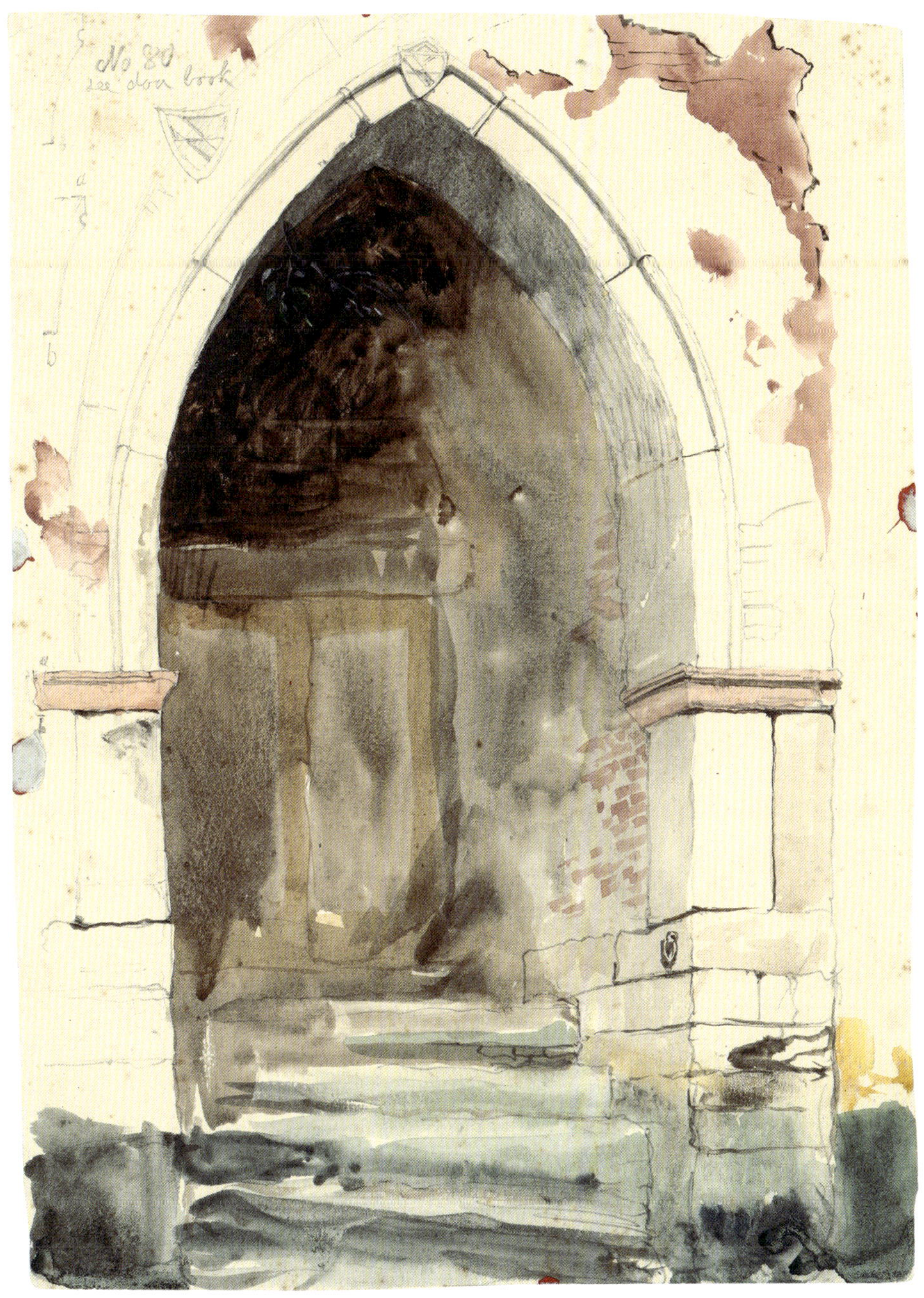
No 80
see door book

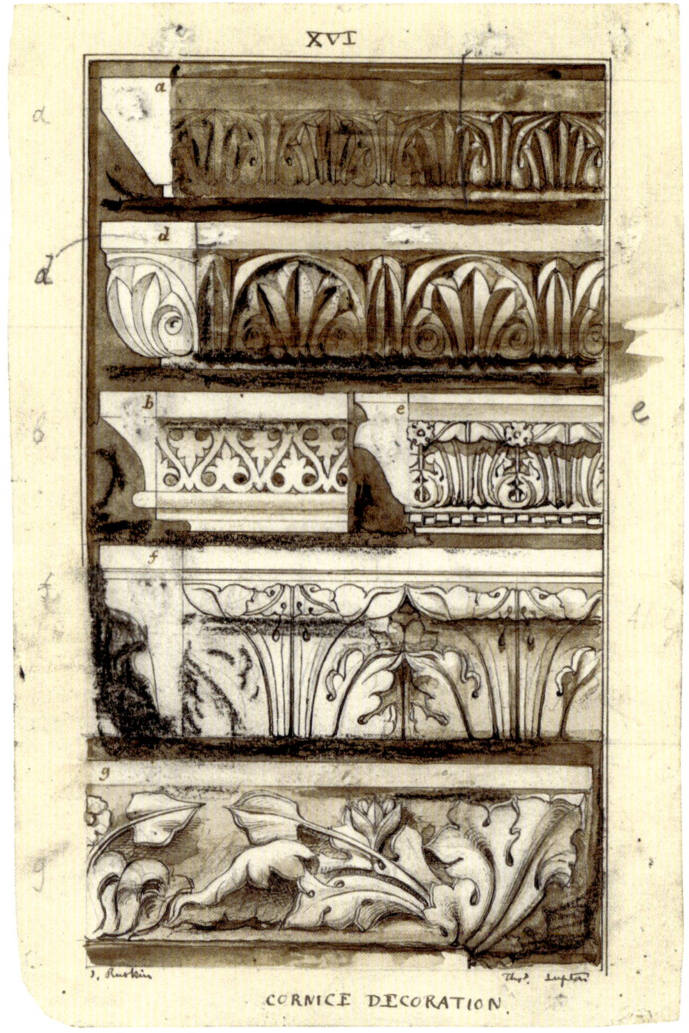

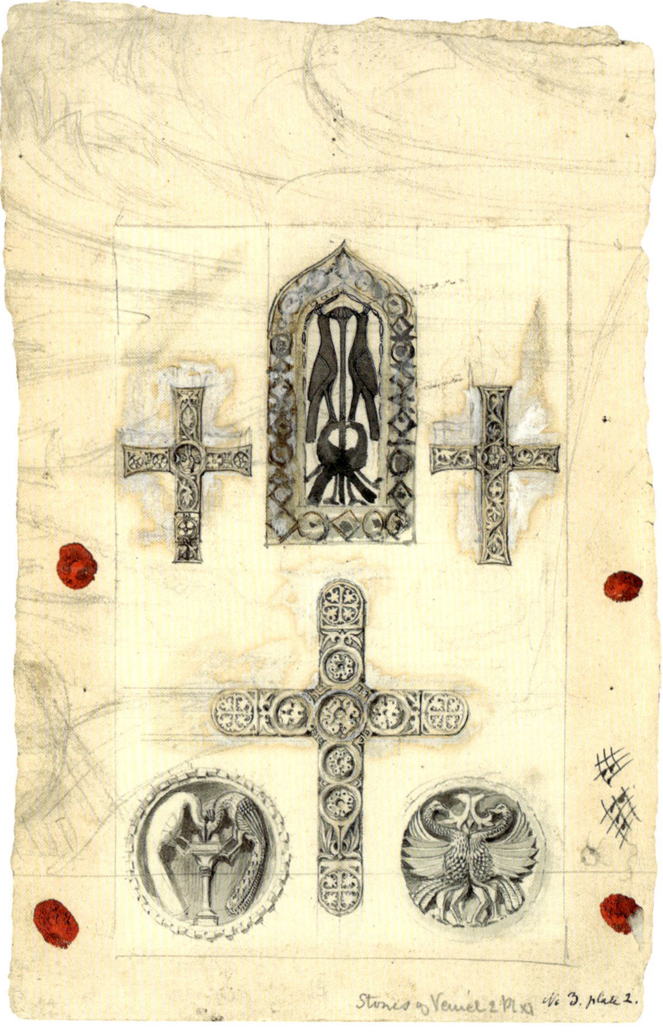

THE STONES OF VENICE: CORNICE DECORATION, 1851
pencil, ink, ink wash on paper, 240 × 162 mm
inscription: "XVI / J Ruskin / Thos. Lupton / CORNICE DECORATION"
Lancaster, The Ruskin, Lancaster University, inv. 1996P1036

THE STONES OF VENICE: BYZANTINE SCULPTURE, 1851
pencil, ink wash, watercolour, bodycolour on paper, *circa* 206 × 136 mm
on the verso, *Female face* (Portrait of Effie Gray?), pencil on paper
inscription: "No. 3. Plate 2"
Lancaster, The Ruskin, Lancaster University, inv. 1996P1028

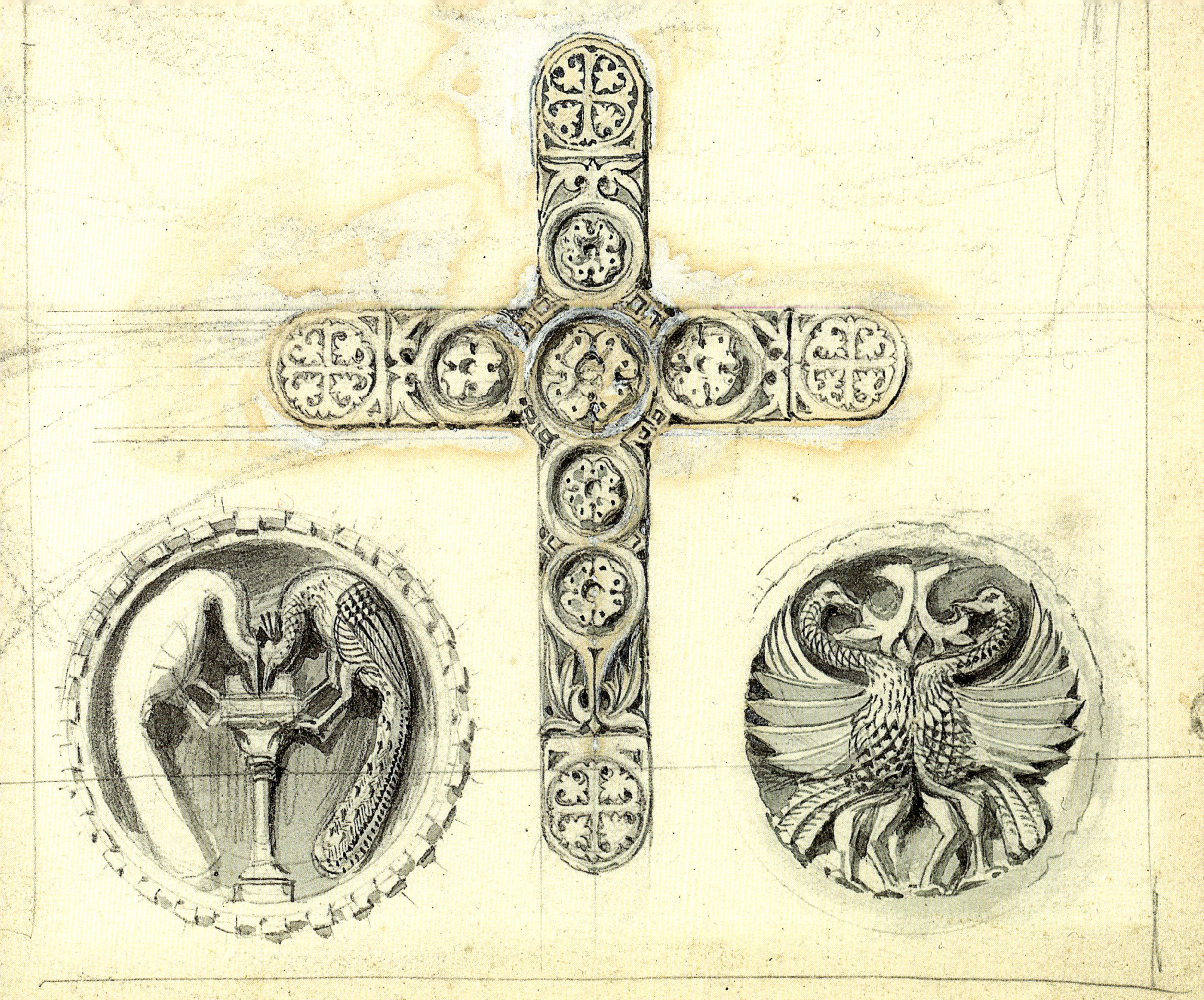

Stones of Venice 2 Pl XI No 3.

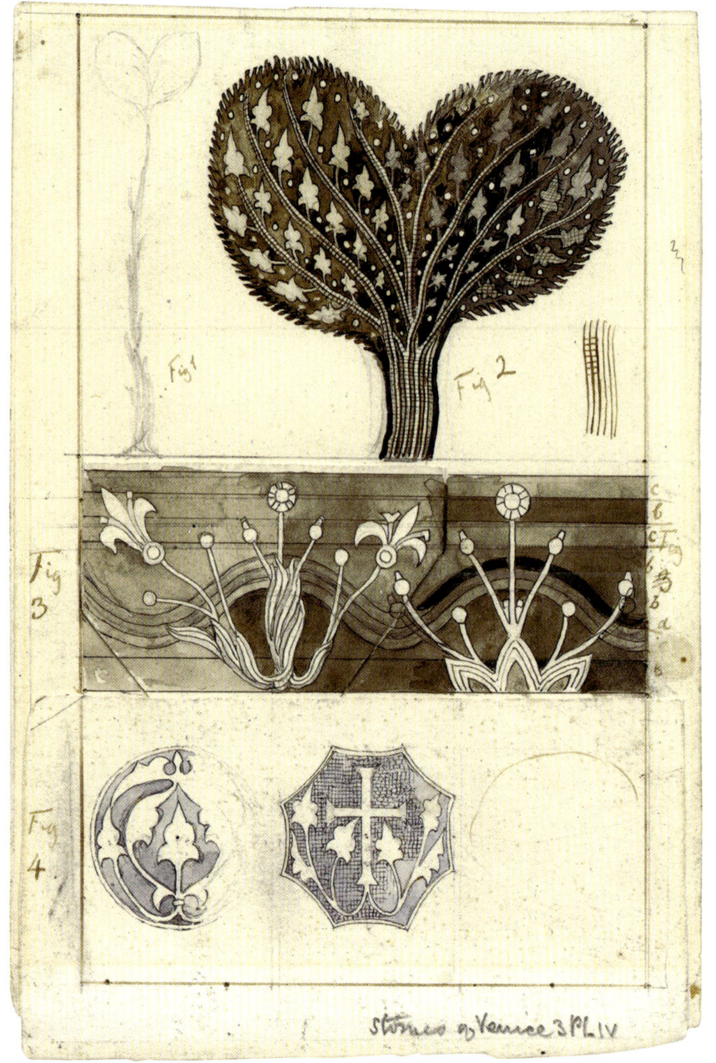

THE STONES OF VENICE: MOSAICS OF OLIVE TREE AND FLOWERS, 1852
pencil, watercolour on paper, 230 × 157 mm
inscription: "Stones of Venice 3 PL IV"
Lancaster, The Ruskin, Lancaster University, inv. 1996P1059

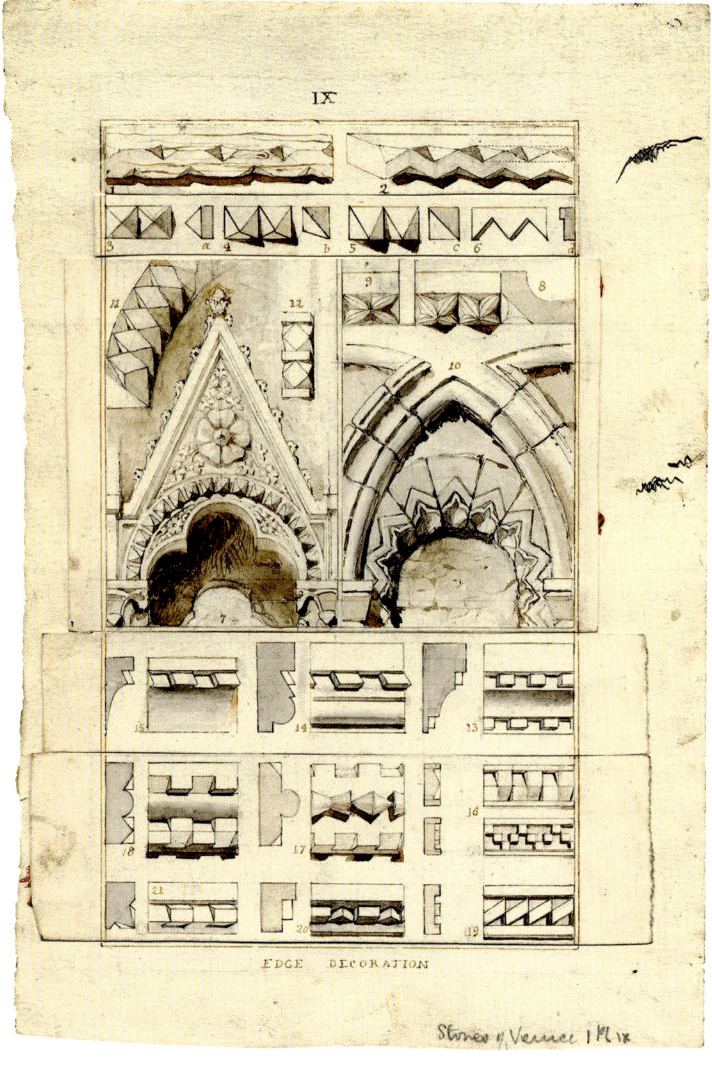

THE STONES OF VENICE: EDGE DECORATION, 1849–51
pencil, ink, ink wash on six joined sheets, 235 × 135 mm
inscription: "IX EDGE DECORATION Stones of Venice 1 PL IX"
Lancaster, The Ruskin, Lancaster University, inv. 1996P1042

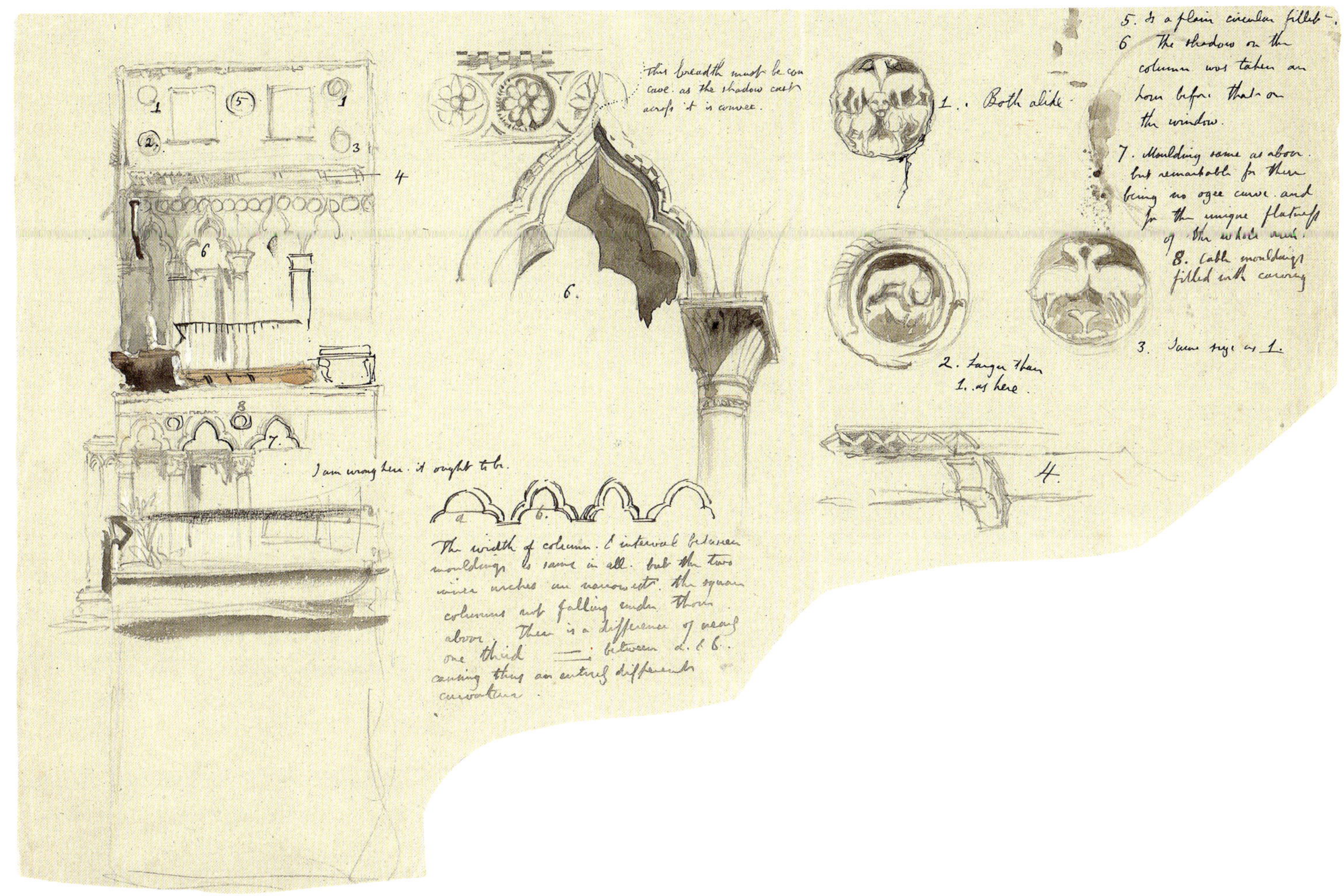

SHEET FROM RUSKIN'S *STONES OF VENICE* MANUSCRIPT: SKETCHES OF COLUMNS AND FILLETS WITH MANUSCRIPT ANNOTATIONS BEGINNING "THIS BREADTH MUST BE CONCAVE AS THE SHADOW CAST ACROSS IT IS CONVEX", 1851–53
pencil, ink, watercolour on paper, 250 × 386 mm
New York, The Morgan Library & Museum, inv. MA 398#1

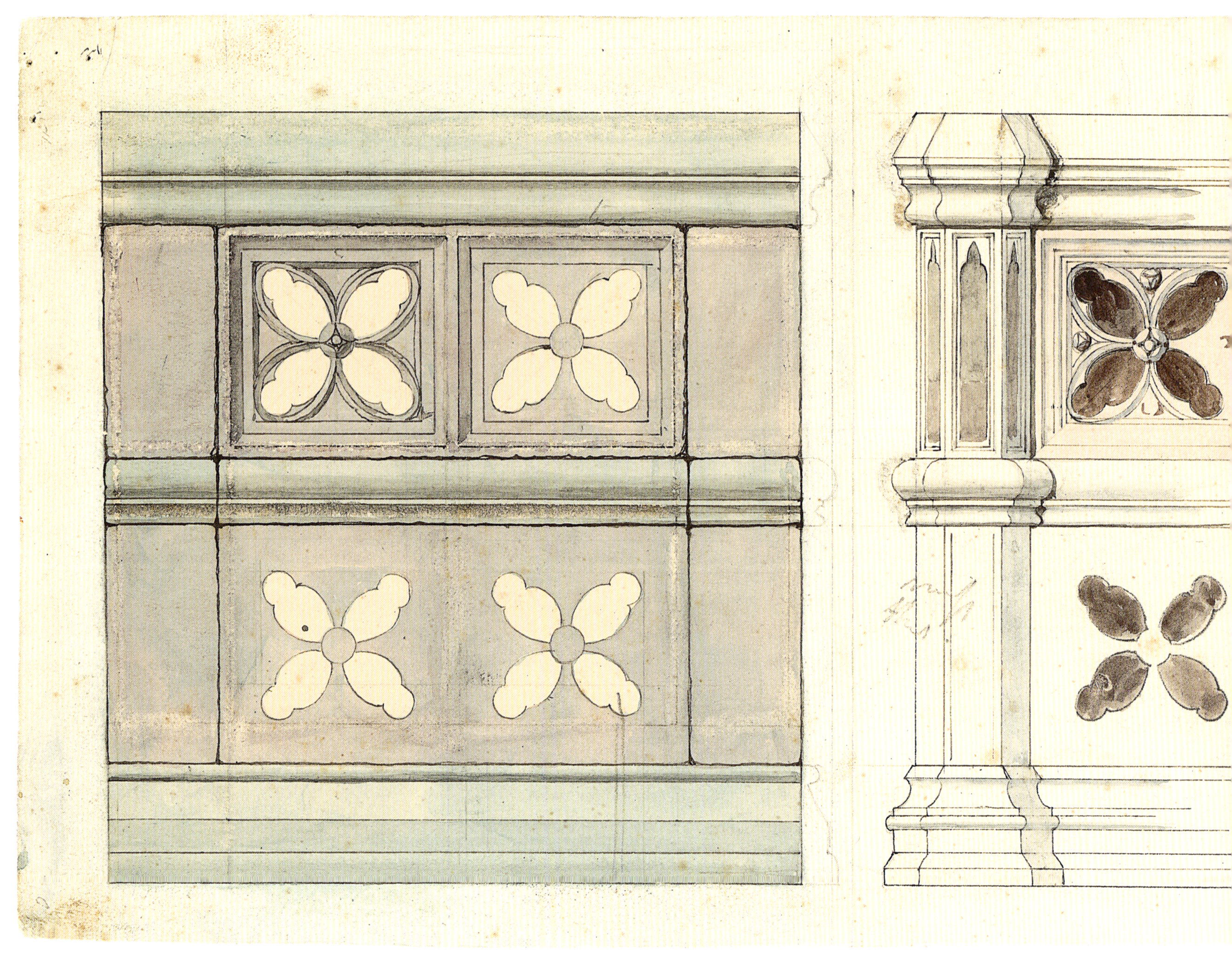

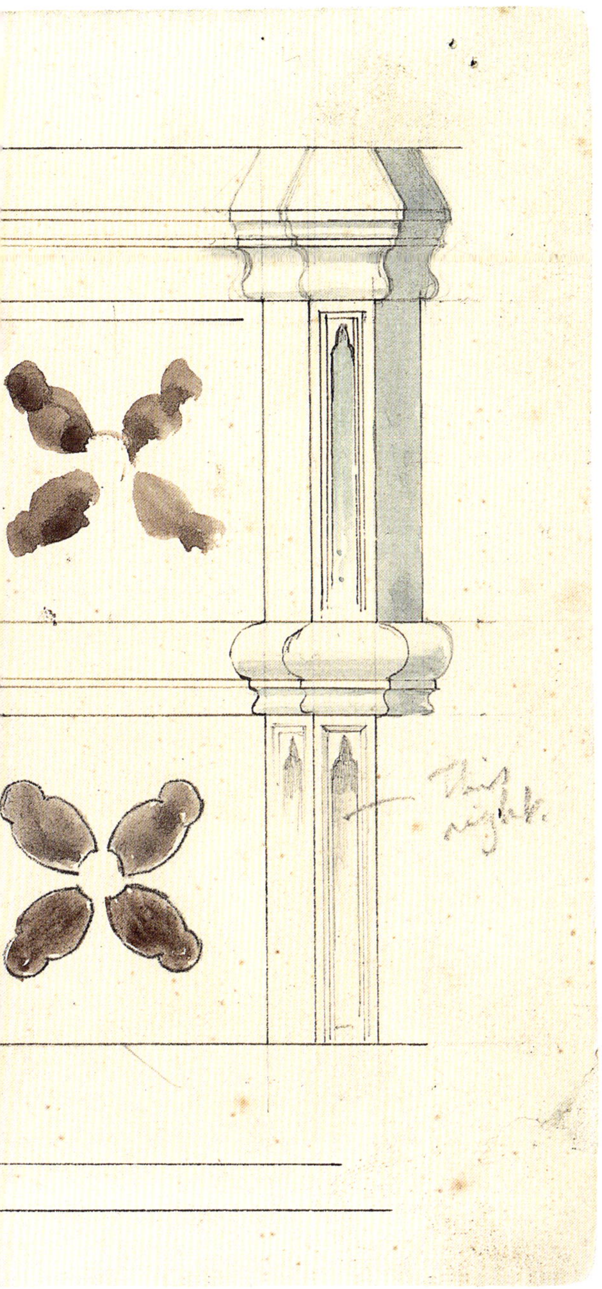

SHEET FROM RUSKIN'S *STONES OF VENICE* MANUSCRIPT
WATERCOLOUR DRAWING OF TWO SQUARE ARCHITECTURAL ELEMENTS WITH DECORATIVE DETAIL, 1851–53
pencil, ink, watercolour on paper, 178 × 340 mm
New York, The Morgan Library & Museum, inv. MA 398#4

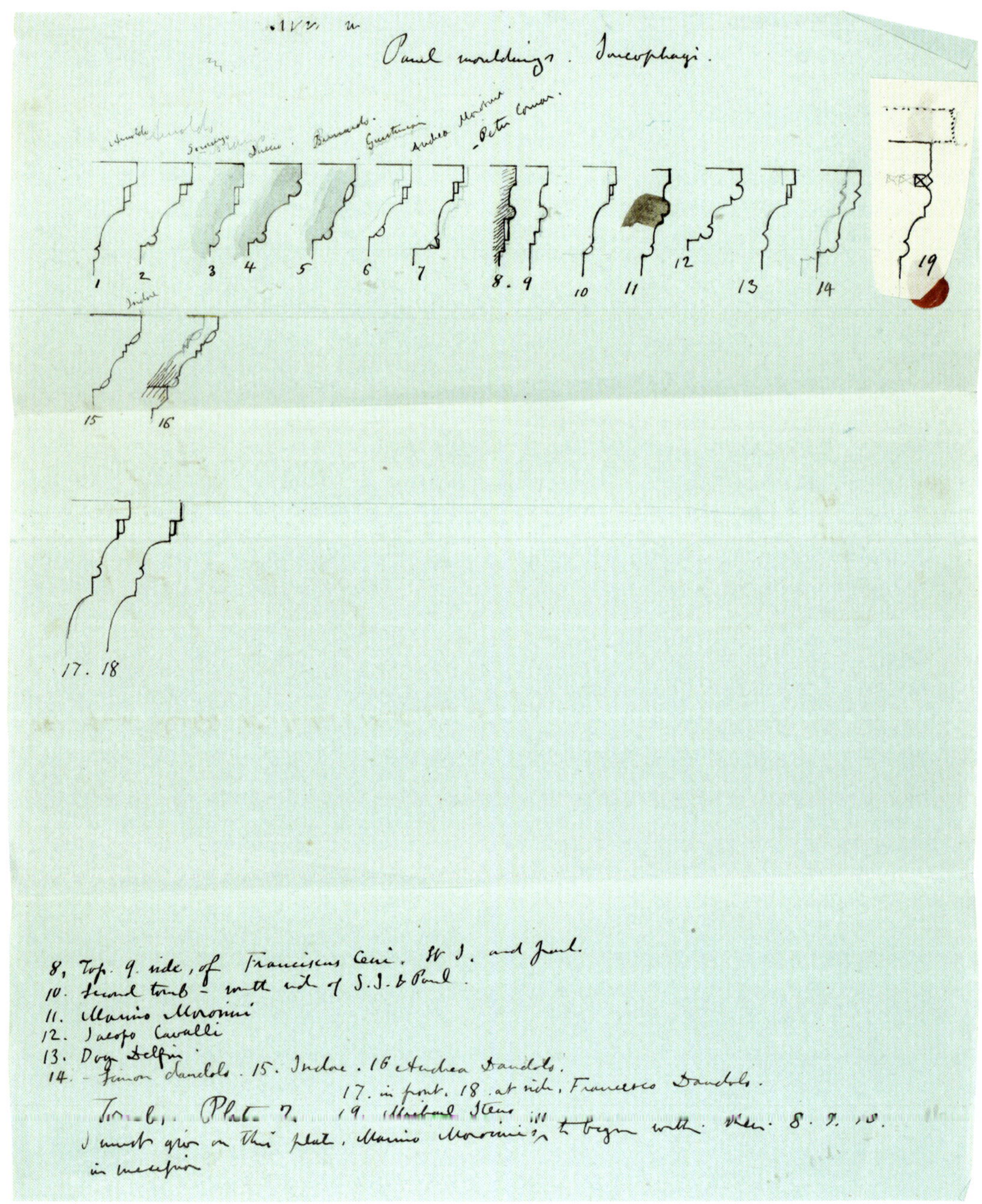
Panel mouldings. Sarcophagi.
1 2 3 4 5 6 7 8. 9 10 11 12 13 14 19
15 16
17. 18
11. Marino Morosini
12. Jacopo Cavalli
13. Doge Delfin
16 Andrea Dandolo.
17. in front. 18. at side. Francesco Dandolo.
Plate 7.

PANEL MOULDINGS, SARCOPHAGI, 1849–52
black and brown ink and graphite on thin blue wove paper; attached piece of white paper, 271 × 223 mm
Harvard, Harvard Art Museums / Fogg Museum, transfer from the Fine Arts Department, Harvard University, inv. 1926.33.127

ARCHITECTURAL DETAIL, 1849–52
graphite, grey wash, and brown ink on cream card, 192 × 158 mm
Harvard, Harvard Art Museums / Fogg Museum, transfer from the Fine Arts Department, Harvard University, inv. 1926.33.122

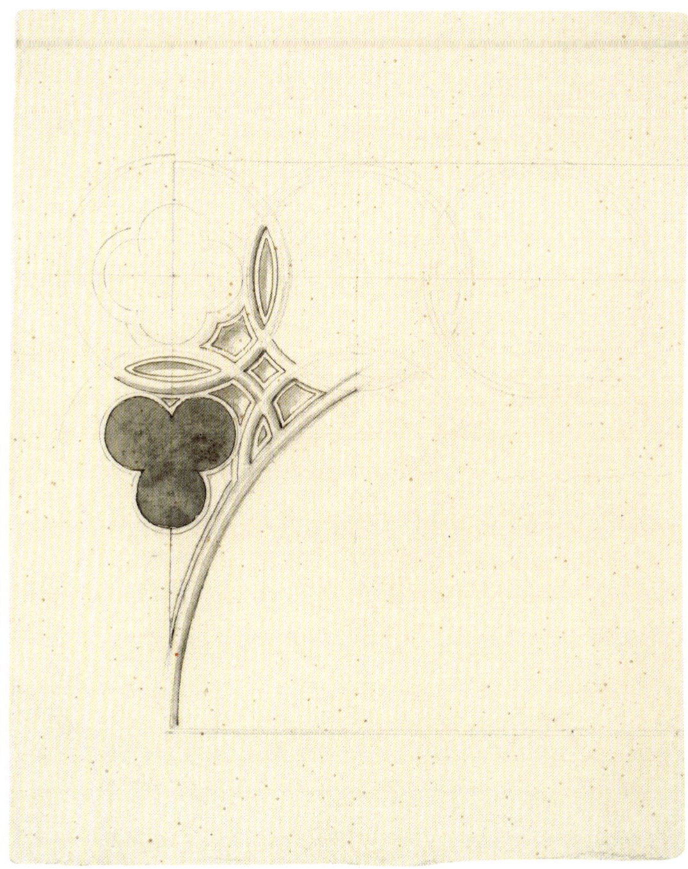

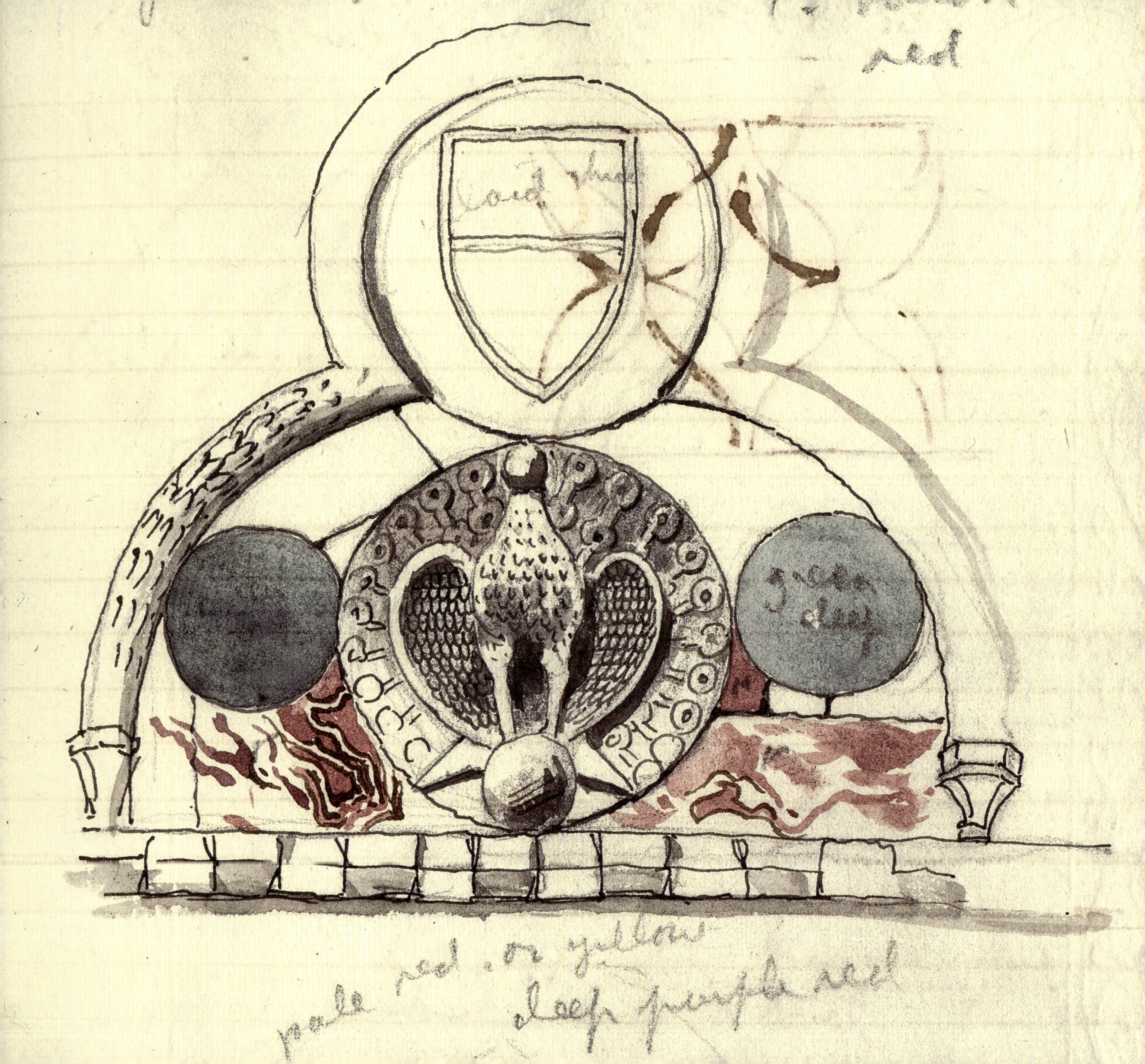
red
green deep
pale red . or yellow
deep purple red

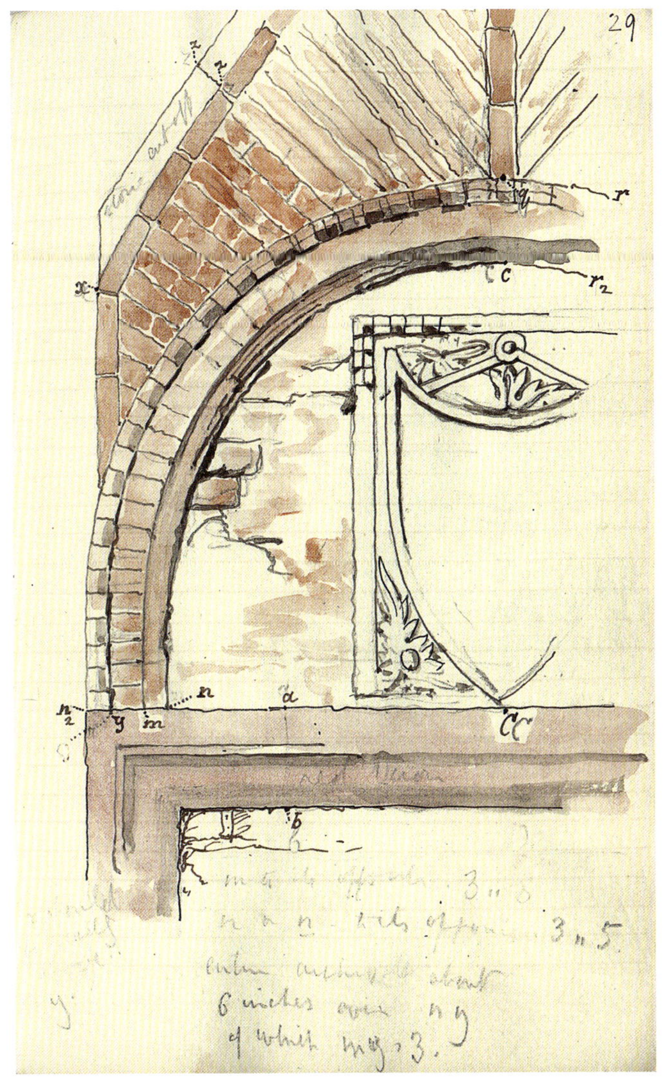

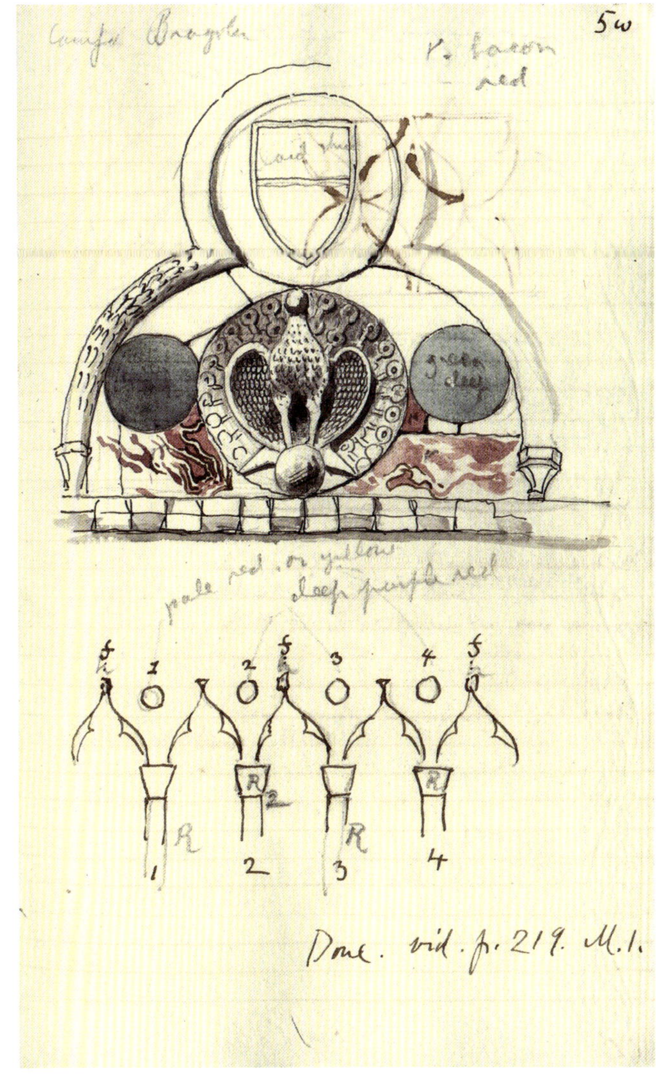

CARVING OVER DOOR, BRANCH OPPOSITE MOCENIGO
SHEET 29R FROM BIT BOOK, 1850
manuscript notebook, green marbled binding, 194 × 122 × 11 mm
inscription: on the cover, on label "Bit Book"
Lancaster, The Ruskin, Lancaster University, inv. 1996P1614

CAMPO BRAGORA, PALAZZO DEI BADOARI PARTECIPAZZI
[BADOER PARTECIPAZIO], SHEET 77V FROM BIT BOOK, 1850
manuscript notebook, green marbled binding, 194 × 122 × 11 mm
inscription: on the cover, on label "Bit Book"
Lancaster, The Ruskin, Lancaster University, inv. 1996P1614

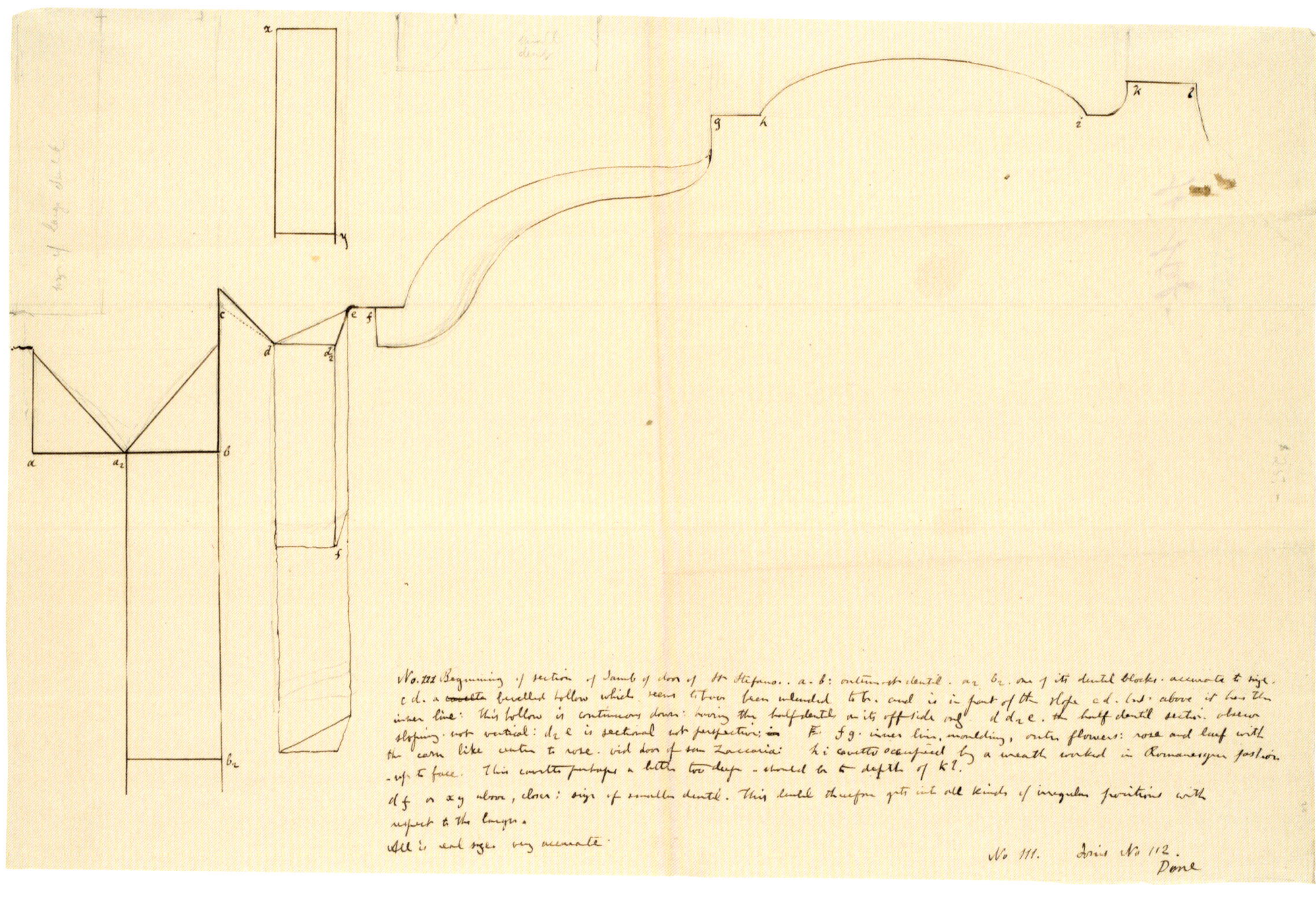

ARCHITECTURAL SKETCH: SECTION OF DOOR JAMB, SAINT STEFANO, 1850
brown ink and graphite on thin cream wove paper, 285 × 445 mm
Harvard, Harvard Art Museums / Fogg Museum, transfer from the Fine Arts Department, Harvard University, inv. 1926.33.126

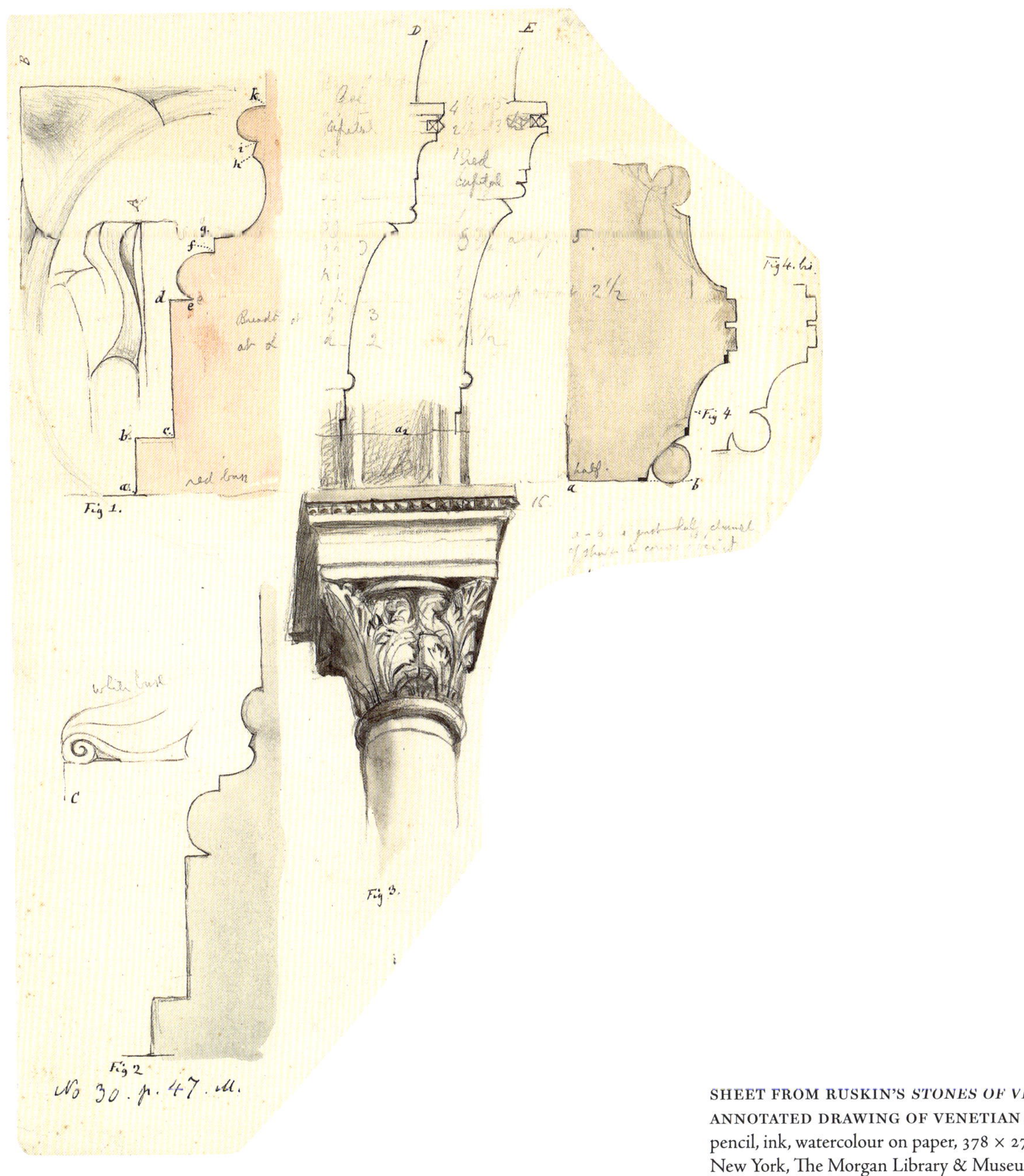

SHEET FROM RUSKIN'S *STONES OF VENICE* MANUSCRIPT
ANNOTATED DRAWING OF VENETIAN CAPITALS, 1851–53
pencil, ink, watercolour on paper, 378 × 277 mm
New York, The Morgan Library & Museum, inv. MA 398#3

STUDIES FROM PAINTERS

JOSEPH MALLORD WILLIAM TURNER, *THE SUN OF VENICE GOING TO SEA*. STUDY, 1843
pencil, gouache (or chalk?) on grey paper, mounted on paper, 234 × 270 mm
Birmingham, Birmingham Museums Trust / Birmingham Museum & Art Gallery, inv. 1907P142
presented by an anonymous donor, 1907

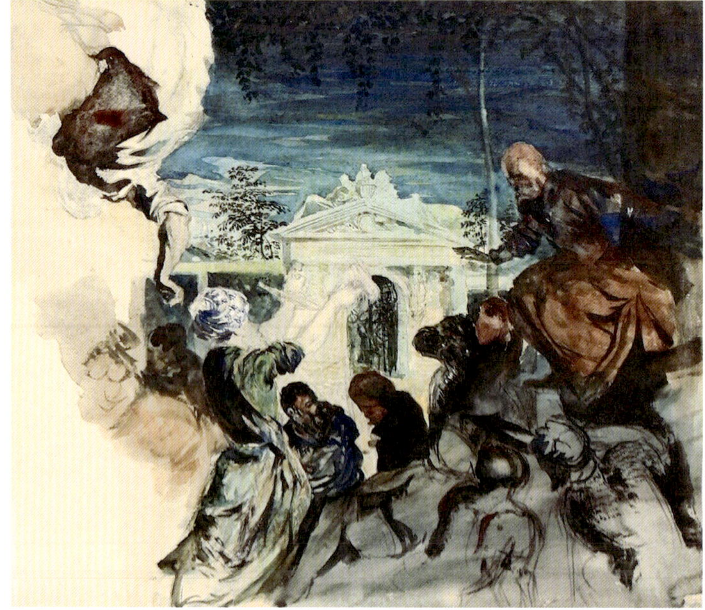

Venice, September 24th [1845]

My Dearest Father
I have had a draught of pictures today enough to drown me. I never was so utterly crushed to the earth before any human intellect as I was today, before Tintoret. Just be so good as to take my list of painters, & put him in the school of Art at the top, top, top of everything, with a great big black line underneath him to stop him off everybody – and put him in the school of Intellect, next after Michael Angelo. He took it so entirely out of me today that I could do nothing at last but lie on a bench & laugh. Harding said that if he had been a figure painter, he never could have touched a brush again, and that he felt more like a flogged schoolboy than a man – and no wonder. Tintoret don't seem to be able to stretch himself till you give him a canvas forty feet square – and then, he lashes out like a leviathan, and heaven and earth come together.

Harold Shapiro (ed.), *Ruskin in Italy. Letters to His Parents*, 211–12.

PART OF THE *MIRACLE OF ST. MARK*, AFTER TINTORETTO, 1845
watercolour, bodycolour on cream paper, 375 × 420 mm
Coniston, The Ruskin Museum, inv. ConRM1989.748

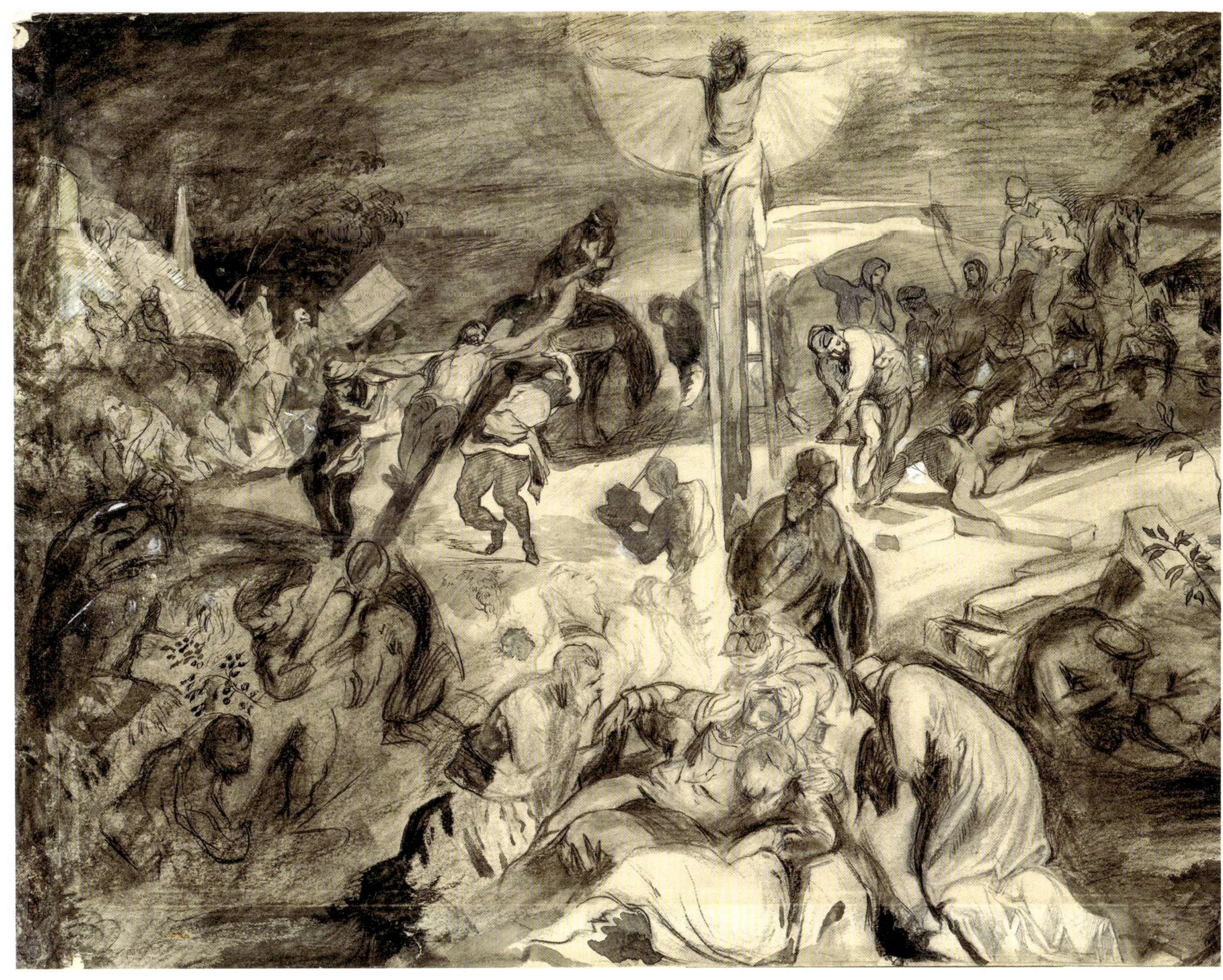

STUDY OF THE CENTRAL PORTION OF TINTORETTO'S *CRUCIFIXION*, 1845
pencil, chalk, ink, watercolour, bodycolour on paper, 370 × 535 mm
Lancaster, The Ruskin, Lancaster University, inv. 1996P1553

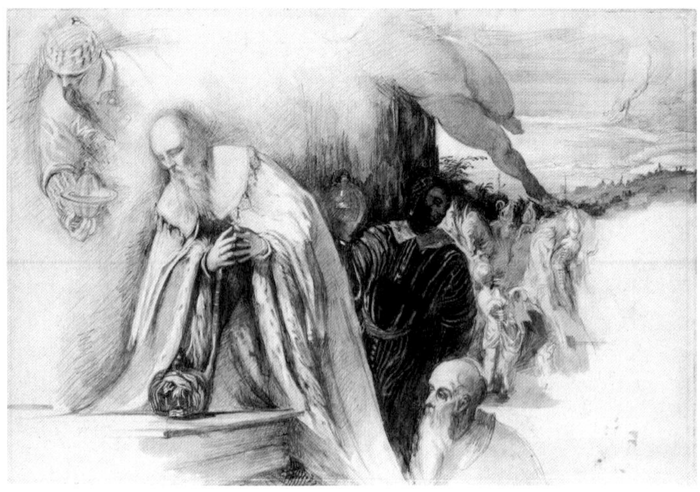

ADORATION OF THE MAGI, AFTER TINTORETTO: MAGI, 1845
pencil, ink wash on paper, 333 × 495 mm
Lancaster, The Ruskin, Lancaster University, inv. 1996P1552

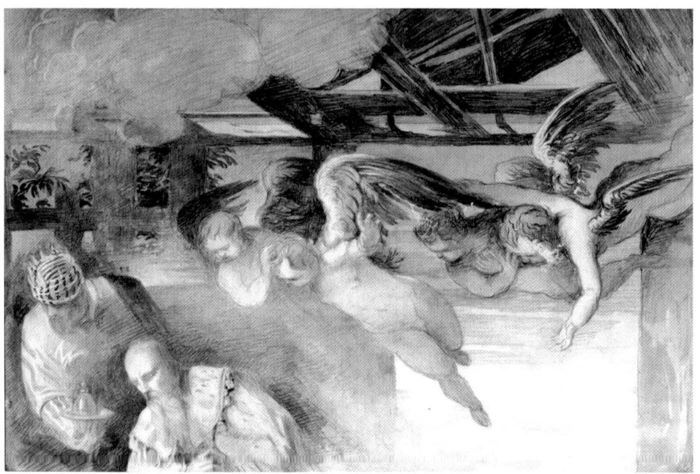

ADORATION OF THE MAGI, AFTER TINTORETTO: CHERUBS, 1852
pencil, ink wash on paper, 370 × 550 mm
Lancaster, The Ruskin, Lancaster University, inv. 1996P1009

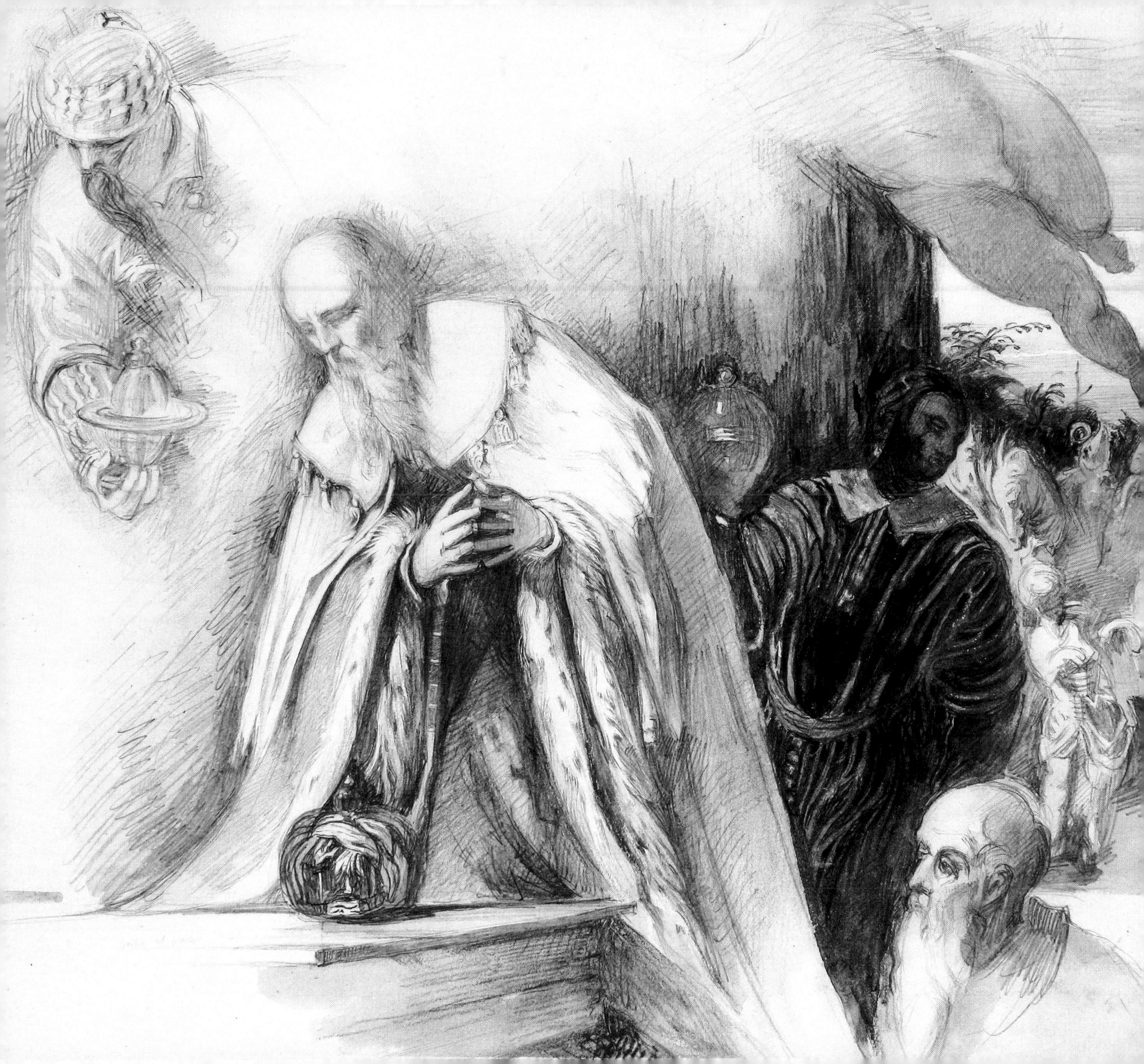

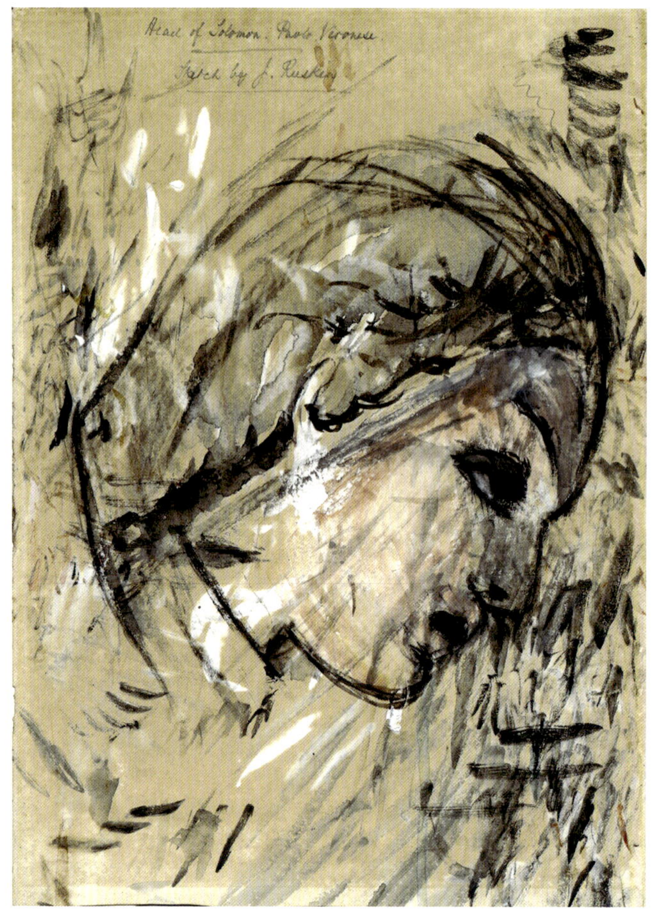

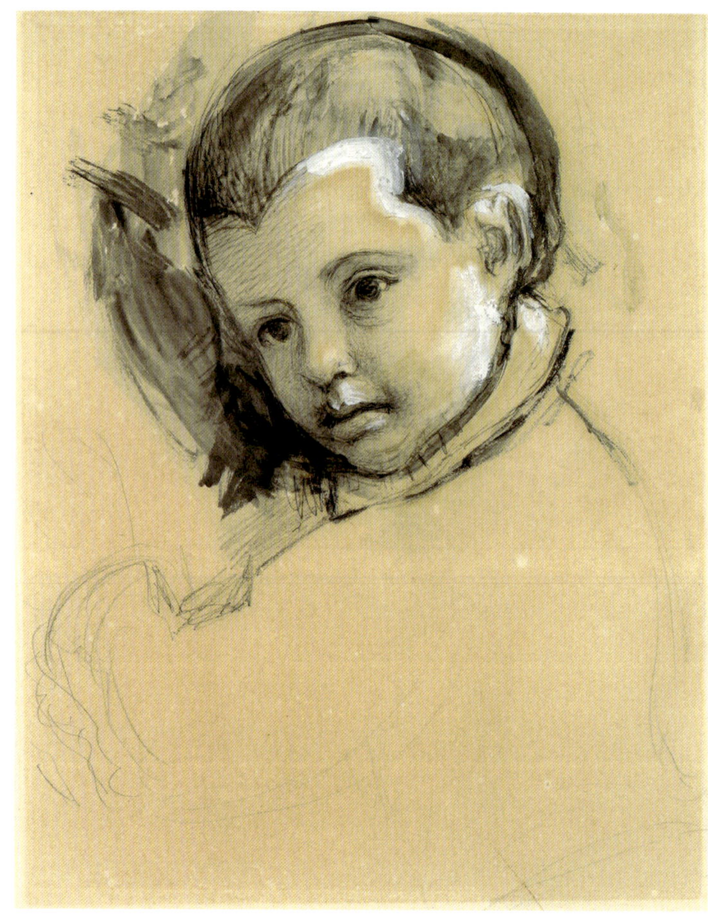

HEAD OF SOLOMON, FROM VERONESE'S
SOLOMON AND THE QUEEN OF SHEBA, 1858
bodycolour, ink wash, watercolour, pencil on cream paper, 375 × 277 mm
inscription: "Head of Solomon, Paulo Veronese, sketch by J. Ruskin"
by Charles Eliot Norton
Lancaster, The Ruskin, Lancaster University, inv. 1996P1671

HEAD OF A BOY, FROM VERONESE'S *CUCCINA FAMILY*, 1859
ink, ink wash, bodycolour, pencil on paper, 381 × 335 mm
Lancaster, The Ruskin, Lancaster University, inv. 1996P1670

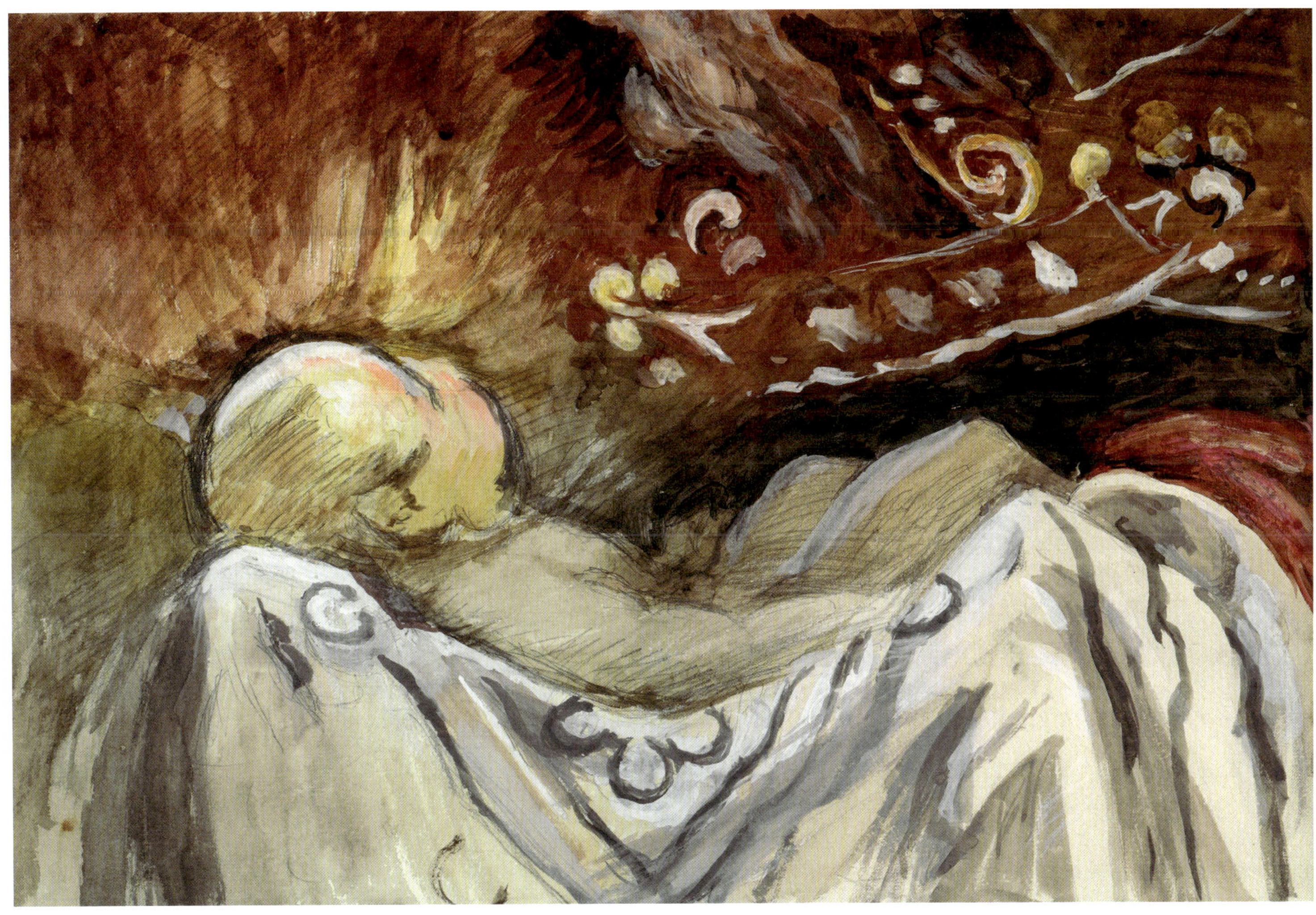

STUDY OF THE CHILD IN TINTORETTO'S *CIRCUMCISION*
IN THE SCUOLA GRANDE DI SAN ROCCO, 1869
watercolour, bodycolour, pencil on paper, 341 × 506 mm
Oxford, Ashmolean Museum, University of Oxford., inv. WA.RS.REF.096

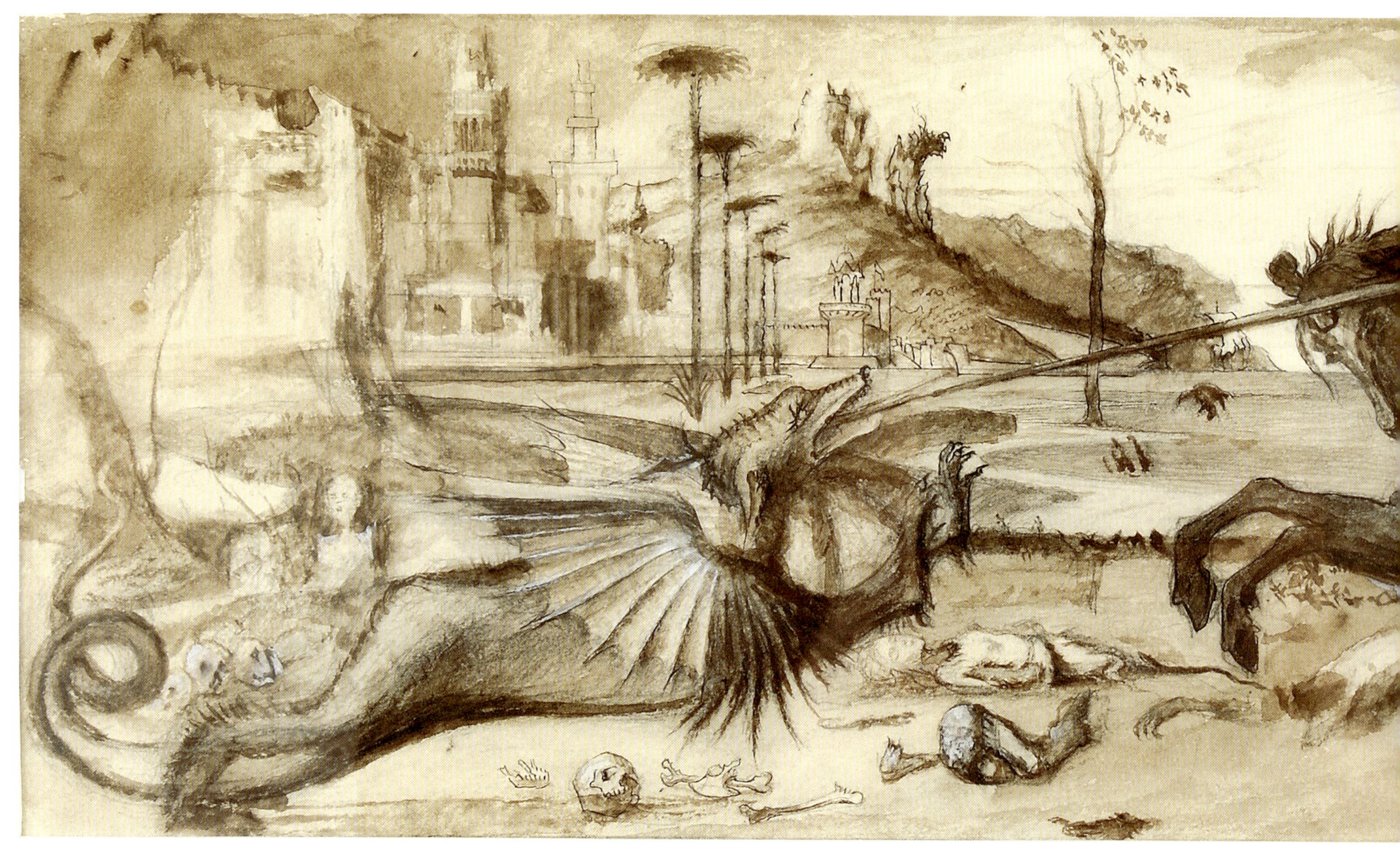

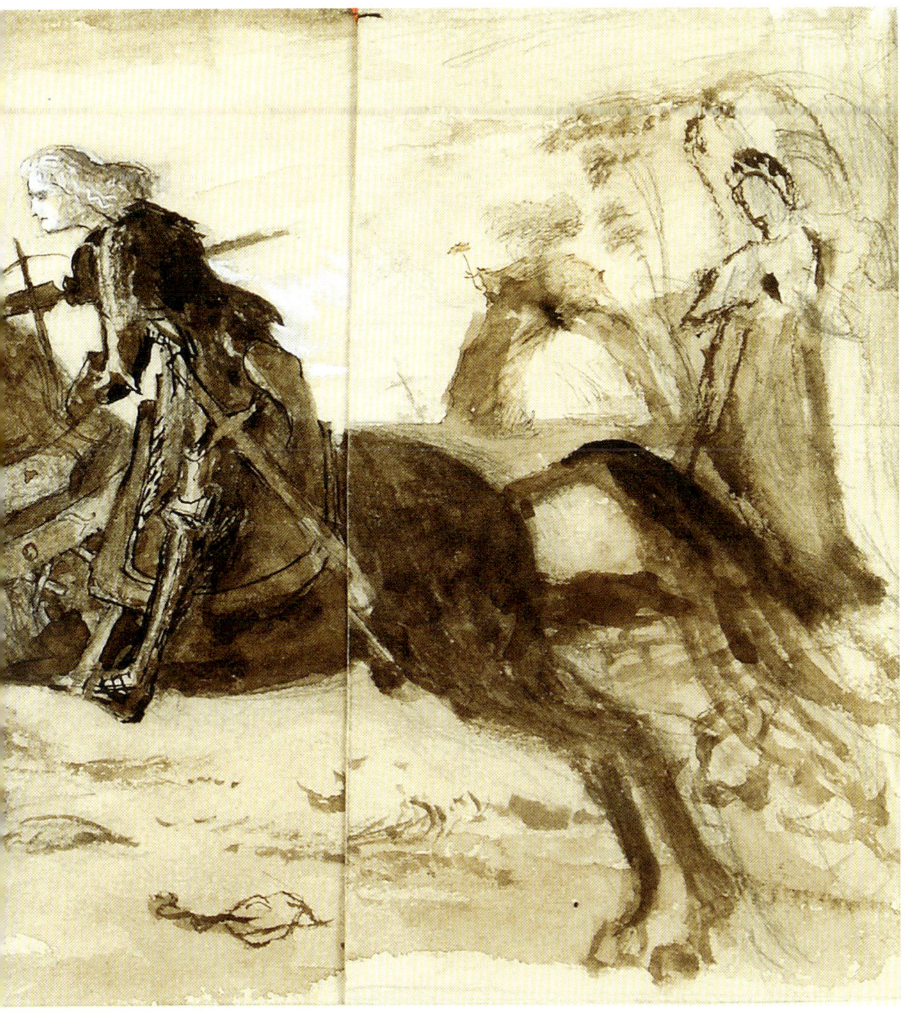

SAINT GEORGE AND THE DRAGON AFTER CARPACCIO, 1872
sepia, pencil and ink with white highlights on paper, 182 × 462 mm
Sheffield, Sheffield Museums Trust, Collection of the Guild of St. George
inv. CGSG00191

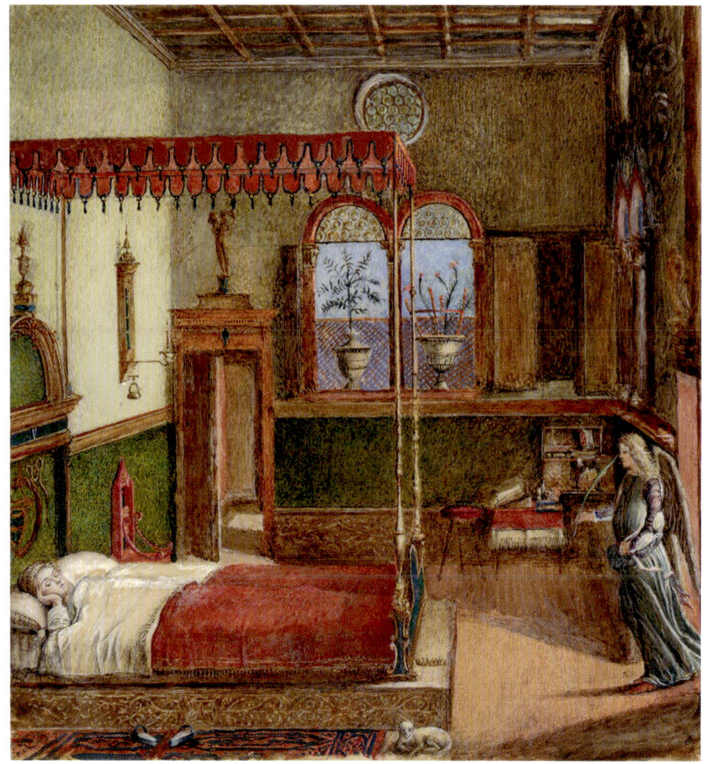

Saturday March 3rd, 1877

Yesterday lovely light showed me how to finish St. Ursula, and I got the angel's palm done.

The Diaries of John Ruskin, vol. III, 941.

March 17th, 1877

Sad… perceiving the goodness of the past, and divinity of Carpaccio.

The Diaries of John Ruskin, vol. III, 943.

DRAWING OF CARPACCIO'S *DREAM OF SAINT URSULA* FROM THE *LEGEND OF SAINT URSULA*, 1876
watercolour, bodycolour, pencil on wove paper, 294 × 277 mm
Oxford, Ashmolean Museum, University of Oxford, inv. WA.RS.WAL.09

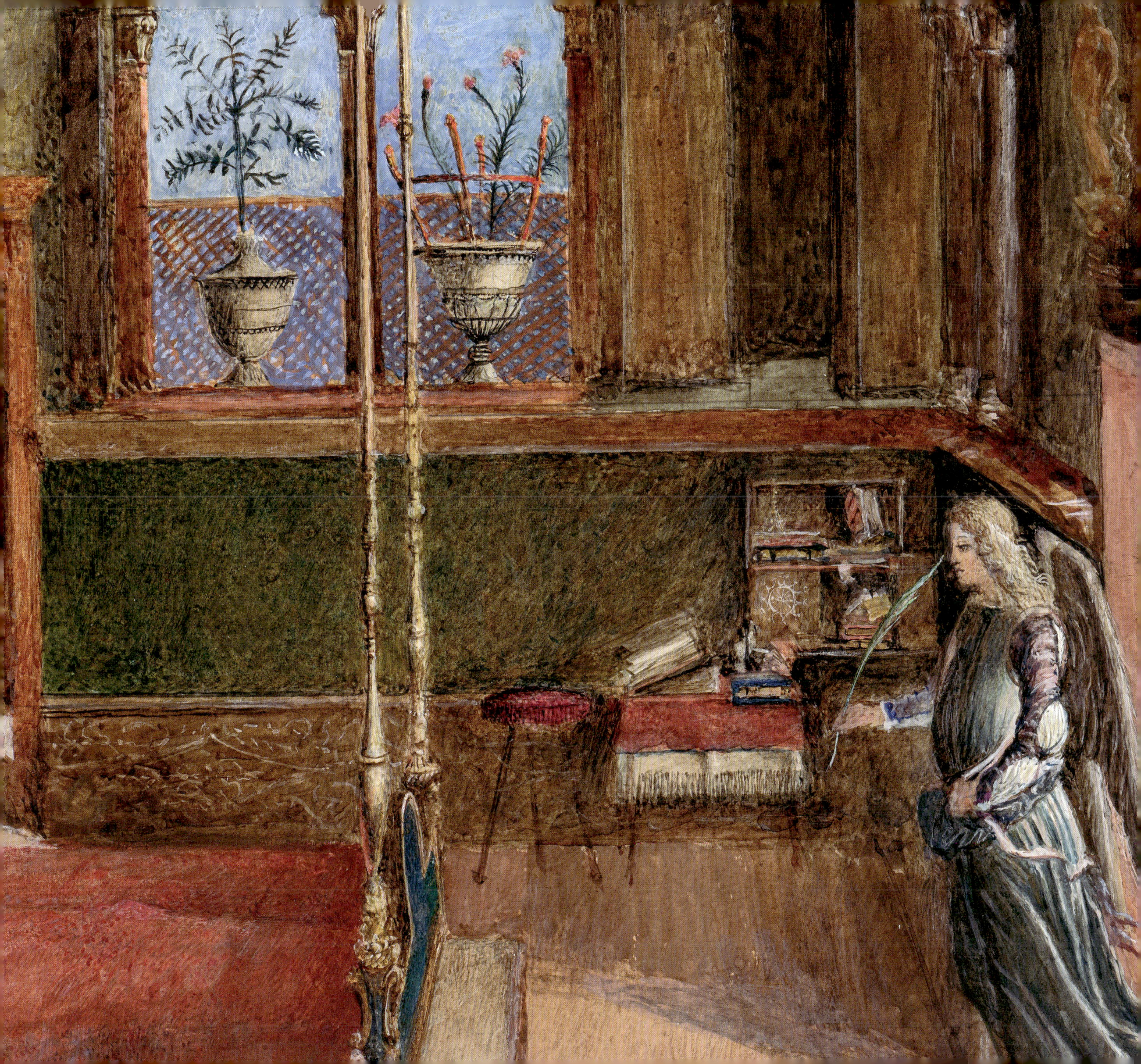

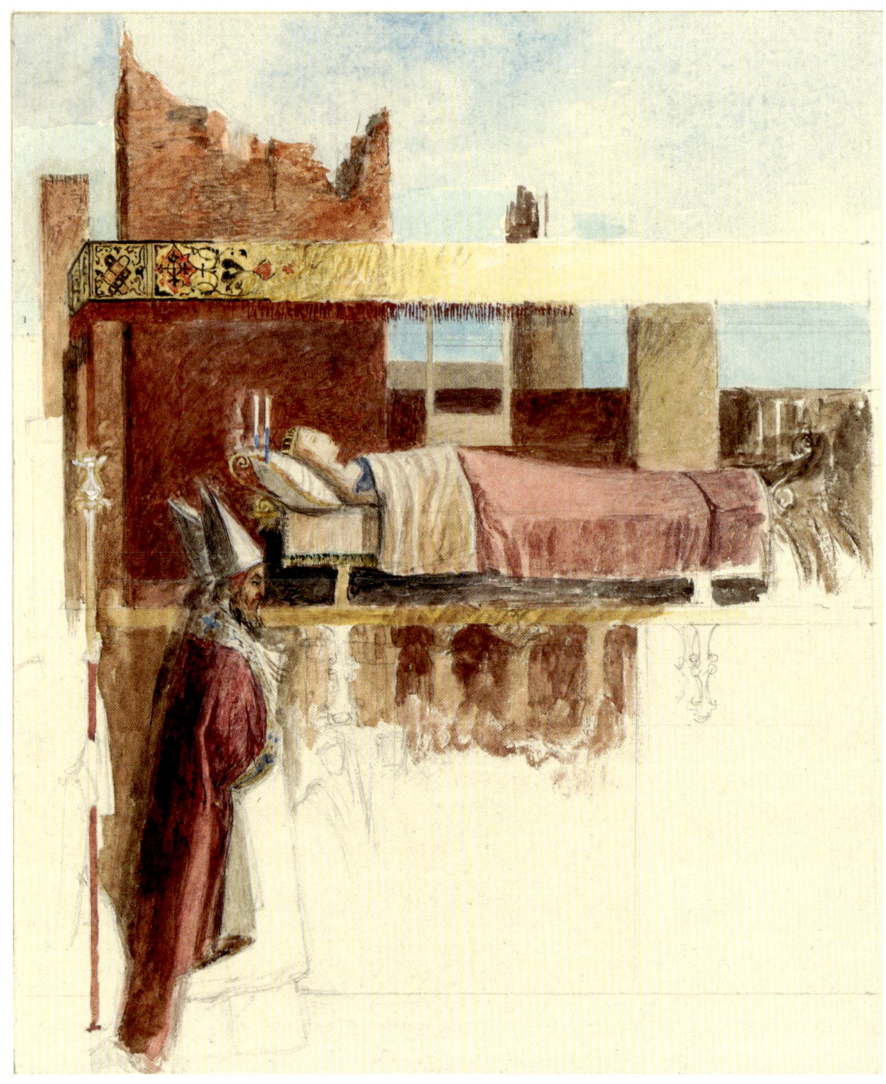

SAINT URSULA ON HER BIER: DRAWING OF CARPACCIO'S *MARTYRDOM OF THE PILGRIMS AND FUNERAL OF SAINT URSULA* FROM THE *LEGEND OF SAINT URSULA*, 1876
watercolour, bodycolour, pencil on paper, 277 × 236 mm
Oxford, Ashmolean Museum, University of Oxford, inv. WA.RS.RUD.106bis

Thursday March 29th 1877

But this a better morning after prosperous beginning of St. Mark's in divine morning yesterday; though morning is now to me only a part of sunset, but one is still lively at work. Got on with 15th century ladies's shoes at the Correr: how lucky as a piece of teaching with St. Ursula's!

The Diaries of John Ruskin, vol. III, 945.

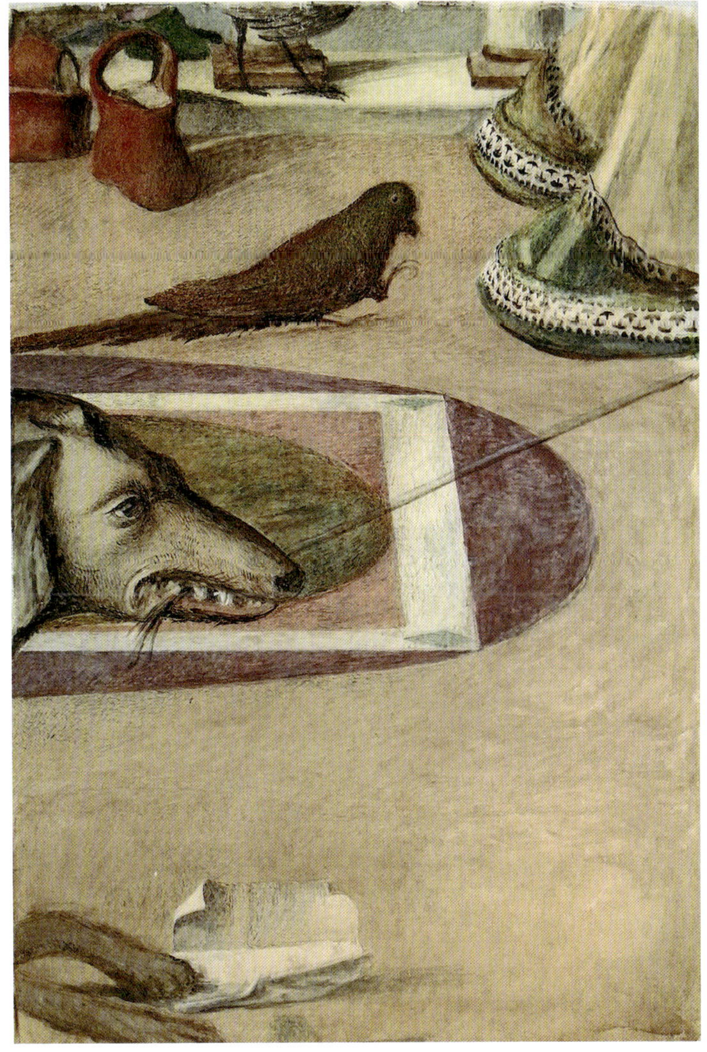

DETAIL FROM CARPACCIO: *TWO VENETIAN LADIES AND THEIR PETS*, 1877
watercolour, bodycolour on cream paper, 435 × 305 mm
Coniston, The Ruskin Museum, inv. ConRM1989.753

VIEWS
OF THE
LAGOON

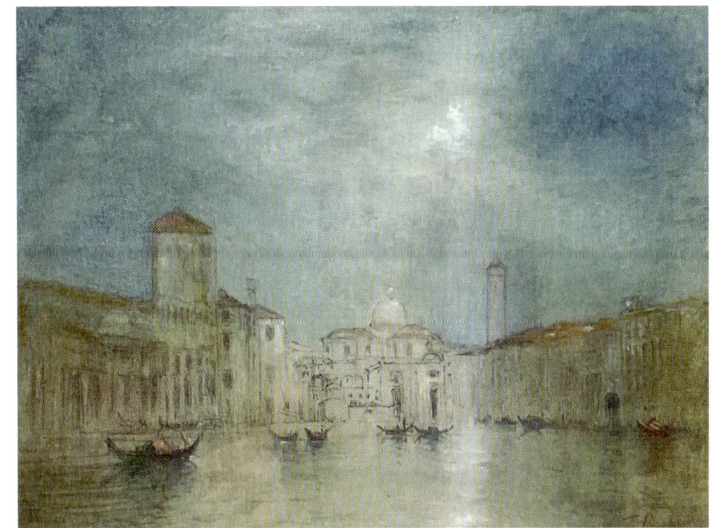

Venice. 10th Sept. Hotel de l'Europe [1845]

What makes me sadder is, that the divine beauty of the yet uninjured passage about the Salute & Piazzetta has struck me more intensely than ever. I have been standing (but the moment before I began this letter) on the steps at the door – the water is not even plashing in the moonlight, there is not even a star twinkling, it is as still a as if Venice were beneath the sea, but beautiful beyond all thought.

Harold Shapiro (ed.), *Ruskin in Italy. Letters to His Parents*, 199.

VENICE BY MOONLIGHT, undated
watercolour and pencil signed, 160 × 220 mm
Private collection (courtesy of David Duggleby)

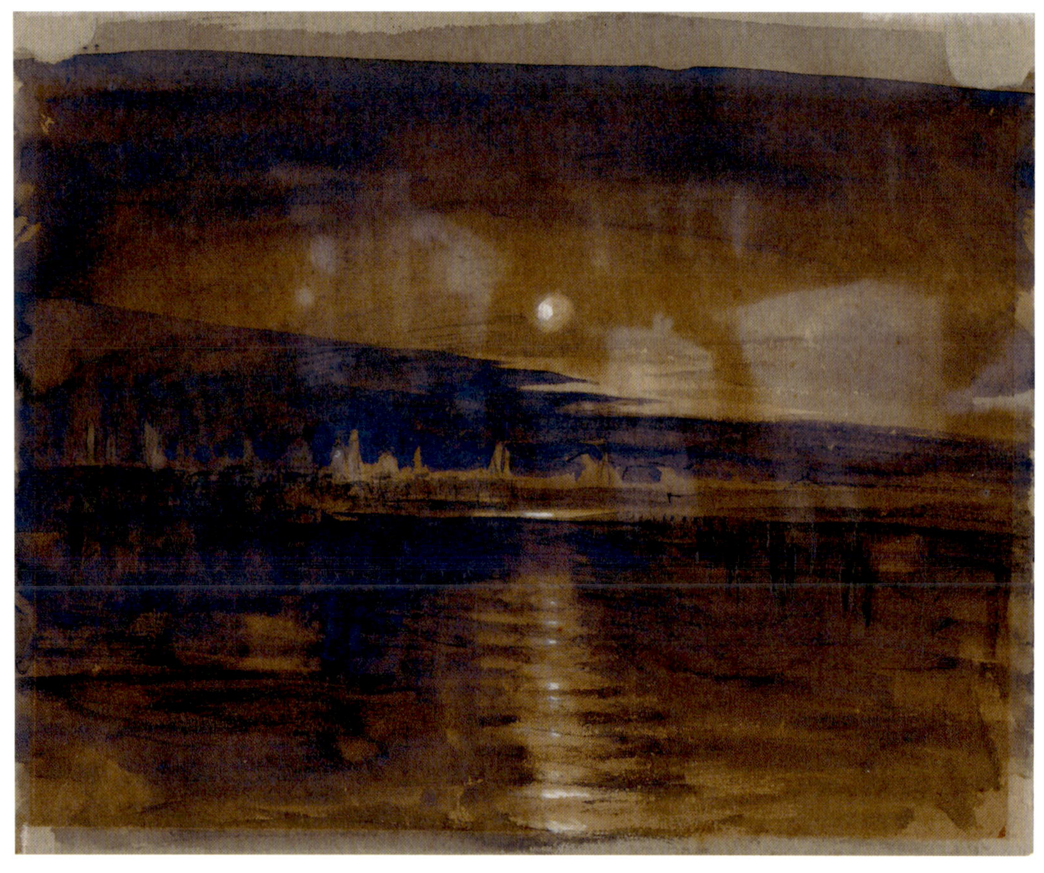

MOONLIGHT ON THE LAGOON, 1849
watercolour, bodycolour on grey paper, 165 × 228 mm
on the verso: *Sails of Fishing Boats* [page 15]
Lancaster, The Ruskin, Lancaster University, inv. 1996P1049

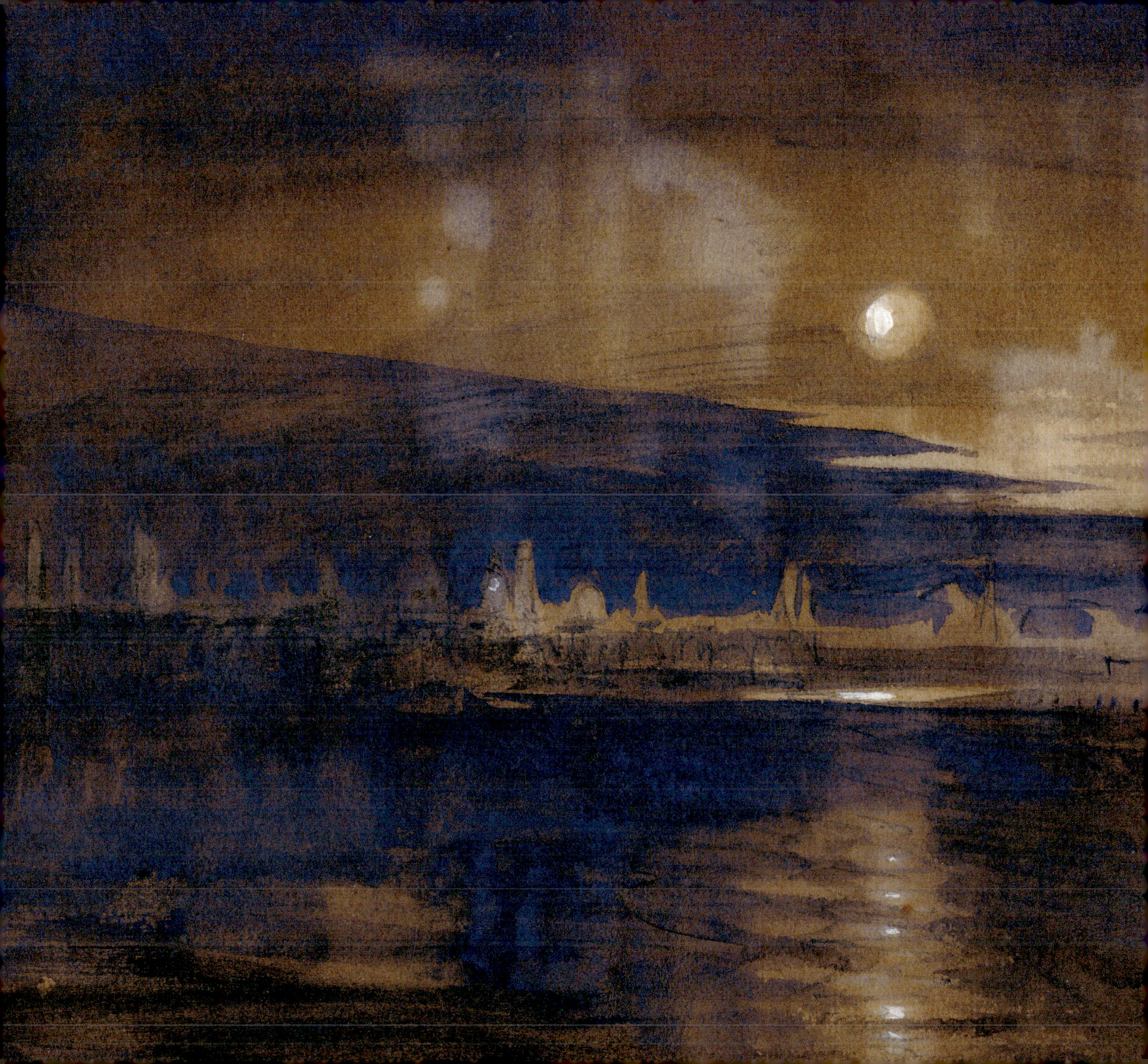

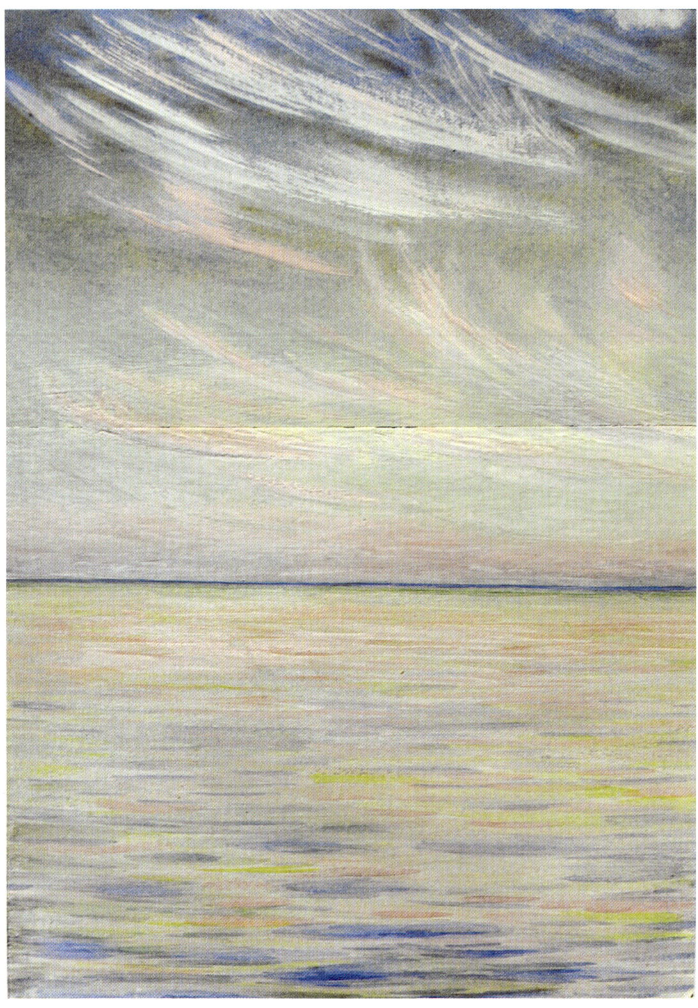

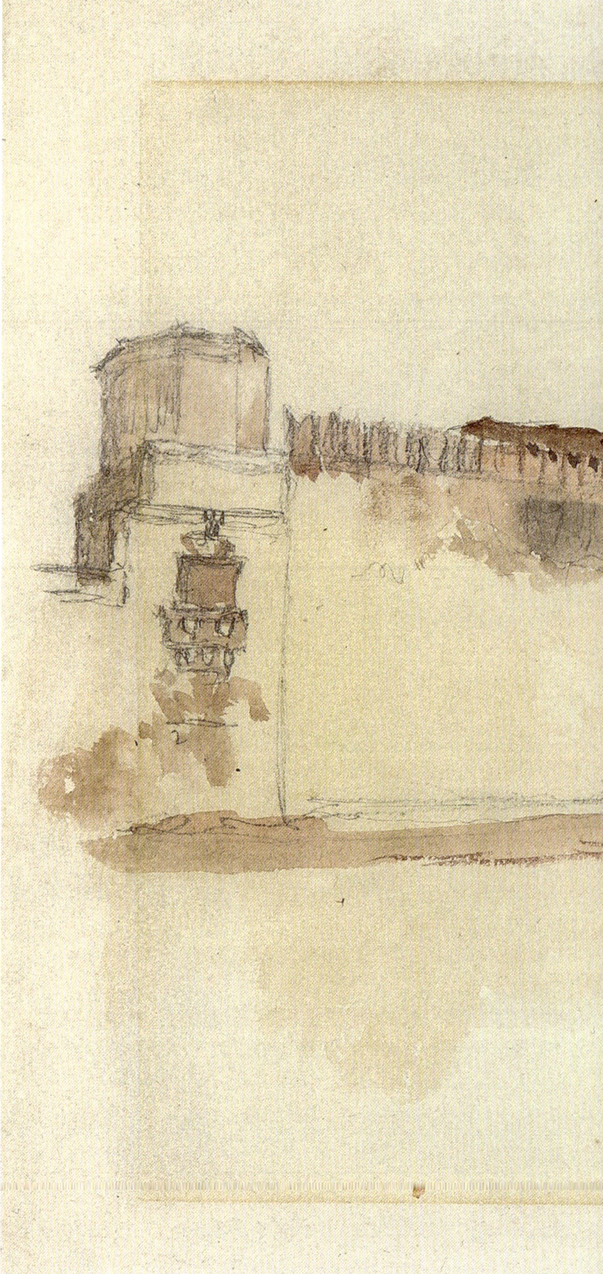

SUNRISE OVER THE SEA, 1873
watercolour on paper, 172 × 124 mm
Kendal, Abbot Hall, Lakeland Arts Trust,
given by Mrs D. E. Barton, inv. AH1159/73

SEA WALL, 1876–77
pencil, watercolour on paper, 220 × 424 mm
Lancaster, The Ruskin, Lancaster University, inv. 1996P2053

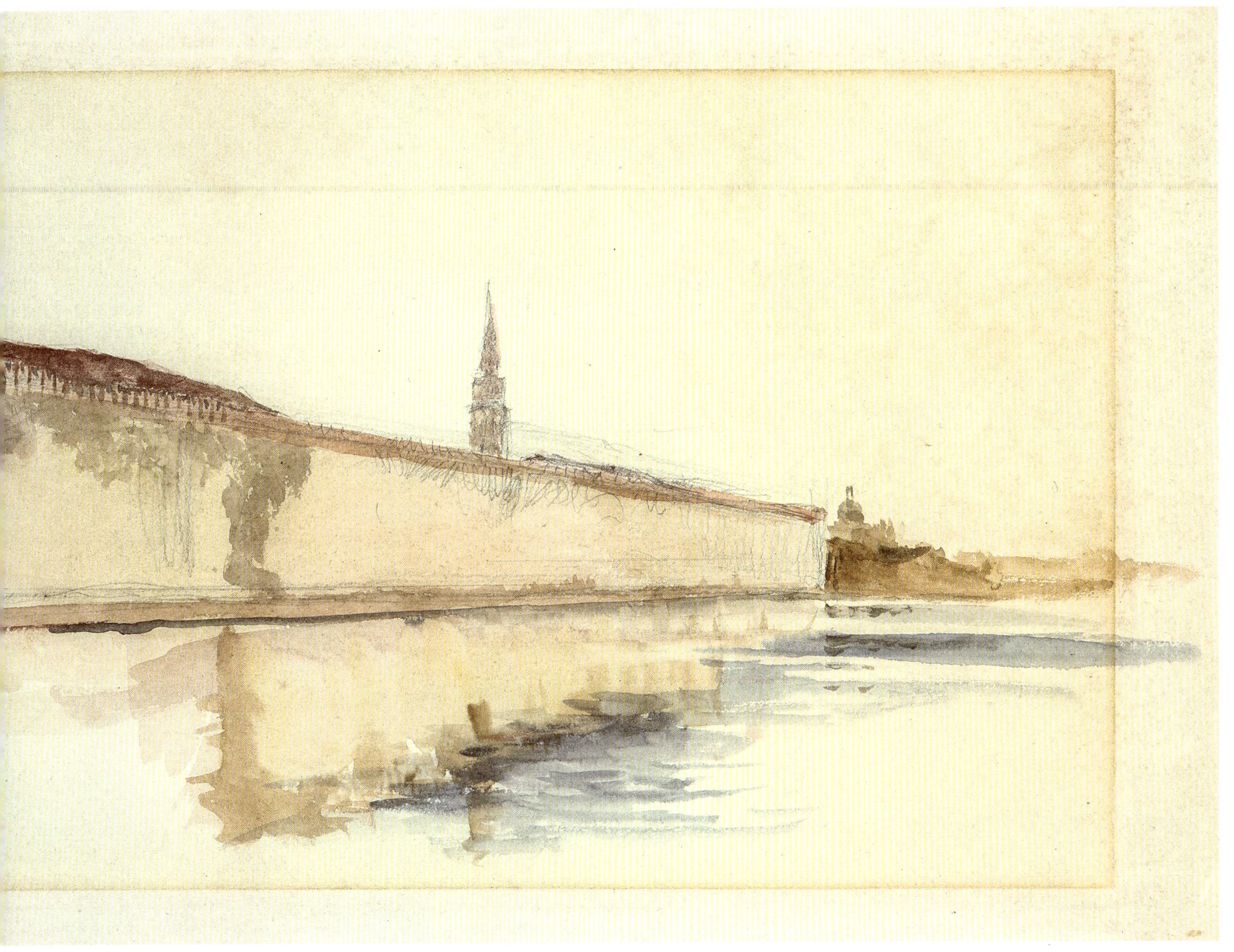

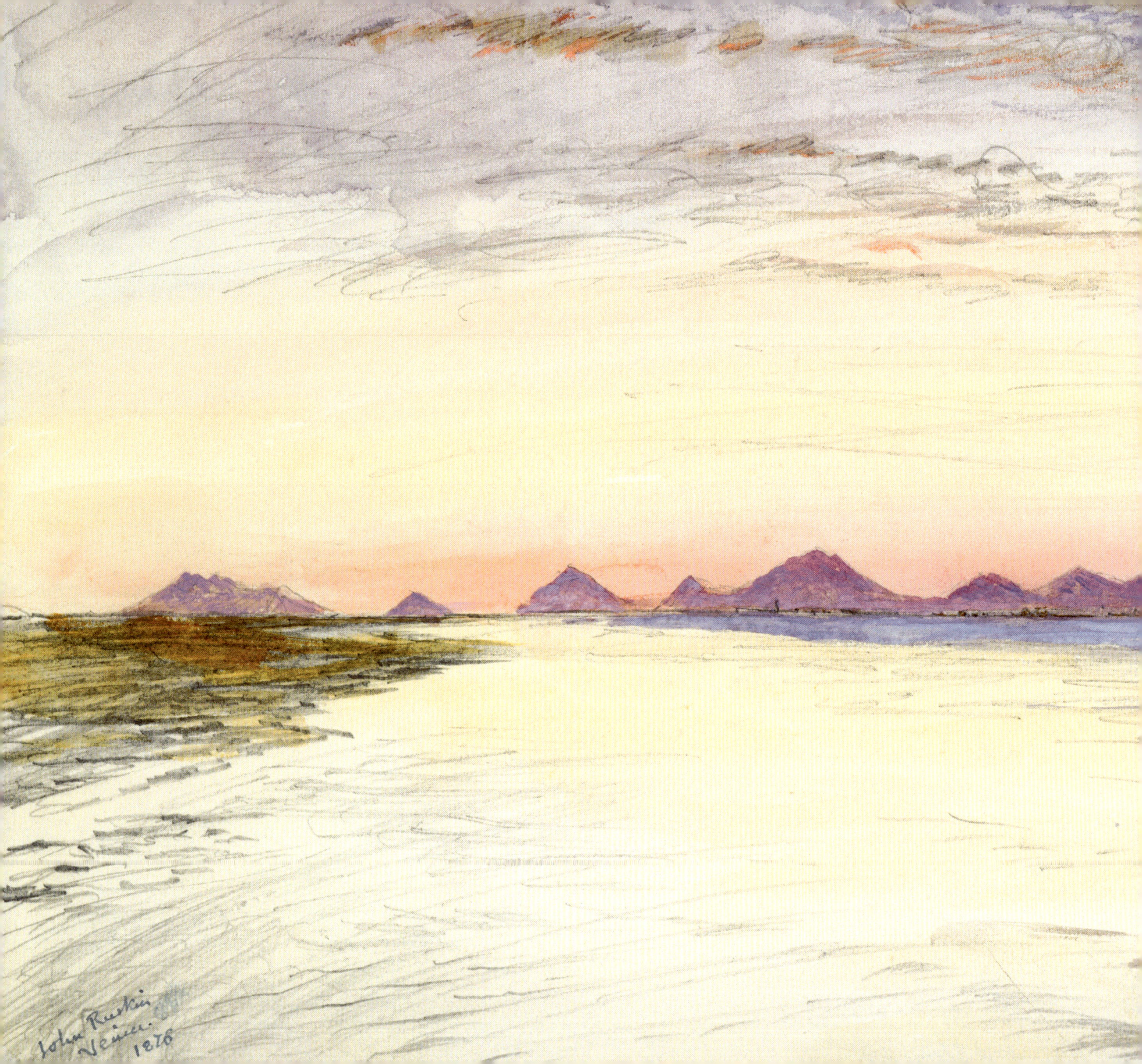
John Ruskin
Venice.
1876

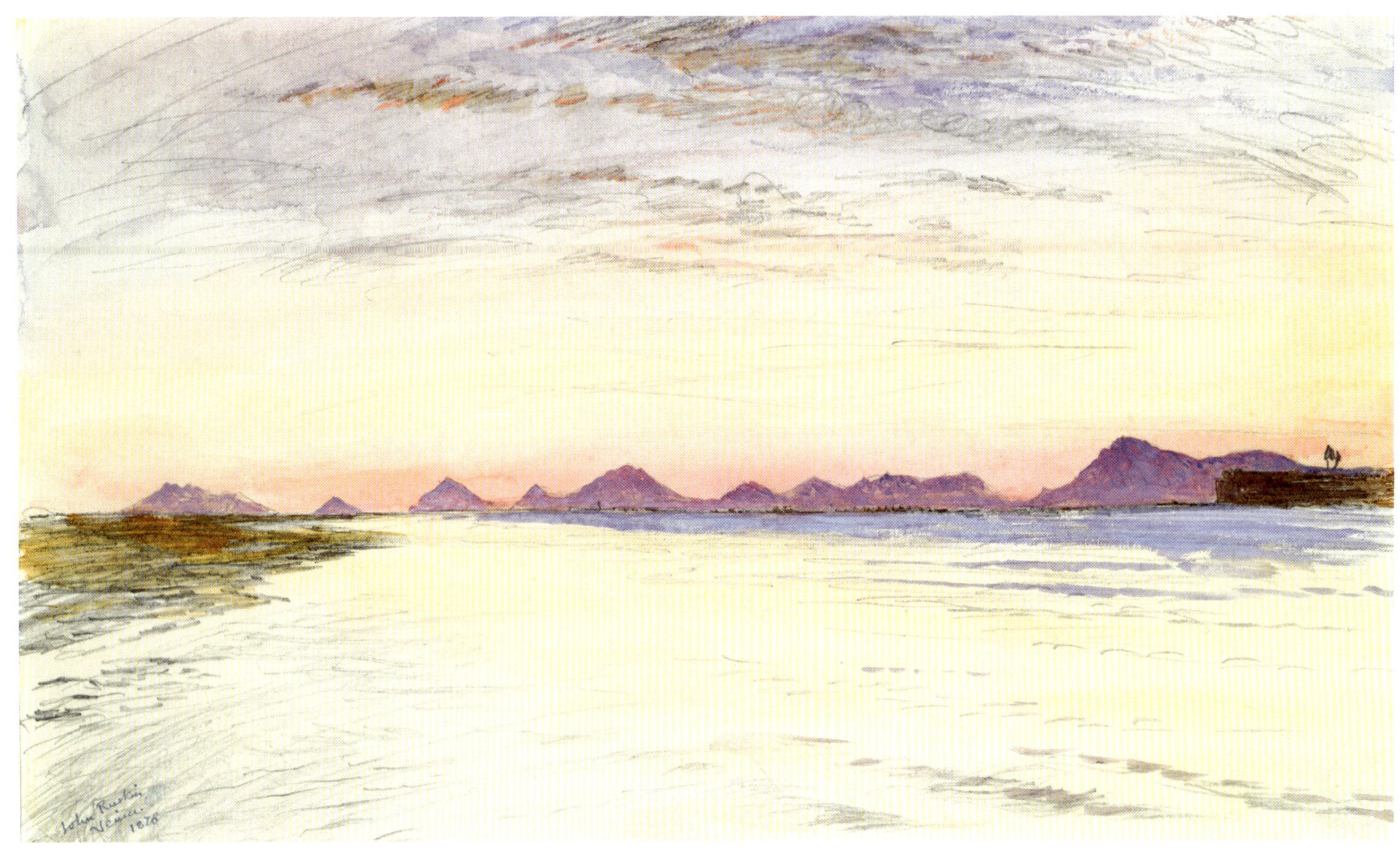

THE EUGANEAN HILLS FROM THE LAGOON
SEEN AT SUNSET, 1876
pencil, watercolour and bodycolour, 136 × 231 mm
London, Royal Collection Trust, inv. RCIN 913547

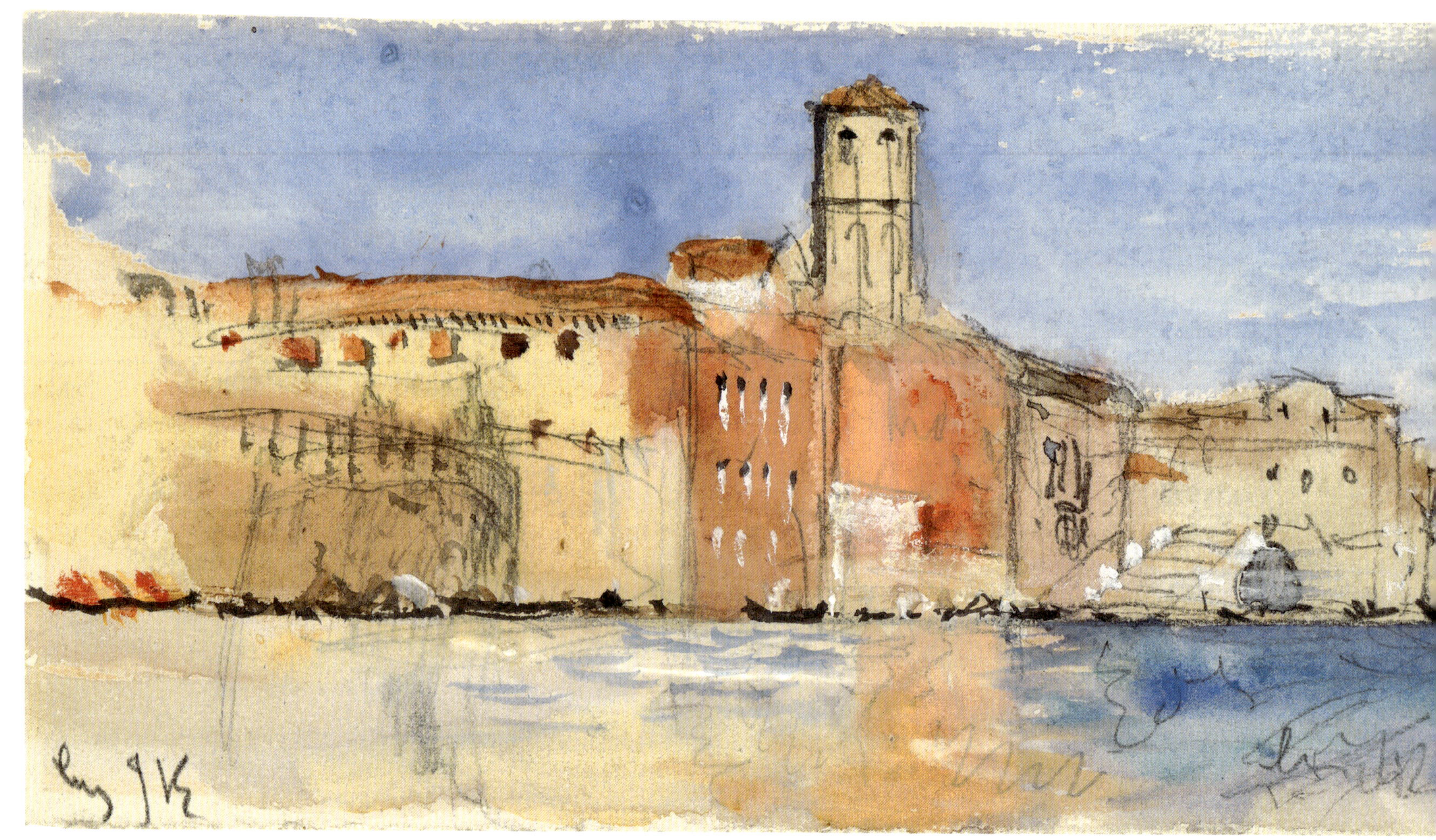

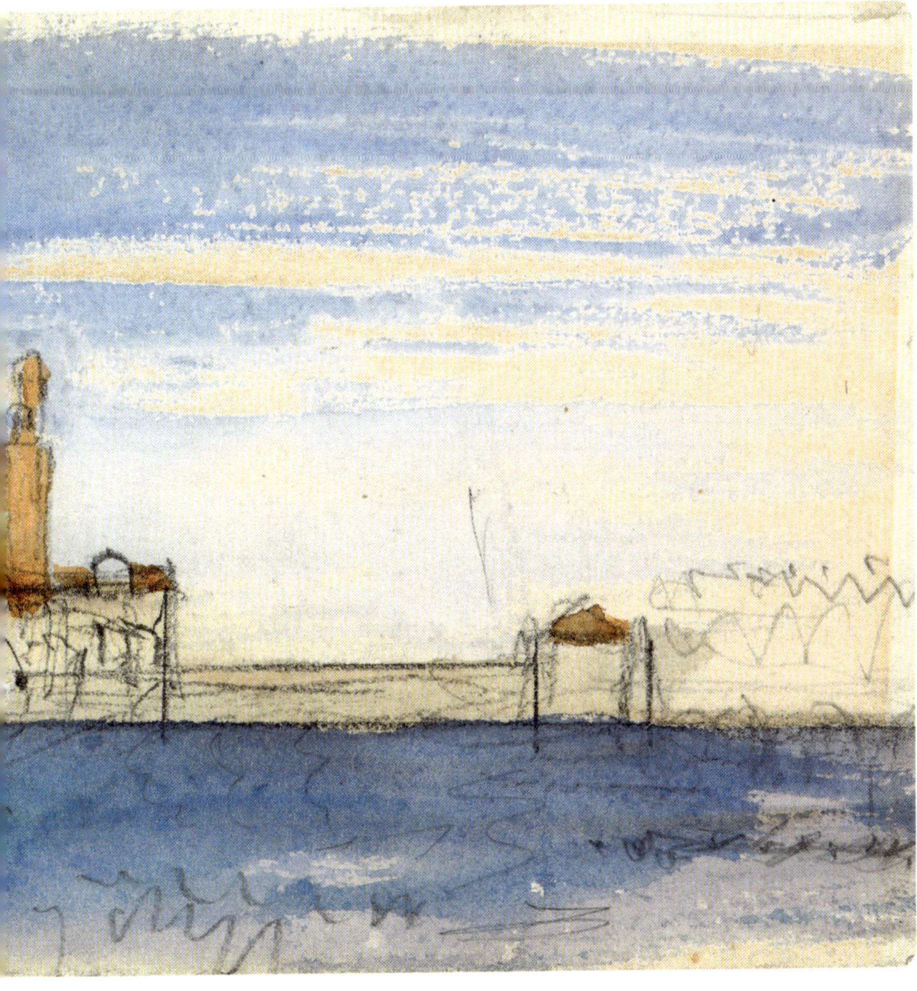

THE FONDAMENTE NOVE, *circa* 1876
pencil, watercolour and gouache 90 × 265 mm
Private collection (courtesy of Lowell Libson & Jonny Yarker Ltd)

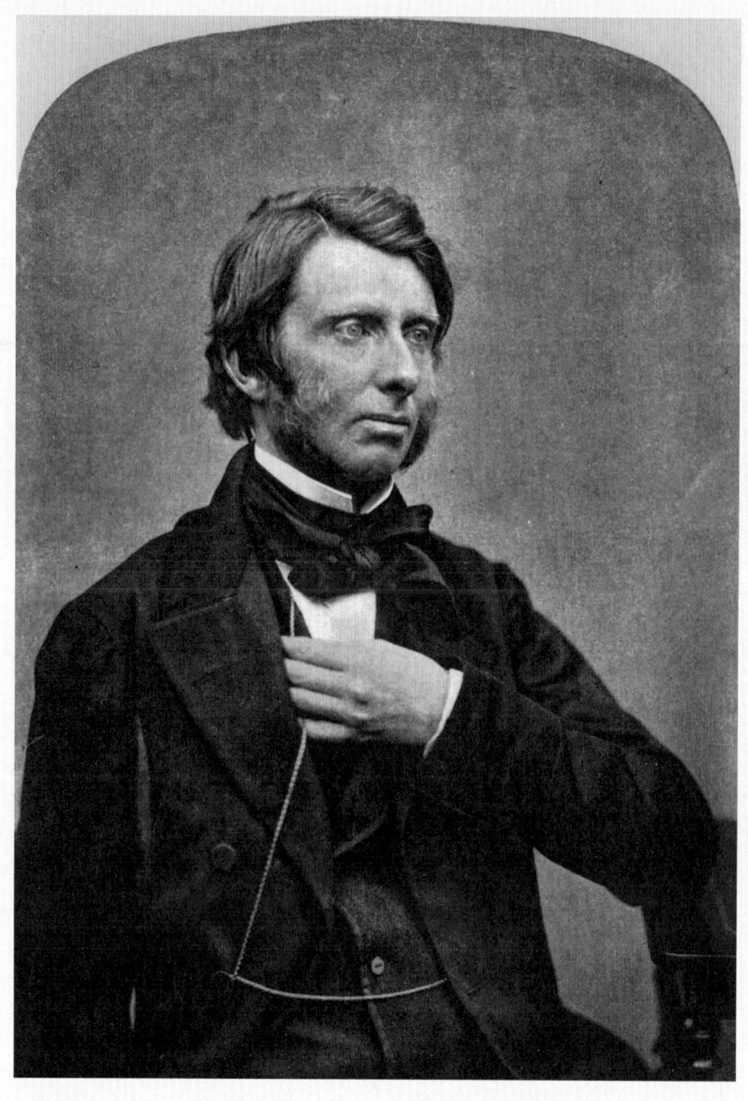

William Jeffrey
THE FIRST KNOWN PHOTOGRAPH OF JOHN RUSKIN, *circa* 1856
Courtesy of K&J Jacobson, UK

SELECTED BIBLIOGRAPHY

Birch, Dinah, "Ruskin and Venice," in M. O'Neill, M. Sandy, S. Wootton (eds.), *Venice and the Cultural Imagination: 'This Strange Dream upon the Water'*, London: Routledge, 2015, 95–108.

Bradley, John and Ian Ousby, *The Correspondence of John Ruskin and Charles Eliot Norton*, Cambridge: Cambridge University Press, 1987.

Bunney, Sarah, "Mementoes of late 19th century Italy: American patronage of John Wharlton Bunney (1828–82)," *British Art Journal* vol. x (Winter/Spring 2009/10), 108–24.

Bunney, Sarah, "John Wharlton Bunney's British Patrons: Pictures Lost and Found," *British Art Journal* vol. xv (1, Autumn), 65–81 (2014).

Bunney, Sarah, "John W. Bunney's 'big picture' of St. Mark's, and the Ruskin–Bunney relationship," *Ruskin Review and Bulletin*, vol. 4, no. 1 (2007), 18–47.

Burd, Van Akin, *Christmas Story. John Ruskin's Venetian Letters of 1876–1877. Edited with and Introductory Essay on Ruskin and the Spiritualists, His Quest for the Unseen*, Delaware: Associated University Presses, 1990.

Clegg, Jeanne, *Ruskin and Venice*, London: Junction Books, 1981.

Clegg, Jeanne, *John Ruskin. An Arts Council Exhibition*, exhibition catalogue (Sheffield, Mappin Art Gallery; Kendal, Abbot Hall, Oxford, Oxford Museum of Modern Art, 25 May–13 November 1983), London 1983.

Clegg, Jeanne and Emma Sdegno, "Le pietre di Ca' Foscari: Ruskin e il Palazzo," in *Le lingue occidentali nei 150 anni di storia di Ca' Foscari*, Anna Cardinaletti, Laura Cerasi, Patrizio Rigobon (eds.), Venice: Edizioni Ca' Foscari, 2018, 19–41.

Collingwood, W.G. *Ruskin's Relics*, London: Ibster, 1903.

E.T., Cook and Alexander Wedderburn, (eds.), *The Works of John Ruskin*, Library Edition, 39 vols, London: George Allen, 1903–12. *Modern Painters*, vols III–VII; *The Stones of Venice*, vols IX–XI; *Praeterita*, vol. XXXV; *Catalogue of Drawings*, vol. XXXVIII.

Costantini, Paolo and Italo Zannier, *I dagherrotipi della Collezione Ruskin*, Venice: Arsenale Editrice, 1986.

Evans, Joan and John Howard Whitehouse (eds.), *The Diaries of John Ruskin*, 3 vols, Oxford 1959.

Hanley, Keith and Emma Sdegno (eds.), *Ruskin, Venice and Nineteenth-Century Cultural Travel*, Venice: Cafoscarina, 2010.

Harvey, Michael, "Ruskin and Photography," *Oxford Art Journal* vol. 7, no. 2 (1984), 25–33.

A. Hélard, "Ce qui commence à Calais: l'Europe, terrain de jeu de Ruskin," Emma Sdegno, Martina Frank, Myriam Pilutti Namer, Pierre-Henri Frangne (eds.), *John Ruskin's Europe. A Collection of Cross-Cultural Essays*, Venice: Edizioni Ca' Foscari, 2020, 169–80.

Hewison, Robert, *Ruskin and Venice*, London: Thames and Hudson, 1978.

Hewison, Robert, Warrell, Ian, Wildman, Stephen, *Ruskin, Turner and the Pre-Raphaelites*, exhibition catalogue (London, Tate Britain, 9 March–28 May, 2000), London: Tate Gallery Publishing, 2000.

Hewison, Robert, *Ruskin on Venice: 'The Paradise of Cities'*, New Haven and London: Yale University Press, 2009.

J. Hobbs, *Diary, 1846, 1849* (unpublished), New York, Pierpont Morgan Library, MA 2539.

Jacobson, Ken and Jenny, *Carrying off the Palaces: John Ruskin's Lost Daguerreotypes*, London, Bernard Quaritch, 2015.

Kite, Stephen, *Building Ruskin's Italy: Watching Architecture*, Aldershot, Ashgate, 2012.

Levi, Donata and Paul Tucker, *Ruskin didatta. Il disegno tra disciplina e diletto*, Venice: Marsilio, 1997.

Newall, Christopher, *John Ruskin. Artist and Observer*, exhibition catalogue (Ottawa, National Gallery of Canada, 14 February–11 May, 2014), London: Paul Holberton, 2014.

Ottani Cavina, Anna (ed.), *John Ruskin. Le Pietre di Venezia*, exhibition catalogue (Venice, Palazzo Ducale, 10 March–10 June, 2018), Venice: Marsilio, 2018.

Pemble, John, *Venice Rediscovered*, Oxford: Clarendon Press, 1995.

Quill, Sarah, *Ruskin's Venice: The Stones Revisited*, London: Lund Humphries, 2015.

Rogers, Samuel, *Italy. A Poem.* Illustrated by J. M. W. Turner and T. Stothard, London: John Murray, 1830.

Ruskin, John, *Résumé of Italian Art and Architecture (1845)*, Tucker, Paul (ed.), Scuola Normale Superiore di Pisa, 2003.

Ruskin, John, *Pittori moderni*, Giovanni Leoni (ed), 2 vols, Turin: Einaudi, 1998.

Ruskin, John, *Guide to the Principal Pictures at the Academy of Fine Arts Venice (1877) with Other Texts*, Paul Tucker (ed.), Venice: Edizioni Ca' Foscari, 2023.

Giuseppe Sandrini (ed.), John Ruskin, *Lettere da Verona*, Verona 2013.

Sdegno, Emma (ed.), *Looking at Tintoretto with John Ruskin. A Venetian Anthology*, Venice: Marsilio, 2018.

Seddon, Martin, "A Bridge by Any Other Name': the Search for the 'Ponte dei Pugni', Venice," *The Ruskin Review and Bullettin* vol. 8: 1, 2012, 46–55.

Shapiro, Harold (ed.), *Ruskin in Italy. Letters to his Parents 1845*, Oxford: Clarendon Press, 1972.

Tanner, Tony, *Venice Desired*, London, Blackwell, 1992.

Unrau, John, *Looking at Architecture with Ruskin*, London: Thames and Hudson, 1978.

Unrau, John, *Ruskin and St. Mark's*, London: Thames and Hudson, 1984.

Walton, Paul, *Master Drawings by John Ruskin*. Selections from the David Thomson Collection, London: Pilkington Press, 2000.

Wildman, Stephen, "'Scrawls and rags'? John Ruskin's Venetian Drawings of 1876–77," *Master Drawings*, vol. 47, no. 3, 2009, 329–345.

Wildman, Stephen, *Ruskin and the Daguerreotype*, Lancaster: Library Exhibition Catalogues, 2006.

Wildman, Stephen, *Ruskin's Venice*, Lancaster: Ruskin Library Exhibition Catalogues, 2010.

Wildman, Stephen, *'A noble invention': Ruskin's Daguerreotypes of Venice and Verona*, Lancaster: Library Exhibition Catalogues, 2013.

Photographic credits
Reproduced by courtesy of Abbot Hall, Lakeland Arts Trust, England
© Ashmolean Museum
© Ashmolean Museum, University of Oxford
Photo by Birmingham Museums Trust, licensed under CC0
© Collection of the Guild of St George, Sheffield Museums Trust
Courtesy of David Duggleby
© Fitzwilliam Museum / Bridgeman Images
© Gallery Oldham / Bridgeman Images
Courtesy of K&J Jacobson, UK
Courtesy of Lowell Libson & Jonny Yarker Ltd
© Manchester Art Gallery / Bridgeman Images
The Metropolitan Museum of Art, New York
The Morgan Library & Museum, New York
President and Fellows of Harvard College
Royal Collection Trust / © His Majesty King Charles III 2023
The Ruskin Museum, Coniston
© The Ruskin, Lancaster University
Photograph Courtesy of Sotheby's, Inc. © 2023
South London Gallery Collection / Southwark Council
Tate, London
© The Trustees of the British Museum
© Victoria and Albert Museum, London

Reproduction and printing
Grafiche Antiga s.p.a., Crocetta del Montello (Treviso)

for
Marsilio Editori® s.p.a., Venice